1993

Heretics and Hellraisers

American Studies Series
William H. Goetzmann, Editor

Heretics & Hellraisers

Women Contributors to *The Masses*, 1911–1917

MARGARET C. JONES

University of Texas Press, Austin

Requests for permission to reproduce material from this work should be sent to Permissions, University of Texas Press, Box 7819, Austin, TX 78713-7819.

(∞) The paper used in this publication meets the minimum requirements of American National Standard for Information Sciences — Permanence of Paper for Printed Library Materials, ANSI Z39.48-1984.

Library of Congress Cataloging-in-Publication Data

Jones, Margaret C., 1949–
    Heretics and hellraisers : women contributors to The Masses,
 1911–1917 / Margaret C. Jones. — 1st ed.
        p.   cm. — (American studies series)
    Includes bibliographical references and index.
    ISBN 0-292-74026-3 (alk. paper). — ISBN 0-292-74027-1 (pbk. :
 alk. paper)
        1. American literature — Women authors — History and criticism.
    2. Feminism and literature — United States — History — 20th century.
    3. Literature and society — United States — History — 20th century.
    4. Women and literature — United States — History — 20th century.
    5. Women authors, American — 20th century — Biography.   6. Amer-
 ican periodicals — History — 20th century.   7. Social problems in literature.   8. Masses (New York, N.Y.)   I. Title.   II. Series.
 PS151.J65   1993
 810.9'9287'09041 — dc20   92-42215

For Essam:
a very dear heretic

Contents

Preface

I WAS FIRST attracted to the feminist socialist magazine called *The Masses* by its wit, its irreverence, its committed and intelligent treatment of social issues. At the time of this first encounter I was completely ignorant of how the magazine had been represented in subsequent histories; hence I enjoyed the art of Cornelia Barns equally with that of Art Young, Adriana Spadoni's fiction alongside of John Reed's, Helen Marot's articles on labor issues as much as the essays of Floyd Dell, without any sense that I was paying disproportionate attention to merely "minor"—which is to say, female—contributors.

Precisely because I had been so deeply impressed with the work of women of *The Masses*—as by that of many interesting male contributors—when I began to read the literature about *The Masses,* I was at once forcibly struck by a sense of something missing. Most of these histories and anthologies—William L. O'Neill's *Echoes of Revolt* is an admirable exception—deal eloquently and perceptively with the work of *Masses* men, but (except for occasional allusions to the more colorful excesses of feminine Greenwich Village bohemianism) hardly mention *Masses* women at all. As for women's intellectual contribution to the magazine, it apparently was nonexistent. Where are the pointed, witty, speculative essays of Elsie Clews Parsons? The stories of Helen Hull and Mary Heaton Vorse? The verse of Elizabeth Waddell and Jean Starr Untermeyer? Cornelia Barns' marvelous, original drawings?—so profusely scattered through the *Masses'* pages that to imagine them removed is immediately to imagine a duller magazine?

The present book, then, represents an attempt to accord the women contributors of *The Masses,* if not justice, at least the kind of attention hitherto devoted only to their male counterparts—to examine not only the work of those contributors whose careers began and ended with *The Masses,* but the subsequent lives and writings of those, like Helen Hull, Mary Vorse, Dorothy Day, Elsie Parsons, Inez Irwin, who enjoyed productive careers thereafter.

The book has a second purpose: to examine the ideas and ideals of women who contributed to a leftist, feminist periodical for their relevance to the present—most notably, in their conceptions of the relations between feminism and the needs and aspirations of society's working-class majority. The women of *The Masses* offer access to a paradigm long forgotten—that of a feminist radicalism, a class-conscious feminism. Often playful, irreverent, and funny, they took their political commitments very seriously. Some of them made painful personal sacrifices for those commitments. They had important things to say, and said them with eloquence. We owe it to them, and to ourselves, to give their work a second glance.

Acknowledgments

WARMEST THANKS to the Interlibrary Loan staff of the Eisenhower Library of Johns Hopkins University, of the library of the State University of New York (SUNY) at Stony Brook, of the Polytechnic University at Farmingdale, and of the library of Central Washington University. A special debt of gratitude is owed to Donna Sammis at SUNY, and to Mae Morey at Central Washington University. Without their industry, patience, and kind helpfulness, the writing of this book would not have been possible.

For access to manuscript material, I would like to thank the staff of the Butler Library of Columbia University, the Schlesinger Library, Radcliffe College, the Marquette University Archives, the Walter Reuther Library, Wayne State University, and the library of the American Philosophical Society. Thanks also to the librarians of the New York Public Library and of Goucher College.

I am most grateful to Professors Bernard Benstock of the University of Miami, Frank Cioffi of Central Washington University, and William H. Goetzmann of the University of Texas at Austin, for their careful and constructive readings of and comments on my manuscript. These proved a most useful learning experience for me. I appreciate their taking the time to read so carefully.

I would also like to thank all those at the University of Texas Press who have offered invaluable help with the production of *Heretics and Hellraisers*. In this connection, warmest thanks are due to Carolyn Wylie, Liz Gold, and Vicki Woodruff for their meticulous and constructive copyediting. I would like, above all, to thank Frankie Westbrook, sponsoring editor at the Press, who has believed in *Heretics and Hellraisers* from the beginning.

1

Women Are People

SCENE: *The Office of 'The People,' a morning in March, 1917 . . . a long table strewn with manuscripts and papers, a desk. On the walls are revolutionary posters; wads of paper are thrown about on the floor—the office of a publication which is radical and poor. . . .*

A moment later the woman appears. . . . Her manner is a little shrinking and yet as she stands in the doorway looking about the bare room, her face is the face of one who has come a long way and reached a wonderful place.[1]

IT SEEMS FITTING that this wondering pilgrim in Susan Glaspell's *The People,* a one-act play in celebration of *The Masses,* should be female. After all, the historical original of *The People* was not only the liveliest radical periodical of its day—it was also a feminist magazine. The offices in Nassau Street, and later in the three-story building at 91 Greenwich Avenue that also housed the *Masses* bookstore, were the home of an unflagging commitment to women's rights. *Masses* contributors worked for woman suffrage, but also for birth control education, against gender stereotypes and oppressive laws, for the rights of minority women and of women in the workplace. And *The Masses* provided an empowering forum for a particular kind of woman contributor. As Mabel Dodge said of "New Women" of the type who edited, wrote, and drew for the magazine, they were for the most part "unorthodox women," women "who did things and did them openly . . . fine, daring, rather joyous and independent women."[2]

For the founding of a magazine of the type of *The Masses,* 1911 must have seemed a propitious time. For *Masses* fiction editor Inez Haynes Irwin (then Inez Haynes Gillmore), the years between 1900 and 1914 were some of the most exciting of her life. As she was to recall decades later, existence then seemed

. . . full of hope and freedom. Great movements were starting every-where. In the United States, the loudest voice in the land was that of the liberal. Everyone was fighting for something. Everyone was sure of victory. I used to say that a speaker with a megaphone could go to the intersection of Forty-Second Street [and] Broadway . . . and announce, "I am here to gather recruits for a movement to free . . ." and before he could state the object of his crusade, he would be in the center of a milling crowd of volunteers.[3]

Among the movements Irwin no doubt had in mind was the suffrage movement, in which she herself played an active part. It gained both in momentum and in militancy as the Woman's Party, founded in 1914, emu-lated the dramatic tactics of the British suffragettes. The terms *feminism* and *New Woman* became current in the United States in those years, and *The Masses* did much to lend them currency among intellectuals. Middle-class women, even those who did not consider themselves feminists, were, in the resonant phrase of the satirical suffrage writer Alice Duer Miller, coming "out of the kitchen."[4] Between 1900 and 1920, the number of women earning PhDs more than doubled, while the first three decades of the century saw an increase of more than 87 percent in the numbers of women in professional employment.[5]

The first twenty years of the century were also a period of intense labor radicalism—of the Industrial Workers of the World (IWW) and their leg-endary leaders Bill Haywood, Elizabeth Flynn, Carlo Tresca, Mary Jones—and of legendary labor conflicts, too: Lawrence, Paterson, the New York garment strikes. It was a period in which the Socialist Party enjoyed un-precedented, never-repeated success, with nearly one million votes for So-cialist presidential candidate Eugene Debs in 1912, and Socialist represen-tatives in office in a number of U.S. cities. In her autobiographical novel *The Eleventh Virgin* (1924), Dorothy Day's listing of the stories typically covered by a young journalist working for a radical newspaper conveys something of the hectic fervor of the times:

There was much to do—meetings to attend of protest against labor, capital, the high cost of living, war-profiteering. . . . There were meet-ings to start strikes, to end strikes, to form unions, to fight against other unions. Food riots came. The city hall was stormed—if you can call it storming (as the papers did) when a crowd of fat Jewish women from the East Side with babies in their arms stood in front of the city hall and scolded that institution. . . . There were birth control meet-ings—trials of birth control leaders, meetings of the Anti-conscription League, the Emergency Peace Federation—and interviews galore. (113–114)

Clearly, there was much in such a milieu for *The Masses* to address. While its editors aimed to be radical, they aimed to be so in a pluralistic, nondogmatic spirit. Thus, they published stinging anticapitalist polemic, but also a good deal of work that was overtly, playfully, apolitical. They were intellectually eclectic, as interested in psychoanalysis as in socialism, in feminism as in free verse. Such eclecticism, what Leslie Fishbein has called a refusal "to discriminate among pleasing ideas"[6] has drawn criticism from chroniclers of *The Masses* who charge that such lack of intellectual rigor in the long run rendered *Masses* radicals incapable of dealing with the ideological and political crises of the period during and after the First World War. On the other hand, by this very eclecticism, they did, it might be suggested, escape the doctrinaire rigidity of some later, Stalinist-influenced American leftists. Max Eastman, *Masses* editor-in-chief for five years of the magazine's short life, grasped the value of the nondogmatic approach to those socialists who also considered themselves feminists, and vice versa: "This freedom enabled us to join independently in the struggle for racial equality, for women's rights, for intelligent sex relations, above all (and beneath all) for birth and population control."[7]

The Masses was founded by Piet Vlag, a Dutch anarchist, manager of a cooperative restaurant in Greenwich Village. It was Vlag who brought together three of the original women members of the *Masses* editorial collective, Inez Haynes Irwin, Mary Heaton Vorse, and Alice Beach Winter, with Charles Winter, Art Young, John Sloan, and Louis Untermeyer. After a little more than a year, this original *Masses* went bankrupt. The founding members invited Max Eastman to be editor, in the memorable lines, endorsed by the entire committee: "You are elected editor of *The Masses*. No pay." Major factors in the choice of Eastman were the feminist background of his family (his mother was a celebrated church minister known for her eloquent oratory) and his own record as a speaker on woman suffrage who had organized a Men's League for Woman Suffrage. Eastman immediately set about putting the magazine on a more solid financial footing, with the very practical aid of the office manager Dolly Sloan, "a tiny, vital, scrappy, devoted, emotional organizer of socialist locals." Until Eastman's arrival, or so he claimed, "There was no one in that bunch of utopians with whom she could even discuss such a question, for instance, as paying the rent. . . ."[8] Eastman may exaggerate a little here; certainly neither Irwin nor Vorse, judging by the evidence of their subsequent careers in journalism and labor organizing, was as impractical as Eastman's generalization would suggest. No doubt, however, the more practical elements on the *Masses* board were too preoccupied with the numerous other social causes for which they worked to pay the financial affairs of *The Masses* much-needed attention.

In a period when socialist and other radical magazines could be numbered in the hundreds, *The Masses* quickly became recognized as one of the most controversial. Its manifesto declared it

> a revolutionary and not a reform magazine; a magazine with a sense of humor and no respect for the respectable; frank, arrogant, impertinent, searching for the true causes; a magazine directed against rigidity and dogma wherever it is found; printing what is too naked or true for a money-making press; a magazine whose final policy is to do as it pleases and conciliate nobody, not even its readers. (Eastman, *Enjoyment*, 421)

Arturo Giovannitti called it "the recording secretary of the Revolution in the making." For Floyd Dell, *Masses* Associate Editor, the magazine stood for "fun, truth, beauty, realism, freedom, peace, feminism, revolution" (558–559).

Masses editors and contributors were interested in numerous (mostly controversial) social causes, but also in art and literature. They aimed to be occasionally funny and irreverent, but fundamentally serious about their subject matter. They succeeded so well that *The Masses* acquired a fame—indeed a notoriety—out of all proportion to its circulation, which at its peak never exceeded tens of thousands. As Max Eastman succinctly expressed it, *The Masses* was

> kicked off the subway stands in New York, suppressed by the Magazine Distributing Company in Boston, ejected by the United News Company of Philadelphia, expelled from the Columbia University library and bookstore, stopped at the borders by Canada, and swept out of colleges and reading rooms from Harvard to San Diego. (*Enjoyment*, 474)

Masses readers sometimes wrote in to complain when they thought the magazine overstepped the bounds of propriety. When it published a poem about the puzzlement of Joseph over the pregnancy of the Virgin Mary, a reader named Mary Sanford was only one of those who demanded "*Please* do not let me receive the paper again." On the other hand, socialist writers Upton Sinclair and George Bernard Shaw were loyal allies of *The Masses*. Shaw wrote in to praise—and on one occasion to scold—*Masses* editors for a perceived "falling off" in standards. John Dos Passos recalls how, as a young man, he would eagerly await the appearance of each new issue of *The Masses* hot from the press. When, in 1913, the Associated Press charged *The Masses* editors with criminal libel, Charlotte Perkins Gilman and the suffragist leader Inez Milholland spoke in the magazine's defense.[9]

The Masses paid nothing for published contributions, yet was inundated

UNTITLED CIRCUS SCENE, CORNELIA BARNS.
(Courtesy General Research Division, The New York Public Library, Astor, Lenox and Tilden Foundations.)

with manuscripts. In February 1917 the editors printed a plea for stamped self-addressed envelopes to accompany submissions. "We get almost a thousand MSS a month," the editors complained, "and we are becoming swamped!" (41).

Apart from these unknown, or little known, contributions, *The Masses* published some famous writers and artists: Amy Lowell, Pablo Picasso, John Reed, Bertrand Russell, Sara Bard Field, Mary White Ovington (a founder of the National Association for the Advancement of Colored People), and international pacifist Rosika Schwimmer. Dorothy Day later recalled how, as editor's assistant in the summer of 1917, she "answered the mail and sent back the work of some eminent poets with rejection slips." As Day explains in her autobiography *The Long Loneliness,* "It was considered an honor to have one's work published by *The Masses.*"[10]

It seems worth pondering the irony of a feminist magazine's being remembered primarily for its male contributors. True, the majority of editors and contributing editors on the *Masses* permanent staff were men, but of the minority of women, three—fiction editor Inez Haynes Irwin, contributing editor Mary Heaton Vorse, and contributing editor Alice Winter—were among those Eastman believed "really cared about the magazine" (*Enjoyment,* 399). The well-known labor analyst and activist Helen Marot was another cooperative owner and regular contributor. The anthropologist Elsie Clews Parsons and the poets Sarah Cleghorn, Lydia Gibson, and Jean Starr Untermeyer published articles and verse throughout the magazine's lifetime. Others, like Dorothy Day, Helen Hull, and Susan Glaspell, published early work in *The Masses,* establishing reputations later. Some of the most effective and wittiest cartoons were the work of female artists. Then there were the dozens of single contributions by unknown women, for whom the magazine provided a publication opening.

Some feminist work in *The Masses* would have been too controversial for publication in less radical journals of the time—a poem by Helen Hoyt about menstruation, for instance, or Elizabeth Grieg's drawing of an unmarried mother, captioned "Well, every baby can't have a regular father, I suppose" (Feb. 1914: 13). Even feminist statements of the most general kind might be viewed with caution by mass-circulation magazines. When, in 1912, Inez Haynes Irwin wrote for *Harper's Bazaar* on the exclusion of women from full participation in social life, the editors published the piece with a disclaimer: "The opinions expressed in this article are those of the writer. They are not the opinions of the editors, nor are they in harmony with the editorial policy of [the *Bazaar*]. They are published because experience shows that our readers always enjoy a new point of view, even when they do not share it."[11] When, in August of the same year, *The Masses* published "As Mars Sees Us," Irwin's satiric sketch on masculine

"AT THE CITY HOSPITAL," ELIZABETH GRIEG.
"Well, every baby can't have a regular father, I suppose."
(Courtesy General Research Division, The New York Public Library, Astor, Lenox and Tilden Foundations.)

stereotypes of femininity, no such disclaimer was necessary. Women poets wrote for *The Masses* about the sexual frustration of single women, about the oppression of daughters and wives, about the goddess Artemis as lover of her female devotees—topics that, in the late 1900s, could be handled in the pages of a few small-circulation poetry magazines, but not in the mass-circulation press, nor in more orthodox (and often puritanical) left-wing papers.[12] *The Masses* thus has to be understood as a feminist magazine not only in name, but for what women themselves made of it.

One explanation for the neglect of women's part in shaping *The Masses* and its content may lie in an image of the magazine constructed by its chroniclers. Indeed, the extent to which historians have neglected discussion of *Masses* women is quite remarkable. Daniel Aaron, in his *Writers on the Left* (1961), devotes some twenty pages to *The Masses*. He deals with Eastman, Dell, and Reed at considerable length, while mentioning the founding members Irwin and Vorse in a single line (22). Even more remarkable is Irving Howe's introduction to William L. O'Neill's 1966 *Masses* anthology, *Echoes of Revolt*. While O'Neill himself does include a representative selection of work by *Masses* women in the anthology, Howe achieves the remarkable feat of writing his entire introduction without mentioning a single female contributor. Howe concludes resoundingly: "For who among us . . . would not change places with the men of *The Masses* in their days of glory?" (27) More recent histories redress the balance somewhat—notably Judith Schwartz's study of women of the Greenwich Village Heterodoxy club, many of whose members had ties with *The Masses,* and *Art for "The Masses,"* Rebecca Zurier's 1987 anthology of the work of *Masses* artists.[13] Nancy Cott's frequent allusions to *Masses* women in *The Grounding of Modern Feminism* (1987) indicate how very central to that grounding, to the shaping of turn-of-the-century feminist discourse, *Masses* women were. But in many imaginations, *The Masses* remains the project of Eastman, Dell, Reed, Art Young, and Charles Winter.

Of those women who actually took part in the editing of *The Masses,* one of the most committed and earliest to join the staff was Inez Haynes Irwin (then Inez Haynes Gillmore). Piet Vlag chose her as fiction editor for her already established reputation as a writer of popular fiction; but no doubt also for her credentials as a reporter on labor struggles in rural California. Among conservatives these activities had earned Irwin the name, in which she took a certain humorous pride, of "the reddest woman in America." As Irwin recalled, the experience of editing gave her both an unaccustomed sense of power, and a new perspective on the relations of editor and magazine contributor. She had almost as much qualification for the position of magazine editor, she wrote years later in her autobiography, "as for work on the atomic bomb." However, this initial sense of inexperience did not prevent her from accepting the post "with enthusiasm" ("Adventures," 323). While, as a writer, she had always "hated the fiction editor who suggested cuts or changes" in her work, Irwin confessed that, as soon as she became an editor herself, she "began cutting down and rewriting the stuff that came in," as if she "had been born in an editorial chair" (391).

Like Irwin, Mary Heaton Vorse already enjoyed an established literary reputation when she became one of the first editors and cooperative owners of *The Masses.* Although she had written articles on social issues, Vorse's fame as a labor reporter and foreign correspondent still lay largely in the future. Thus, it was mainly for novels such as *The Autobiography of an Elderly Woman* (1911), and for her stories in *Harper's, Scribner's,* and *Atlantic Monthly,* that Gillmore invited her to write for *The Masses.* Vorse later gave a lively account of the editorial decision-making process at *Masses* manuscript selection sessions, which were often held at her house. An intense rivalry existed between *Masses* writers and artists, as the latter "would try to get all the space in the magazine. . . . The writers had to

Inez Haynes Irwin. (The Schlesinger Library, Radcliffe College.)

fight for any room at all."[14] Some writers suffered acute embarrassment at having their work dissected before an exacting and sometimes unsympathetic audience:

> It might be the work of an outsider, or it might come from one of the editors. As Floyd read along, Sloan would give a groan. . . . A voice would say, "Oh, my God, Max, do we have to listen to this tripe?"
> . . . The poor author would feel more and more like a worm. You could see him looking wildly around to see if there was a swift exit.
> (*Footnote to Folly,* 42)

"Nothing more horrible can be imagined," Vorse considered, than this "dismemberment" of one's work by the artists. On the other hand, "there was no greater reward than having them stop their groans and catcalls and give close attention, then laughter if the piece was funny, finally applause" (*Footnote to Folly,* 42).

During the period of her connection with *The Masses,* Vorse was variously involved with strike reporting, membership in suffrage committees, war reporting and anti-war activism, the legal defense of the birth control educator Margaret Sanger, and the writing of light fiction to support her children, about whose inevitable neglect she felt acutely guilty. Little wonder that, as Eastman recalls, Vorse, although "abounding in energy," wore "a permanently weary look" (*Enjoyment,* 399). Yet she still found time both to contribute actively to those famous *Masses* meetings and to write regularly, unpaid, for the *Masses* fiction pages.

Other women called upon to take part in the *Masses* editorial process were Cornelia Barns and Alice Beach Winter, as contributing art editors; Mabel Dodge, whom Max Eastman asked to edit an issue in the spring of 1914 (Dodge, *Movers and Shakers,* 154), and Dorothy Day, in her brief tenure of the editor's chair during the summer of 1917. Day's task was to select poems and drawings from the "slush pile" of all submitted manuscripts for later evaluation at meetings—a task which Floyd Dell had delegated to Day because he wanted time to work on a novel. Dell remembered Day as "an awkward and charming young enthusiast, with beautiful slanting eyes, who had been a reporter and subsequently was one of the militant suffragists who were imprisoned in Washington."[15] Day took her responsibilities fairly lightly, taking "not more than a few hours every morning" for her work, and finding time to enjoy leisured afternoons and evenings with Greenwich Village friends (*Long Loneliness,* 66–67).

One irony about the day-to-day running of *The Masses* was the degree to which the magazine depended on wealthy women who acted as its financial backers. The irony of a group of millionaires lending their financial support to the survival of a magazine whose long-term end was to render

their class obsolete was not lost on Max Eastman. Eastman gives an amusing account of some of those to whom he turned for help to pull *The
Masses* out of its recurrent financial crises. The wealthy, and formidable,
backer of the militant suffrage movement, Mrs. O. H. P. Belmont, was
one. "She doesn't know anything about socialism. Just tell her it's a fight
and she'll like it," was the advice of the suffragist Inez Milholland before
introducing Eastman to this prospective patron. A donor who gave with a
better sense of the uses to which her gift would be put was Aline Barnsdall,
who wrote a $5000 check to *The Masses* with the words "Congratulations
on your stand against the war" (*Enjoyment,* 463). "Such," wrote Eastman,
"was the economic character of *The Masses,* a luxurious gift to the working-
class movement from the most imaginative artists . . . and the most imaginative millionaires in the Adolescence of the Twentieth Century" (*Enjoyment,* 463).

Between Piet Vlag's editorial tenure and that of Max Eastman, a change
in the magazine's tone is apparent—particularly in the style of its nonfictional prose. Articles in *The Masses* in the year before Eastman's editorship
tend to be not only serious, but solemn. Typical of the early style in this
respect are the articles contributed by the socialist orator Lena Morrow
Lewis. Lewis, praised in a *Masses* article by Ethel Lloyd Patterson for her
"wonderful work for socialism," was a staunch, indefatigable activist, who
could claim never to have spent more than fourteen consecutive days under the same roof for the space of seventeen years, so dedicated was she to
spreading the socialist message.[16] Lewis' *Masses* articles, published between December 1911 and April 1912, have titles like "Jeffersonianism vs.
Social Democracy," "Working Class Politics in America," and "The Sex
and Woman Questions." "The Sex and Woman Questions" begins, "The
tendency of some people to confound the woman question with the sex
question evidences a lack of scientific knowledge." It concludes porten-
tously, "The Co-operative Commonwealth will give us a new and higher
standard of morality" (Feb. 1912: 9).

Very different are the writings of a majority of later prose writers for
The Masses. Although these writers are no less committed to social change
than their predecessors, their polemical methods are more often those of
the satirist than of the preacher. In "San Francisco and the Bomb" (October 1916), the poet and suffragist Sara Bard Field writes on the very grim
subject of the bombing that year at a militaristic "Preparedness" parade in
San Francisco, in which nine bystanders were killed and some forty others
injured. The incident proved to offer a pretext for wholesale repression of
the San Francisco labor movement, and resulted in the jailing of Warren
Billings and Thomas Mooney, even though the evidence pointed to the innocence of both labor leaders. In writing of the Preparedness Day bombing, Field captures some of the paranoia, and the cynicism, of the public

response by a tone which treads a fine line between facetiousness and grim satire: "O divine Providence! O beloved Bomb! You have exploded at the right time. You are the missing link between what we, Big Business, wanted to do and how it is to be done. . . . Profitable indeed to capital has been this tragedy" (16). In similar vein, Helen Marot, in discussing the fight of railroad workers for an eight-hour day, employs a dry irony. The Atcheson and Topeka Railroad had announced that it would disregard the Act of Congress which mandated the eight-hour day, and would appeal to the Supreme Court. "They probably know their Supreme Court," Marot comments. She adds, "I wonder if they remember that the seeds of rebellion have flourished in the hearts of just such gentle and righteous people as Mr. Garretson and his Railroad brotherhoods represent?" ("Railroads and Revolution," Nov. 1916: 5).

The actual number of nonfiction prose pieces by women seems to have dropped after Max Eastman became editor-in-chief; but this decrease was partly offset by the addition of a new woman artist, Cornelia Barns, by the continuing participation of women fiction writers, and by an expansion of the *Masses* poetry section, to which numerous women contributed. It was during Eastman's editorship, too, that Elsie Clews Parsons and Dorothy Day became regular journalistic contributors.[17]

The regular *Masses* staff after 1914 included two women artists. Alice Beach Winter was one of the oldest contributors. While her husband, Charles Winter, drew images for *The Masses* of titanic, muscular workers, Alice Beach Winter, who had received her artist's training at the St. Louis School of Fine Arts before becoming a painter of society portraits, inclined more to pathos—indeed, to sentimentality. She employed her gift as "the Norman Rockwell of the Left"[18] in the service of socialist causes, and was a dedicated member of New York's Branch One of the Socialist Party. Less sentimental, and more original, is the work of Cornelia Barns. Besides her work for *The Masses,* Barns, who had studied at the Philadelphia Academy of Fine Arts, drew illustrations for *Sunset* magazine, *The Suffragist,* and the *New York World,* and drew and edited for the *Birth Control Review.* Eastman called her work "brilliantly comic . . . not like anything else in the world." He considered her to possess "an instinct for the comic in pictorial art that few artists have ever surpassed."[19] "Art and Humor," an essay by Edmond McKenna in *The Masses* for June 1915, devotes a section to Barns' work. Despite some quite startlingly sexist remarks about feminists' alleged lack of a sense of humor, McKenna's overall assessment is an enthusiastic tribute to Barns' own sharply feminist sense of the absurdity of the American male's pretensions to self-importance—as McKenna points out, a fit revenge on generations of artists who treated women as the butt of sexist jokes:

"LORDS OF CREATION," CORNELIA BARNS.
"Moisten your lips a little—there—that's perfect."
(Courtesy General Research Division, The New York Public Library, Astor, Lenox and Tilden Foundations.)

She saw the young American Male, callow, sallow, silly. She made pictures of this Lord of all he leered at and sneered at. In cigar stores, by the soda fountain, in street cars and in pool rooms she tracked this callow cub and set him down just as he is, as an example and for a warning. (10)

For this achievement alone, McKenna considers, Barns deserves "a triple crown" (10).

Like Alice Beach Winter, Barns was a member of the Socialist Party. Her left-wing and pacifist cartoons, like her drawings of oafish-looking males, were a hallmark of *The Masses*. But she produced much work that was exuberant, playful, without overt political purpose—for example, her strikingly original view of a woman declaring to her companion, "My Dear, I'll be economically independent if I have to borrow every cent!"

"LOOK WHAT I GOTTA CARRY," ALICE BEACH WINTER.
"Quit cher bellerin'! Look what I gotta carry! Look what we all gotta carry!"
(Courtesy General Research Division, The New York Public Library, Astor, Lenox and Tilden Foundations.)

"MY DEAR, I'LL BE ECONOMICALLY INDEPENDENT IF I HAVE TO BORROW
EVERY CENT!" CORNELIA BARNS.
(Courtesy General Research Division, The New York Public Library, As-
tor, Lenox and Tilden Foundations.)

(March 1915) or her somewhat amateurish-looking bareback rider, teeter-
ing nervously and excitedly on the rear of an implacably cantering horse,
that appeared on the cover of *The Masses* for November/December 1917.
Tuberculosis forced Barns to leave New York for California in that year,
but she continued to do regular work for the *Oakland Post Enquirer,* and
to draw for *Sunset* magazine, the *Liberator* (successor to *The Masses*), *New
York World,* and *The Suffragist.*

Masses fiction writers were, if anything, as diverse in their styles and
approaches to their subject matter as *Masses* artists. They wrote stories of
social protest, like Helen R. Hull's "Mothers Still," about an upper-class
family's mistreatment of a pregnant servant woman, or Dorothy Weil's "A
New Woman?" about an unmarried mother—and many others in a similar
vein. They published gentle, and sometimes not-so-gentle, satires on domestic life—Mary Heaton Vorse's "Tolerance," for instance, which deals

with the relationship of an Irish and a German immigrant family in an industrial town. Another story by Vorse, "The Happy Woman," is an amoral tale which tells how a couple successfully evades the clutches of the law after the husband has embezzled money from his firm. More predictably, Vorse's "The Day of a Man" recounts the final day in the life of a homeless social outcast, who redeems his dignity by dying to save a boy from drowning. More surprisingly, writers published "society fiction," such as Inez Haynes Irwin's "The Other Way" and "Henry," featuring very unproletarian characters: "Grefe-Saunders was somebody no matter where you found him. . . . Two years after leaving, Harvard had returned him monocled, hyphenated, accented and so well-dressed that his mere clothes constituted a bond between him and every woman he met . . ." ("Henry," Dec. 1911, 15). They probed the experience of unhappy love, as in Mabel Dodge's "A Quarrel" and "The Parting." They wrote stories of immigrant life, like Adriana Spadoni's "A Rift of Silence" and Hull's "Yellow Hair." Arguably, some of the best fiction in *The Masses* was brought to it by women—and certainly much of its variety.

Women poets brought an even more dazzling variety to *The Masses* than the magazine's fiction writers. There are dramatic monologues like Amy Lowell's "In the Grocery" and Mary Aldis' "The Barber Shop." "The Barber Shop" (Apr. 1916) portrays a puritanical and lonely upper-class male who discovers passion during a visit to the manicurist:

> I looked at her young wet eyes,
> At her abashed bent head,
> Looked at her sweet deft hands
> Busy with mine . . .
> But—
> Not for nothing
> Were my grandfather and four of my uncles
> Elders in the Sixth Presbyterian Church
> Situated on the Avenue—
> Oh not for nothing
> Was I led
> To squirm on those green rep seats
> One day in seven—
> And now
> The white-tiled, sweetly-smelling barber shop
> Is lost to me.
> What a pity!

(23)

There is humorous doggerel, like Mary Field's "Justice": "Sing a song of lawyers, / Pockets full of dough, / Four and twenty legal lights / Defending rich John Roe . . ." (June 1916: 23); or Laura Simmons' vision of Whitman at the lunch counter: "O High Cost of Everything! Oh Grafters! Oh, Food-Sharks! / I will have ham instead. . . ." ("Blades of Grass," Oct. 1917: 43). There are overtly polemical pieces. Elizabeth Waddell's call to revolution, "The Sword of Flame," for instance, appropriates for radical socialist purposes Christ's assurance that he came to bring not peace, but a sword. Waddell's poem represents that sword "Pointing its own burning way to a better Paradise to come . . ." (Dec. 1913: 3). In Babette Deutsch's "Extra," a middle-class woman in her comfortable apartment hears the cry of newsboys in the street. To her, the sound evokes images of the sufferings of workers and prisoners, and of "twisted bodies in the bloodstained dirt." Abruptly, these images are supplanted by that of a female voice, crying from "some Amazonian throat" for "bread, / and roses too . . ." (the famous demand of the workers in the 1912 Lawrence textile strike). This female cry is, in turn, conflated with that of "a world in torment." Its antidote will be, in Deutsch's words, "the conquering fires / Of unappeasable desires," in their power to "Quicken men's raptures and men's agonies" (Nov./Dec. 1917: 37).

Much *Masses* poetry written by women functions as both intimate autobiography and public manifesto. In their verses, *Masses* women seek to fashion new feminine/feminist identities in challenge to a contested patriarchal order. In "Zanesville," the name of her birthplace, Jean Starr Untermeyer writes of a woman's refusal to be treated like the clay of the "unaspiring" hills, to be shaped by the will of Man into "vases and cups of an old pattern." She will, rather, be her "own creator, / Dragging myself from the clinging mud," to mold herself into "fresh and lovelier shapes" (Oct. 1916: 20). "Comparison," by Helen Hoyt, on the other hand, seeks to reshape, not the feminine psyche, but traditional conceptions of the female body. In "Comparison," a woman gazes at her male lover's body, contrasting it with her own. In tones of awe, she describes the male body as like "the shaft of a strong pillar, / Or brawny tree-trunk, firm and round and hard," and adds, "How frail I look next thee!" Then, reversing this denigration of her own body in comparison with the male's phallic attributes, she adds, "And yet, I think I like my own self better: / What has thy body lovely as my breasts?" (Sep. 1915: 16).

Masses women poets also examined the sometimes heavy price exacted from women who sought self-realization outside of traditional feminine domestic roles. The social isolation of many turn-of-the-century women who left the confines of family life in quest of self-identity finds expression in Mary Bradley's "A Stranger in the City":

It is loneliest when the lights spring out,
When the city turns from working to pleasure,
And the shop girls put on rouge before the mirrors,
Anticipating, expecting. . . ."

Her working day over, the lonely stranger finds herself excluded from participation in the meetings of lovers and the affairs of workers with "the
look of home-going in their eyes." Her own destinations after the day's
work are "my room in the boarding house or the movies—alone— / I go
up the stairs slowly!" (Mar. 1917: 40). In Jeannette Eaton's "Rebellion," a
professional woman wanders isolated in a city crowd, reflecting ironically
on her career achievement, as assessed in material terms: "Success is mine,
quoted at market rate." Amid this apparent fulfillment, however, biology
takes its revenge: "I hate my barren years, / When heart and soul and blood
long for a mate!" It should be added that the speaker's ideal of a sexual
partner appears surprisingly conventional. She yearns for "A mate, greater
than I, of splendid mould. . . ." That this ideal is presented not without
irony, however, may be surmised from the poem's close. Returning to her
office from the crowded street the speaker reflects—gratefully, this time—
"I am alone—alone." Solitude now becomes a condition of possibility—"I
can take my seat / Before the piled up work awaiting me"—and of liberation—"Far out beyond my window lies the sea, / Freedom—great spaces
where the wind blows sweet" (Aug. 1917: 23). Still, the reader is left with
the troubling implication that a satisfactory sexual relationship would, by
definition, preclude access to such freedom.

A number of poems recuperate traditionally denigrated female biological functions in the name of the new feminism. As Cary Nelson has suggested, the apparent sentimentality of much *Masses* poetry is better understood within the verse's sociocultural context.[20] Helen Hoyt's "Menaia,"
which celebrates menstruation, is a case in point. Admittedly, the poem
does indulge in essentialist mystification:

Always returning,
Comes mystery
and possesses me
And uses me
As the moon uses the waters.
                    (Sept. 1915: 16)

However, such mystification may be read in the light of a contemporary
superstitious dread of female biological functions—of what one contem-

porary medical authority, quoted in *The Masses* as the butt of editorial satire, called "the reverberations of woman's physiological emergencies."[21] Given this context, Hoyt's poem may be seen as an empowering gesture, a spirited assertion of resistance to a tradition of furtive secrecy and of repression of feminine sexuality.

For some *Masses* poets, the quest for self-fashioning demanded new role models, some of whom might be found among contemporaries. Josephine Bell's "Mighty Fires" praises the dancer Isadora Duncan as one such source of inspiration, for her liberation of the body from shame, for "Giving us back our happy bodies," and for dispelling "All our ancient, awkward, hooded modesty . . ." (June 1917: 43). In "Woman Returning," on the other hand, Marguerite Wilkinson invokes an idealized, imaginary figure of pre-patriarchal, primeval woman, formerly a "queen dethroned, a faith un-honored," but now "Strong to seek her own and reign" (Oct./Nov. 1915: 6). A third source of inspiration for feminist self-fashioning is that of classical mythology. "Artemis," by Lydia Gibson, finds in the virgin moon god-dess, the "childless and husbandless," a fit "mother" and "lover" of strong and liberated women who have outgrown dependency on Mary, the ideal mother of centuries of patriarchal tradition: "Ye pray to your motherly Marys; but I am the ultimate one" (Mar. 1915: 11).

Gibson's "Artemis" is fairly unusual in *The Masses* in its celebration of homosexual desire. More often, *Masses* women rest content with celebrat-ing heterosexual desire, defending it against sociocultural construction as evil or shameful. For example, Helen Hoyt's "Golden Bough" calls for lovemaking to take place in outdoor surroundings, "Free as when love first loved beneath the sky" (Aug. 1916: 14). Nan Apotheker's "In the Hallway" protests the secrecy in which a younger sister has to meet her lover, "Start-ing at every sound she hears / In the midst of her shy, sweet kisses," and rejoices in the triumph over social repression represented by the sight of her sister undressing, later that evening, before the mirror: "Her lips touched with a sweet expectancy . . . / Her soul lit with the sheer, young joy of living . . ." (Sept. 1917: 42).

For some *Masses* contributors, publication in *The Masses* might be a "guest appearance," as it was for the NAACP founder Mary White Ovington, or for international feminist and pacifist Rosika Schwimmer, or for Susan Glaspell, in her obituary poem for Mary Heaton Vorse's husband, Joe O'Brien, who died in 1915:

Much I do not know, but this I know—
You saw things straight; nobody put it over very hard on you. . . .
Strong clear violet; the flash of steel;
The life of the party—a tree way off by itself. . . .[22]

Another "guest" was Amy Lowell, who contributed her poem about a poem:

It was only a little twig
With a green bud at the end;
But if you plant it,
And water it,
And set it where the sun will be above it,
It will grow into a tall bush
With many flowers,
And leaves that thrust hither and thither. . . .
                        (Apr. 16: 21)

On the other hand, some contributors, like Barns, did their best work for *The Masses*. For others still—for Helen R. Hull, or the poets Babette Deutsch or Sarah N. Cleghorn—publication in *The Masses* marked only the beginning of long, productive careers. In her autobiographical novel *The Spinster* (1916), Cleghorn portrays the rapturous excitement with which a young woman receives the news that "The Proletarian" has published her poem, the first to appear in print. She goes off to sleep that night, happily treasuring the letter of acceptance.

For a number of contributors *The Masses* was a diversion from other activities. When not writing for the magazine, its most regular contributors, like their male counterparts, tended to be busily involved with a bewildering variety of causes. Dolly Sloan, like Alice Beach Winter and Cornelia Barns, was active in the Socialist Party, and distributed Socialist literature on street corners. Mary Heaton Vorse, Elsie Clews Parsons, and Rose Pastor Stokes fought on behalf of Margaret Sanger, prosecuted in 1916 for teaching working class women about birth control. Helen Marot, through the Women's Trade Union League, organized strikers, earning praise in contemporary reports for her skillful management of the 1909 New York garment workers' strike. Mabel Dodge, who was later to join her friend Elsie Clews Parsons as a fighter for the rights of Native Americans, conceived of, and aided John Reed and Dolly Sloan in staging, the famous Paterson Pageant in New York in 1913, in which striking silk workers from Paterson reenacted their struggles in dramatized form, to a deeply moved audience of New Yorkers. Dorothy Day, Louise Bryant, and Inez Irwin worked in the woman suffrage campaign.[23] The poet Sarah Cleghorn took part in peace marches. She writes dramatically of one such Socialist-organized postwar march in her autobiography, *Threescore* (1936):

Our celebration was to end in a meeting at Carnegie Hall. No sooner had we turned the corner than a little body of men in uniform attacked us. My partner was wounded in the hand, and blood flowed from it. . . . I saw two more khaki uniforms coming towards us, and ran over to them and seized one of them by the sleeve, without premeditation saying in ladylike tones, "Please don't!" They hesitated and then turned back. I was rather thrilled to have been in the mêlée, small as it was. (215)

In a number of their activities, as in their personal lives, *Masses* women strongly supported one another. One focal point for such cooperation and support was the Greenwich Village club known as Heterodoxy, sole membership condition for which was that a woman should hold unorthodox views. Not surprisingly, a disproportionate number of Heterodoxy members were also *Masses* contributors: Vorse, Irwin, Elizabeth Gurley Flynn, Alice Duer Miller, Helen Hull, Mabel Dodge, Elsie Clews Parsons, Rose Pastor Stokes, Margaret Widdemer, and Susan Glaspell. At Heterodoxy they met other independent-minded women: Charlotte Perkins Gilman, Crystal Eastman, Mary Ware Dennett. At Heterodoxy Irwin enjoyed Vorse's analyses of contemporary politics and colorful stories of her European travels, and appreciated what she calls the "silver-dirk wit" of *Masses* poet Margaret Widdemer. "A safe refuge" is how Mabel Dodge recalled such gatherings. To Helen Hull, they offered to women who had "stepped out of their grooves" the "solidarity feeling" that workers seek in their unions, "and women so much lack."[24]

For some, the bonds women formed in their years in Greenwich Village endured for decades. Mary Heaton Vorse and Elizabeth Gurley Flynn, for instance, worked closely together during the years of their association with *The Masses* and for many years after as labor organizers and publicists. In September 1939, Flynn wrote to Vorse from the Mesaba Range in Minnesota, scene of past labor battles, sending "love as always, dear Mary, from one who thinks fondly of you and our fighting past in such spots as this. . . ."[25] Flynn also advised and supported Vorse in 1920, during her unhappy relationship with Robert Minor.[26] The two remained friends well into the 1950s. Mary Vorse and Babette Deutsch retained close ties, Deutsch reading and commenting enthusiastically on Vorse's writing.[27] Long after the demise of *The Masses,* Elsie Clews Parsons and Mabel Dodge found a new common interest in their shared fascination with the Native American culture of New Mexico.[28]

Some discussion seems in order here of the relations of *Masses* women with *Masses* men. Much has been made in some histories of *The Masses* of women's alleged sexual exploitation by the freeloving Greenwich Village male. Relations *were* rendered complicated between *Masses* women and men like Louise Bryant, Mabel Dodge, John Reed, and Max Eastman, who actually lived in Greenwich Village and participated in its bohemian lifestyle. (Max Eastman, for instance, pursued other women compulsively while his marriage to Ida Rauh steadily fell apart, while Louise Bryant seems to have been less than totally faithful to John Reed.[29] On the other hand, many *Masses* contributors of both sexes remained more or less monogamous; some, like Elsie Clews Parsons, exercising their feminist rights in occasional extramarital affairs. Others, like Helen Hull, who remained faithful to Mabel Louise Robinson through a lifetime, formed long-standing gay relationships. Dorothy Day, during the time of her association with *The Masses,* shared an apartment with a group of men purely as a convenient economic arrangement.[30]

The predominantly male editors of *The Masses* were as capable of patronizing and sexist attitudes toward the women who drew and wrote for the magazine as were less would-be liberated men. Max Eastman deeply admired the work of Cornelia Barns, but apparently experienced no sense of incongruity in referring to this woman of twenty-four as "an elf-eyed girl" (*Enjoyment,* 407) who "came through the door of the *Masses* like a child into a playroom" (*Love and Revolution,* 23), or in characterizing the well-known labor analyst, organizer, and editor Helen Marot as "a charming and sophisticated old maid" (4). In this respect, they were at least no worse than most of their contemporaries.

It must also be said that the men of *The Masses* did for the most part express a warm respect for their fellow-workers' qualities of character and intellect. Max Eastman recalls his first impressions of Elizabeth Gurley Flynn as he saw her in 1913, speaking to the striking workers of Paterson. He admired her "earnest and sensible" speech and demeanor, her clear-headed and thorough attention to mundane organizational details: "Stand firm and come to me with your problems, you can trust me, she seemed to be saying" (*Enjoyment,* 447). Flynn later appeared as a character in Eastman's autobiographical novel, *Venture.*[31] Art Young writes in his memoir *On My Way* (1928) of the deceptively unimpressive and unassuming external appearance of Mary Heaton Vorse. It was knowing "her work, and herself better than slightly, that made her admired of the many who made up our meetings," wrote Young of his time with Vorse on the staff of *The Masses* (286). Later, he would write to Vorse herself that he felt even this sympathetic portrait had not really done her justice: " . . . How little I said in my book about you—compared to the intense admiration I have had for you and your work these many years. I am really afraid of getting sentimental and even 'mushy' about you—when I take my pen in hand. . . ."[32] No doubt Young's affectionate feelings about Vorse were blended with a certain nostalgia for the heady days of the boldly experimental, ideologically fearless, and inevitably short-lived *Masses.*

The events leading to the demise of *The Masses* have been recounted often. In April 1918, Max Eastman, Floyd Dell, Merrill Rogers, and Josephine Bell were prosecuted under the wartime Espionage Act, on a charge of conspiracy to "obstruct the recruiting and enlistment service" of the United States. The inclusion of Bell in the conspiracy charge was particularly absurd, since she had only recently begun publishing in *The Masses,* and had never met any of the other defendants until the day of the trial.[33]

The charge was a serious one. The labor activist and *Masses* contributor Rose Pastor Stokes was later to receive a ten-year prison sentence under the Espionage Act for writing to a Kansas newspaper, "I am for the people and the government is for the profiteers" (Eastman, *Love and Revolution,* 35).

The Masses had, in any case, lost its mailing privileges, over publication of part of the material which eventually brought about indictment of the editors—a ban which made it virtually impossible to continue circulating a magazine which depended so heavily on subscriptions. This first crisis occurred when Dorothy Day, who, in her capacity as temporary editor during Eastman's and Dell's absence, had been given the job of "selecting material, making up the paper" for August, included two drawings by H. J. Glintenkamp, and a poem by Josephine Bell. Bell's poem, "A Tribute" to Emma Goldman and Alexander Berkman, jailed for their stand against U.S. entry into the World War, read in part:

> Emma Goldman and Alexander Berkman
> Are in prison tonight,
> But they have made themselves elemental forces,
> Like the water that climbs down the rocks:
> Like the wind in the leaves:
> Like the gentle night that holds us:
> They are working on our destinies:
> They are forging the love of the nations. . . .
>   (Aug. 1917: 28)

As Day explains, it was material in this issue which eventually led to the *Masses* prosecutions. At least as she tells the story, no one on the magazine staff was unduly surprised by these actions by the authorities: "Suppression had been threatened for the past few months, and it was only a matter of time before the paper had to cease publication, so no one felt that I had precipitated matters."[34]

Dorothy Day, Dolly Sloan, and Inez Irwin were among those subpoenaed as witnesses for the prosecution. In fact, Day worked closely with the defendants' lawyer, Morris Hillquit, who coached her in order to make the best possible impression in the defendants' favor. "I was a bad witness for the state and a good one for the defense," Day recalled later (*Long Loneliness,* 85).

Continuation of *The Masses* under its old name and with its old form of quasi-cooperative organization was now out of the question. In fact, even before a second trial and acquittal of *Masses* editors in October 1918—before the final issue of *The Masses* in November 1917—Eastman made plans to start a new magazine, owned jointly with Crystal, his sister. The first issue of *The Liberator* appeared in March 1918.

A good deal of continuity existed between the two periodicals. Like *The Masses, The Liberator* came out monthly. It retained Floyd Dell as Associate Editor, and many other former *Masses* contributors on the editorial board. Mary Heaton Vorse wrote both nonfiction and fiction for *The Liberator*—the latter a more radically polemical, less humorous type of story than she had written for *The Masses.*[35] Cornelia Barns drew extensively for the new magazine. Inez Irwin reported for it, on her experiences in France, and Louise Bryant from Russia. Lydia Gibson published more for *The Liberator* than she had in *The Masses,* becoming an art editor. Dorothy Day contributed a review of Floyd Dell's new novel and a prose sketch about a victim of poverty; Helen Marot, labor articles. There were new women's voices, notably that of the poet and artist Genevieve Taggard. The journalist and novelist Agnes Smedley, and Crystal Eastman, reported extensively from revolutionary Hungary. NAACP leader Mary White Ovington described labor and race relations in Texas. Helen Keller's name was added to the masthead, in a purely honorary capacity. She contributed one article, a defense of the Industrial Workers of the World (IWW).[36]

Eastman claimed that *The Liberator* pursued a more cautious editorial policy than that of *The Masses,* taking care not to antagonize the authorities in a period of intense upper-class anxiety about the possibility of proletarian revolution at home and abroad. In practice, contributors shrank neither from hailing the Bolshevik victories in repelling U.S. invasion of the newly founded Soviet Union, nor from confidently predicting a radical social transformation in the States. Moreover, they energetically defended those who, like the IWW labor leaders, fell victims to antiradical paranoia at home.[37] If *The Liberator* retained some of the old commitment, though, it gradually lost something in wit and fervor. The overall tone of *The Liberator* was somber compared with that of *The Masses.* In its reports on the progress of revolution in Russia and Hungary, it assumed the role Giovannitti had once claimed for *The Masses,* that of "the recording secretary of the Revolution." As editors came and went, *The Liberator* became ever more qualitatively different from its parent magazine. A new stylistic note crept in, no doubt influenced by Soviet revolutionary rhetoric. No one would ever have written an obituary for *The Masses* like one that appeared

Sarah N. Cleghorn. (H. W. Wilson Company.) (Courtesy General Research Division, The New York Public Library, Astor, Lenox and Tilden Foundations.)

in *The Liberator* for October 1923, describing the deceased Clarissa S. Ware as "intellectually capable, yet [sic!] glorious in her womanhood" (7). Eventually, after a series of mergers and changes in editorship, *The Liberator* became *The New Masses,* and semiofficially the literary magazine of the U.S. Communist Party.

For those writers and artists whose reputations were already established, the closing down of *The Masses* made no difference to the success of their future careers. For others, like the poet Elizabeth Waddell, it seems to have ended them before they began. A third group, of those who, like Hull, Spadoni, Dodge, Day, Cleghorn, Deutsch, had only just begun to find acceptance for their work, and for whom *The Masses* had provided a valuable opening, were able to find new outlets for their gifts. Hull and Spadoni both published extensively as popular novelists. Mabel Dodge became well known for her four-part autobiography, *Intimate Memories.*

Babette Deutsch.
(H. W. Wilson Company.)

Dorothy Day continued to work intermittently as a journalist, until in 1932 she discovered her vocation as a founding member of the Catholic Worker movement, and editor of its newspaper of that name. Sarah Cleghorn took up a teaching post at an experimental school run on libertarian lines for the children of socialists and pacifists. She published volumes of verse, including *Portraits and Protests* (1917) and *The Ballad of Gene Debs* (1926); an autobiography; and, in 1945, *The Seamless Robe,* a book of religious meditations. Deutsch established her reputation as a poet. For all these women, *The Masses* helped to launch careers.

But *The Masses* and its contributors are important for broader reasons than its significance to each of those who worked for it. Not least among these is its stand as a radical magazine: radical in the boldness and creativity of its feminism, radical in its attitudes to the rights of workers. In 1911, as today, this was a rare combination. Nina Bull wrote a memorable "Answer to a Critic" of *The Masses,* which expresses the *Masses'* radical spirit concisely and eloquently:

> You cannot subscribe to *The Masses,* it seems, because
> of its intolerant spirit
> And its recurrent stress on criticism and denunciation. . . .
> It is very modern—this fear of all intolerance . . .
> Jesus did not have it. . . .
>
> (Oct./Nov. 1915: 4)

In Bull's view, two human failings deserve to be treated with intolerance: "The first of these is hypocrisy, and the second is oppression" (4). As feminists who were also class-conscious radicals, *Masses* women contributors waged all-out war on both these obstacles to liberation, whether in their critiques of patriarchal ideology or of capitalism. They remain important and compelling for our own time, not only because many of them led interesting lives and made useful social contributions, but because of the social perspective which all of them—whether they called themselves socialists or Fabians, Wobblies, anarchists, or freethinkers—shared. They brought a controversial feminist perspective to challenge the sexual conservatism of the orthodox American Left—but also a firm sense of the centrality of working-class majority issues to the women's movement. A delicate balance to maintain, but one of which, at the century's end, as at its beginning, we remain sorely in need.

How individual *Masses* contributors explored the intricate relations—and occasional conflicts—between their allegiances of class and of gender will form the subject of the chapters which follow.

2

Patriarchy

"IT SEEMS TO ME that women are just as unemancipated . . . in spirit . . . as ever they were," wrote anthropologist and *Masses* contributor Elsie Clews Parsons in 1913. "Hitherto feminists have been so impressed by the institutional bondage of woman . . . that questions of inner freedom have rarely occurred to them."[1] A number of the women of *The Masses* would have agreed with her. As many of them were quick to recognize, the fight for possession of the right to vote was only one aspect of women's overall struggle for full emancipation. Equally if not more important, many of them realized, was the total revision of customs and laws shaped by a view of women as weak-minded, potentially destructive, and posing a possible threat to male supremacy—in short, by patriarchal attitudes.

These attitudes in turn shaped, and often narrowed, the experience of the working-class majority of women as much or more than they did the lives of those women of the upper classes who questioned them. Such attitudes inspired legislation on issues such as prostitution and birth control instruction with negative effects for working-class women, of which women contributors to *The Masses,* as social radicals, could hardly fail to be aware. In their prose and verse, *Masses* women debated and exposed the social consequences of these laws, as they also debated and exposed the consequences of the unwritten laws of male-female relationships in a patriarchal society. Women contributors to *The Masses* were not likely to underestimate the strength of conservative social attitudes toward gender roles, for instance, if they only glanced about them at the dedicated and actively feminist-oriented editors of the magazine. Literary editor Floyd Dell, for example, in his January 1916 article for *The Masses* "The Nature of Woman," admitted that he had long doubted the possibility of women's possession of creative ability equal to that of men: "I did not believe that women would ever successfully compete with men in distinctly creative activities." It is to Dell's credit that he expresses himself delighted to find his earnest wish to believe in women's potential for "creative genius" actually supported by contemporary findings in biology. Max Eastman—

more disturbingly, perhaps—writes in his autobiography, *Enjoyment of Living,* of Bill Haywood, leader of the IWW, as possessing a "feminine and childlike" mind: "He sensed things better than he understood them, and was more at home in figurative than analytic language" (44–49). The unconscious prejudices of these energetically committed profeminist men are indicative of the power of deeply ingrained social attitudes to imbue the thinking of even the most self-critical and well-meaning. The notions which relegated women to a specific, and often restricted, social position were powerful indeed.

Sexual stereotyping was partly endorsed and reinforced by its internalization by women themselves. In this respect a potent tool for conditioning women to their subjection, in the 1900s as in the 1990s, was the women's magazine. Feminist columnist Jeannette Eaton wrote for *The Masses* what must be one of the most telling indictments of the typical agenda of the women's magazine ever produced ("The Woman's Magazine," Oct./Nov. 1915: 15). The magazine has, in Eaton's words, "glorified the workbasket" and "the egg-beater," and "infinitely stretched woman's belief in the miracles which may be wrought with them." Not only does the women's magazine encourage women to waste their hours churning out useless decorative knick-knacks, but it insults its readers by treating them as ignorant and stupid. "If it were not for this perennial adviser," Eaton comments drily, "it would be hard to imagine how a woman could get up a dinner party, mind her manners, keep her beauty or her husband's love." However, with all its limitations—precisely because of them, in fact—the women's magazine, according to Eaton, performs a vital social function. Through repeated exposure to its ideology, "woman's ambitions, her independence, the assertion of her own free personality" are gradually eroded. The women's magazine is, Eaton concludes, "the one sure antidote to feminism." What she might have said if she could have seen the influences she so deplores multiplied via the power of the soap opera and the television commercial is "hard to imagine."

Satire on women's endorsement of patriarchal values in the pages of *The Masses* did occasionally sound a reactionary note, as in Mary Katharine Reely's sketch "The Helpmeet" (July 1914), which portrays the unequal relations of a young married couple. In the sketch a young male wage slave is depicted as being also the slave of his wife as he runs about to her dictation, fetching the baby's bottle, his socks, and his borax powder, while the husband worries over how to cover the expenses incurred by this addition to their household. To the husband's timid suggestion that instead of sitting passively all evening his wife might like to attend a suffrage meeting, the wife reacts with indignant refusal. These suffragist women are unwomanly; her place is in the home. *The Masses* enthusiastically supported women's fight for the vote, and the chief butt of the satire here is evidently the female antifeminist. Yet the joke backfires badly. The lot of the conservative woman who accepts her domestic role is represented as more pleasant and comfortable than that of the poor bemused wage slave, her husband. Even if the point is taken to be that a society which oppresses its women by extension also oppresses its men—as the female will to power, directed away from the broader sphere of public politics, finds outlet in the home—from a feminist point of view the joke is a poor one. It relies on a stereotype of the domineering manipulative female which stigmatizes feminist and antifeminist women alike.

Such implicitly reactionary statements by *Masses* women contributors are exceptional, however. Another sketch of Reely's, which also deals with the internalization of patriarchal attitudes by women, has a much sharper feminist edge ("Barriers," Feb. 1914: 8). Its main idea is a simple one: a young woman, upon learning of her lover's past relations with prostitutes, refuses to marry him. In response to the puzzled lover's demand for explanation, she acknowledges that her education, which has taught her to think of all extramarital sexuality as "vile," was "all wrong" (a view which the lover is by no means willing to concede). The woman insists, however, that she is unable to overcome her ingrained attitudes. She claims to believe that her lover's past behavior was "all according to nature"; she says she understands and forgives it; and yet she cannot come to terms with the idea of it because she is, after all, "a virtuous woman" who has been raised in naive ignorance of human sexuality. Her mother, she says, had a hand in this training in virtue, but she mainly attributes her indoctrination to the demands and conceptions of the male members of the family, and to the expectations of her current suitor: "You wanted me to be a virtuous woman. I am one. . . . I am what you wanted me to be."

Lucy Reynolds' poem "A Good Man" satirizes the pretensions of male chivalry and, like Reely's sketches, deals with the internalization of social stereotypes by women as well as by men:

> My country calls me to arms! (he said)
> And he left his play and his work.
> I may be wounded or ill or dead
> But never a coward or shirk.
> She paid.
> (Dec. 1914: 19)

The "She" in the final line is a mother who has raised a son, only to have him throw away his life in a senseless war. The son acts out the role of hero which society has provided for him to play, to his evident self-admiration, but also at his own—and the woman's—expense.

The poem's second section deals with a victim of another "good man's" patriarchally conditioned self-image. A "little orphan fool," "roped and branded and caged" by an unhappy marriage, is forced to accept her lover's apparently noble renunciation of his claim to her love, although it turns out to be nothing more than a noble recognition of another male's property claims: "I'll trifle with no man's wife, nor hold / A good girl lightly (said he)" (19).

The poem's third victim is depicted as a woman "Ready in spirit and flesh and mind" for marriage, whose lover refuses to marry her while he lacks enough money to support her. He urges her to "Wait, be true," while he travels overseas to make his fortune. In each of the poem's three situations the man is portrayed as at least as much a victim of his self-delusion as the woman; but it is chiefly the woman who "pays," as her fulfillment is sacrificed to the complacent male's love affair with his own self-image.

The ways in which, through internalization of patriarchal values, women may even come to oppress one another are explored in two other poems by Reynolds, which deal with the repression of sexuality in the interest of maintaining existing psychosocial relations. "Oh That's Different!" depicts four people, each of whom yearns for a particular goal. The first three individuals dream of attaining learning, wealth, and good health, respectively. Others, hearing the dreamers' wishes, tell them scornfully to undertake the necessary efforts in order to realize them:

"God give me health," sighed one who sat and ate,
And longing looked within his brimming plate.
"Go out," we said, "And breathe and bathe and sing,
'Tis only effort that such bliss will bring!"
                                        (Dec. 1914: 19)

The poem's fourth speaker has the temerity to put into writing—although not to speak aloud—her longing for a fulfillment society does not care to encourage:

"I long for love," she wrote the shameful line,
And, shocked, we bade her wait and make no sign!
                                        (19)

"The Old Mother's Death" is a study of the psychological context within which the conditions of emotional and sexual repression of an individual woman are created. Written from the point of view of the dead woman's daughter, it draws the portrait of a matriarch who, paradoxically, derived her power from the patriarchal and puritanical values she endorsed and imposed on others:

My heart is breaking, mother,
And I am thrice bereft, and orphaned, and alone
Recalling how you spoke crisply of your faith in God,
With your shamed form, uncleanly prudish, drugged and swathed;
And how your children were repressed, and made unfrank and cold
And how we grew in fear of sun and rain, and wind and wave
And held our little mouths up for the dose. . . .

(Dec. 1914: 19)

The repressive culture of which the dead woman was both sustainer and victim is evoked in the nature of her funeral. The dead woman, wearing "costlier" clothing than she wore to church when living, is buried "in a casket of dark wood," to "hide and mould, darkly."

The continuing influence of the dead woman upon her offspring is evident. The sons are "dolefully coarse and early trivial and old"; the daughters, like their mother, "self-righteous," but, lacking her determination, "timid" and "futile."

The daughter is "thrice bereft"—of the spontaneity which her upbringing has taken from her; of the idealized, wished-for mother who, the daughter romantically imagines, would have gladly followed "Nature's first sweet urge and guiding" in conceiving her child; and of the opportunity, missed while her mother still lived, to communicate with this "ravisher" of her "violated soul" who is also a victim:

I was mute
And effortless, when it may be you would have listened
A little, and warmed a little, and somewhat understood
If I could, once, have cried out, unashamed, with arms out
    to your heart.

(19)

The line which follows this lament—"Such as you were, the only mother that we had"—suggests that such an attempt might well have been futile, all the same, and that the speaker knows it. The culture remains stronger than the individual, and the mother who has fully endorsed its values remains more subjugated by it than is her would-be rebellious daughter.

Internalization by women of patriarchal values might combine with class prejudice to exclude completely the possibility of sympathy between women of different classes. Such a failure of sympathy is the subject of "Mothers Still," a story for *The Masses* by Helen Hull (Oct. 1914: 14–15). An upper-class woman, neglected by her husband, is morally indignant on learning that the family servant is pregnant, and even more indignant when the servant, Hulda, insists she will not marry the father. When her employer calls her "a strumpet," and orders her to leave the house, Hulda retorts, "Bein' married don't make you good." There is a strong suggestion at the close of the story that the feckless husband of Hulda's employer may be the father of Hulda's baby. Such is the wife's investment in the notion of the sacredness of marriage, however, that she seems unable even to entertain this possibility. She is merely scandalized by her servant's lack of conventional "morality."

Hortense Flexner's "The Fire-Watchers," on the other hand, expresses the longings of women who are aware of restrictions imposed by the traditional domestic role, and who resist them:

> Why always ours to wait, to feed the fire,
> While he, with leap, with joy of strength and life,
> Follows the prey, spends of his fearless youth . . . ?
> (Sept. 1913: 17)

The speaker in the poem also wishes, for the sake of the contemporary minders of the hearth, that the doggedly faithful female guardians of prehistoric fires had, on behalf of their modern descendants, chosen rebellion:

> Oh why, for us,
> The weary after-keepers of the hearth,
> Did you not heed the call of wind and toil,
> Tread the red embers cold and take your way,
> Alone and free . . . ?
> (17)

That indoctrination into acceptance of patriarchal values did not succeed in all cases in 1917 any more than it always does in the late twentieth century is indicated by a poem by Claire Bu Zard, "A Question." "Did you," the speaker in the poem asks, in her depiction of a loveless marriage maintained only by social convention,

> . . . ever serve dinner to a silent man
> Reading a paper;
> And after washing up the dishes
> Sit alone and twist your wedding ring
> And hate it . . .
> (June 1917: 47)

The poem pictures a day in the life of a household drudge, from the moment when she wakes in the morning in her husband's arms—hating him—through a day of household chores, of mending and cooking and wheeling a "golden haired baby" that all the same "had to be fed," till the night, when the wife lies awake, dreading the approach of the "hot and selfish" arms of her husband.

The central situation depicted in Bu Zard's poem is one common to women of all social classes. One reference in the poem, however, to the woman who, while planning her next day's work, sees herself in the mirror "old and wrinkled and so bent / At thirty," makes it safe to assume that the reference is to a working-class woman, worn out by physical toil.

This relevance of the personal—which is also political—to the concerns of the working-class majority of women is often implied or potential in the writings of *Masses* contributors, even when it is not immediately apparent. This statement would apply even to a writer as apparently preoccupied with the manners and mores of the North American upper classes as was sociologist and anthropologist Elsie Clews Parsons. Writing of social attitudes of rejection disguised as "chivalry" toward, among others, women and members of the lower classes, Parsons argues that the chivalrously protective or gracious attitude, "the very protection you afford them," is "barrier in itself against them. It keeps them most rigorously and most subtly in their place" (*Fear and Conventionality*, 1914: 76).

This "place" of woman as a restricted inferior was one which Parsons from an early age was determined to get herself out of as far as possible. In adolescence she insisted on pursuing her pre-university studies against the strong opposition of her mother, a wealthy socialite who believed that a woman's calling in life was to run a household and make herself socially agreeable. A critic of convention even in her teens, Parsons once kept to her room in her mother's house for two days, rather than put on stays. This, she was to explain years later (to her still uncomprehending mother, for whom such behavior was merely rebellious) was to her in part, at least, the meaning of feminism ("Journal," 102).

Besides being a feminist, Parsons was also "the Left's favorite anthropologist" (O'Neill, *Echoes*, 206). Friend and fellow activist of *Masses* contributors Mary Heaton Vorse and Alice Duer Miller,[2] she published her work not only in scholarly journals but also, writing in a more popular vein, in *The Masses* and *The New Republic*. Although she was not much given to party political statements—her declaration in 1940, in the *New Republic*, of support for socialist Norman Thomas is exceptional in this respect—her ideas on such issues as marriage or birth control can be better understood if viewed in this broader context of her liberal/left political allegiances.

As a sociologist and anthropologist, Parsons had a distinguished career.

A founding member of the New School for Social Research, she was at various times president of the American Folklore Society and of the American Ethnological Society, and in 1941 the first woman to be elected president of the American Anthropological Association. Her early writings, *The Family* (1906), *Religious Chastity* (1913), *Fear and Conventionality* (1914), *Social Freedom* (1915), and *Social Rule* (1916), were praised for their perceptiveness and originality by critics as diverse as H. L. Mencken and Randolph Bourne.[3] In these books she took a comparative approach to social customs, with the aim of inducing her readers to examine in a scientific spirit that fear of novelty which she regarded as the chief obstacle to constructive social change. Her use of ethnology was, as her great-nephew biographer Peter Hare writes, "a pedagogical device" whereby she hoped to persuade readers to become "more tolerant of genuine self-expression" (*A Woman's Quest*, 135). Parsons' criticisms of Western social norms were based on her observation that neither Christianity nor democracy allowed for expression of the feeling which, "for lack of a better word," she called "a love for personality" (*Fear and Conventionality*, 217).

Nowhere was Parsons more concerned about the importance to the individual of this scope for self-expression than in the area of women's social lives. Like Lucy Reynolds, Parsons viewed the sexual stereotypes through which both men and women are compelled to express their social identities as confining and potentially destructive. In a comment which anticipates the sociopsychological feminism of the late 1960s and early 1970s, she writes:

> This morning perhaps I may feel like a male; let me
> act like one. This afternoon I may feel like a female.
> Let me act like one. At midday or at midnight I may
> feel sexless; let me therefore act sexlessly.
> ("Journal," 115)

Some women resent "having always to act like women, or be treated invariably as women," Parsons argued, not only because the role assigned them is that of a social inferior, but also because of the psychological confinement such stereotyping imposes—its denial of "greater elasticity for their personality" ("Journal," 116). Such a freeing of social identity and of social relations would, Parsons considered, be to the benefit of both sexes. "Some day," she wrote prophetically, "there may be a 'masculism' movement to allow men to act 'like women'" (116).

Even where she approved of existing social institutions, Parsons considered they should be instruments in the service of the individual, rather than shibboleths to which the individual should be subordinated and sacrificed. In "Marriage: A New Life," an article she wrote for *The Masses* in

September 1916, Parsons discusses the conditioning of the engaged and newly wed in a number of societies, including that of North America, to the acceptance of an unduly rigid view of marriage, as a state which fully transforms the individuals principally involved; as a "life of new duties and responsibilities, of new feelings and desires, a mystical new life" (28). Viewed from such a perspective, marriage becomes, by implication, a condition permanent and irreversible for the individuals involved—a state from which withdrawal is made difficult or even impossible.

Parsons had earlier, in *The Family: An Ethnographic and Historical Outline* (1906), developed what she regarded as a partial solution at least to the confining rigidity of marriage as an institution. She continued to regard monogamy in sexual relationships as desirable, because "conducive to emotional or intellectual development and to health," and remained married to Republican politician Herbert Parsons, in spite of occasional strains in the relationship, until his death in 1925. (Both spouses, at least at an intellectual level, tolerated one another's extramarital affairs.)[4] Parsons' proposal for the avoidance of possible conjugal incompatibility was to "encourage early trial marriage . . . with a view to permanency, but with the privilege of breaking it if proved unsuccessful and in the absence of offspring without suffering any great degree of public condemnation" (348–349). This rather timid proposal, in terms of today's sexual and social norms, caused a storm of controversy in 1906 when *The Family* was published, reaching well beyond the circle of the book's 3,904 readers. The idea of trial marriage was denounced in the press, caused a certain amount of political embarrassment for Herbert Parsons, and was even used as a legal defense by a man accused of elopement with a minor, who claimed to have acted under the influence of Parsons' theories (Hare, *A Woman's Quest*, 11–12).

Another step advocated by Parsons that seemed radical in relation to the sociosexual norms of her time was the separation, both conceptually and in practice, of mating, on the one hand, and parenthood, on the other. Parsons proposed substitution of "parents' courts" for divorce courts, and the signing by parents of a contract with the state in which one or both of them would undertake to raise their children.[5] While parenthood, according to this theory, would remain a public concern subject to the intervention of the state on behalf of the child, the sexual relationship would otherwise be reserved as purely a private matter. Parsons went so far as to argue that parents should have no right to give or withhold consent to marriage of their children, even in the case of minors (Hare, *A Woman's Quest*, 91). It is in the context of these views that her article for *The Masses*, "Privacy in Love Affairs," may best be understood.

Published in June 1915, "Privacy in Love Affairs" recounts a dinner-table discussion, at which Parsons claims to have been present, where a "Re-spectable Married Woman" asserts that "were she to begin life over again," she would claim the right to keep her intimate relationships private:

> The mating we call marriage is no more the affair of the public, she asserted, than the mating we call adultery. "And by the public I mean not only the state," she added, "not only the community at large, but my acquaintances, my friends, my relatives." (12)

This assertion arouses a good deal of debate among the woman's dinner-table companions. It is on these others that the narrator's attention chiefly centers—upon their reaction to the Married Woman's views. Some have clearly misunderstood the speaker's remark, as applying only to extra-marital relationships. One of the men present argues that men like to know with which male a woman is connected—"a man does not make love to a woman he associates with another man"—or if he does, he knows that such behavior is "Piracy." A "professional feminist" argues that a woman may likewise find it convenient "to have limited automatically the sexual advances made her," through public knowledge of her sexual rela-tionships, so that intellectual and personal relationships with men not of an overtly sexual kind may be possible. "That," she argues, "is one of the best things to come out of feminism." (The Respectable Married Woman rejects this ideal, as denying the element of sexuality inherent in all male-female relationships.) The narrator comments somewhat maliciously on the Respectable Married Woman's wearing of a wedding ring. She notes that "whenever she was addressed by her husband's name [as of course Parsons herself was] it seemed as if a flashlight were turned on the adver-tisement she so resented." Yet, as the narrator points out, the Respectable Married Woman is given the final word in the dialogue. The "tagging" of either a friend or a lover as such by society is, this woman finally argues, "an assertion of monopoly." Those who seek privacy in their relationships are those who "feel that the fine flower of their relationship is bruised by self-exploitation" (12). If the narrator's expressed wish that the Respectable Married Woman might indeed "begin life over again—just to show us," sounds a trifle sarcastic, and if the shaping of the dialogue allows a great deal of ironic credibility to all participants (the narrator included), a num-ber of more explicit comments elsewhere in Parsons' writings seem to identify her own position most closely with that of the Respectable Mar-ried Woman. As Parsons wrote in an article published in 1916, a year after "Privacy in Love Affairs" appeared in *The Masses,*

> With the conditions for privacy more or less formalized and their ob-servance a conventionality, with the advertisement of a sex-relationship

discountenanced, the spirit of monopoly towards another will be condemned. . . . The causes of jealousy will be lessened.[6]

Clearly privacy and the discouraging of "advertisement" in sexual affairs are here presented by Parsons as positive developments, which would result in greater interpersonal harmony.

One undesirable consequence for women of sexual stereotyping, then—particularly for women of Parsons' class—was the degree to which they came under the tutelage and the surveillance of society. At the same time that she deplores the policing of women's sexual lives, Parsons also comments on the repression, furtiveness, and resulting social embarrassment which accompany such surveillance. She shows a remarkable understanding of that strange blend of curiosity about others' sexual behavior combined with public concealment of awareness of human physiology which seems characteristic of many conservative, patriarchal societies. As she points out in her book *The Old-Fashioned Woman* (1913), a pregnant woman dining out in Washington society in the 1900s could cause a scandal—as a friend of Parsons, accustomed to more permissive European manners, discovered to her discomfiture (83). Parsons draws analogies between the taboos of "primitive" and those of "civilized" societies. She indicates that collective attitudes toward women's menstruation are grounded in a superstitious dread of woman as "other"—which in post-Victorian America took the form of complete repression of discourse, though clearly not of awareness, about the subject: "The better to deceive a woman must act normally in every way." Such "normality" is achieved only at the woman's expense. Not only does she "often endure extraordinary discomfort and pain" and sometimes even risk her health to keep up appearances, but in the subterfuges she resorts to in order to disguise her condition, "she spreads the impression of being generally unreliable."[7]

Parsons' article on "Engagements," in *The Masses* for November 1916, deals with another aspect of the social surveillance of young women—and of young men. Parsons' discussion of the "avoidance taboo" laid upon engaged couples in many societies leads her to the conclusion that the separation of the couple is designed not so much to discourage premarital sexual relations as to protect society from the "discomfiture" felt by the sight of a loving couple. In contemporary American society the separation takes the form of discouragement of open physical displays by the engaged couple and of a taboo laid on an upper-class North American girl against "going into general society" in the few days leading up to the wedding. "Lovers may be disquieting," Parsons writes (more than a little ironically, one suspects), and even when engaged, their engagement may be a source of inconvenience and "suspense" to society at large:

In the Islands of Torres Straits the fact that a suitor would keep parents from sleeping at night and would greatly hinder work in the garden by day was given as one of the reasons for female infanticide. (14)

Contemporary American parents and relations proceed in a similar spirit, Parsons concludes, motivated by their unease about the ambiguity of the couple's situation. "Why don't they make up their minds and get married?" society demands. Parsons here, as elsewhere in her writings, champions the interests of the individual against social tyranny. "That lovers should consider themselves," she comments drily, "is quite an unaccustomed thought." When in 1940 Parsons publicly declared her support for Socialist Party candidate Norman Thomas, she appears to have done so mainly on the grounds of a belief in tolerance and personal goodwill, out of a characteristic faith in the potential of the "free" individual. Her statement on Thomas' stand regarding fascism—"He is the only presidential candidate who seems to understand that . . . learning to get on with people you disagree with or dislike makes for progress"[8]—not only seems, viewed with hindsight, more than a trifle naive, but suggests fairly clearly the limits of her radical commitment. Yet the radicalism of her thinking about personal and sexual relations, grounded as it is in a faith in the importance of tolerance and of encouragement of individual diversity, was boldly innovative for its time.

As will also shortly be seen in the case of Parsons' stand in the controversy over birth control, in which she and other *Masses* contributors were deeply involved, if her social analyses did not emphasize working-class issues, they certainly did not exclude them, either. Her study, in *The Old-Fashioned Woman*, of the disparity between men's and women's wages, and also of the disparity between a factory worker's wages and those of a prostitute, makes explicit the differing ways in which women are evaluated in the workplace in terms of the assessed value of their labor power in the two spheres of the factory and the brothel. The study is evidence enough of her sensitivity to such questions.[9]

Parsons was hardly the only *Masses* contributor to have considered women's social situation from an economic perspective—or to have considered the relationship between patriarchal ideology and social attitudes to prostitution. Jeanette D. Pearl's story "Pride" introduces the subject with a description of a young woman addressing a man on the street:

She was young, pretty, not rouged, with clothes louder than her manner. The quick eye of the man she spoke to noted her hesitancy and forced boldness. The contradiction aroused his curiosity. He sensed something unusual. (June 1917: 15)

In the course of the story it emerges that this woman, raised in a sheltered home environment, has been deserted by her husband (whom she had run away from home to marry) and has been rejected by her wealthy family. Lacking skills to earn an adequate living, she has drifted into prostitution. Yet she is indignant when the sympathetic auditor of her story suggests she might ask her family to take her back: "Don't you think I have some pride?" She will play the prodigal daughter for her family's benefit only "if they come for" her—only upon her own terms.

Clearly, the implications of this story for a reader of the 1900s—or, for that matter, of the 1990s—are disturbing. The character in the story is presented as enjoying not only economic "independence," but also greater psychological independence—greater scope for self-respect—in work wherein sale of labor power involves the renting out of her body, than would be allowed within her own family.

Pearl's sketch of the prostitute as a dropout from the upper classes was exceptional, both in *Masses* poetry and fiction and in life. Pearl's woman character is in a sense, even as a prostitute, still presented in her quiet "refinement" as a "lady"—a consolation not open to the majority of fallen women. As a report in *The Masses* for April 1917 suggests, most prostitutes, for whom the alternative was employment at sub-minimum wages, were from the working class. Economic need drove them into a profession which ruined their health and prematurely aged them. "These women do not lead a gay or happy life," *The Masses* reported a prostitute as assuring a meeting of vice crusaders at a church in San Francisco. "Many of them hardly ever see the sunlight." She challenged the local businessmen who claimed to work for the elimination of "vice," if they were sincere, to "give up some of their dividends," and pay their female employees a living wage. "It is too late to try to do anything with us," another woman told the minister responsible for calling the meeting. She urged him rather to consider "the social conditions that are responsible for the spread of prostitution" (22).

Without exception, women contributors to *The Masses* who deal with the subject of prostitution do so in a tone of sympathy for the prostitute as victim of social—usually economic—circumstance. The subject was hardly a new one in American literature by the early twentieth century; Stephen Crane in *Maggie, a Girl of the Streets* (1893), Frank Norris in *The Octopus* (1901), and a host of less well known writers had dealt with it in fiction more or less explicitly. Yet public prejudice and condemnation—not only of the prostitute's way of making a living, but of the prostitute herself as a depraved individual—was widespread then as nowadays, and might even supply fuel to arguments against woman suffrage, as the response of *Masses* contributor Alice Duer Miller to Everett Wheeler's *The Case Against Woman Suffrage* indicates. Wheeler had written:

"Women are often tempted to sexual sin and delight in it. . . . A recent report of a female probation officer relates that some of the girls who, as we say euphemistically, 'had gone astray' owned to her that they enjoyed the life of the evil house." [10]

Miller was best known for her light, witty, but pointed satirical verse. She was the author of a column in the *New York Tribune* and of a series of books of verse on suffrage issues, of which *Are Women People?* (1915) is the most famous. [11] She enjoyed a reputation as a writer of "society" fiction, but also campaigned and lectured for woman suffrage. Her response in rhyming couplets to Wheeler's complacent view projects what is, for Miller, an unusual degree of very unplayful animus. "It may be so," Miller's poem begins, in a tone of calm rationality. It concedes the possibility that "Not all who sin are tempted." The poem then launches an attack on Wheeler, and on all males who share his complacency:

And yet, upon my soul, if I were you—
A man, no longer young, at peace, secured
From all that tempting women have endured
Of poverty and ignorance and fear . . .
If I were you, before I took my pen
And wrote those words to hearten other men,
And give them greater sense of moral ease
In the long score of common sins like these
If I were you I would have held my hand
In fire.
    Ah, well; you would not understand.
    ("To Everett P. Wheeler," Oct./Nov. 1915: 9)

The reference of the speaker in Miller's poem to "all that tempting women have endured" clearly has a double edge. "Women have suffered temptation" might be one way to read the line, but it also implies that women are tempting to men (at least to men younger than the author of *The Case Against Woman Suffrage*)—that men share with women responsibility in the "long score of common sins" and hence have no right to any sense of "moral ease" at women's expense.

Expressions of sympathy for the situation of the prostitute quickly became common in the pages of *The Masses;* by 1914 Floyd Dell was rejecting poems on prostitution as "an overworked subject." [12] Occasionally, women's poems about prostitutes, like those of male contributors, fell into cliché—into endorsements of the late Victorian stereotype of the femme fatale. A poem by Lydia Gibson, "Lies," is one example:

The curve of feather and of eyes,
Their hot light calling to the bed—
The breasts borne temptingly to kiss—
Of what Truth are these things the lies?
                              (Oct. 1913: 15)

Yet the best of the contributions to *The Masses* by women on prostitution—if imbued, like much of the writing on the subject, with a certain
sentimentality—also have touches of sympathetic realism which extend
beyond cliché. A description by Esther Hanna of the backstage of a vaudeville, where the chorus girls tread a fine line between dancer and prostitute,
is a case in point:

> I wondered what happened when their little shred of youth was gone
> from these girls. There was about them none of the sturdy quality of
> successful vice; they would never be able to feather their nests from
> male eroticism. They were tiny, yapping wraiths of vice.
>   ("Amusement," Feb. 1914: 3)

This description is observant and unromanticized, but it also sounds a
characteristic note of pathos. The prostitute of most of the *Masses* portraits is more victim than hardy survivor, more thoroughly a "waif amid
forces"—largely economic in nature—than Dreiser's Carrie ever was.

Sooner or later the prostitute, like the married woman, finds herself
confronted with patriarchal attitudes in the form of the law. Patriarchy
treats women as mere appendages of male-dominated households. It en-
courages the marketing of labor power in general. However, it places pro-
hibitions on the marketing of one form of labor power, in particular, one
much in demand even among those heads of households whose values
sustain a patriarchal system. These contradictions, which surface in the law
courts, are probed and exposed in Miriam Keep Patton's "The Clock":

> With bloated and blotched and pasty face
> You leer over the city . . .
>   (May 1917: 3)

The clock, a "lying old timepiece," constantly breaking down (and
hence lagging behind the times?) is witness to the arrival of the accused.
These include the kitchenmaids indicted for theft, hauled before the Jef-
ferson Market Court by employers "with golden purses in their hands";
drunken and homeless women; and women brought in by young plain-

clothes detectives, men "chosen, like concubines, for their beauty," who "prostitute" their good looks to entrap, "spider-like," the "pitiful moths" of streetwalkers on whom they "pounce and fatten":

> Their fresh young Greek lips curl in incorruptible virtue
> As they hold the flutterers up before
> The judge and the court-room,
> agape.
>
> (3)

In a remarkable set of reversals the courthouse clock, representative of the law and of those who serve in its shadow, is associated with precisely those qualities of corruption which conventional moral value judgments would ascribe to the way of life of the prostitute. The clock is depicted as physically unattractive; its face is "blotched" and "pasty" (like that of a worn-out woman, perhaps) yet also "smug," and it has "prim" hands. The primness, however, fails to obscure a "lascivious" grin. The clock's servants, the handsome young detectives, are ironically prostitutes themselves, as well as predators upon their victims, the streetwalkers.

If *Masses* women were concerned with the plight of the prostitute, caught between economic need and the law, a number of them—Lucy Reynolds, Hortense Flexner, Claire Bu Zard, Elsie Clews Parsons—viewed prostitution as only one aspect of the overall oppression of women under both capitalism and patriarchy.

If workers' control of the means of production was an issue for the majority of *Masses* women, so was their control of the means of reproduction. Like Emma Goldman, they believed that woman could win full liberation, even under the most egalitarian and democratic economic system, only "by refusing the right to anyone over her body; by refusing to bear children unless she wants them. . . ." [13] Most of them would have agreed with the view of Parsons that mating and parenthood should be regarded separately. They also recognized, as did Parsons herself, that for this separation to be feasible at all, deferment of parenthood through the practice of contraception had to be a practical possibility; and, for access to information about contraceptive methods, the majority of North American women were almost totally dependent upon the medical profession.

This dependency may be one reason why, in the pages of *The Masses,* doctors are sometimes presented in an unsympathetic light—as in cartoonist Elizabeth Grieg's drawing, "Now Doctor, I've Had This Trouble for Two Years and—" (Aug. 1916: 11). The caption, in which the patient timidly voices her anxiety, and the doctor ever more irritably interrupts her—"WHAT'S YOUR NAME?"—may or may not have been supplied by

Grieg herself. But even without the caption, the shrunken, stiffly seated figure of the woman craning forward from the chair back, her raw-boned anxious profile, and even the sharp corner of the table—which seems to thrust her at arm's length from the doctor—tell the story of her sense of helplessness before authority. The doctor is a thickset figure, too large for his flimsy chair. His head and shoulders are drawn from the back, so that we share the sense of remoteness from his humanity that is depicted on the woman's face as she watches him writing without looking up at her. The doctor may be taken to represent entrenched male power in its control of the precious knowledge of the medical profession which, working in conjunction with man-made law, could thwart women's aspirations to control their own bodies.

In a short story for *The Masses,* Helen R. Hull, on the other hand, presents a sympathetic image of a doctor—in this case a woman—who wishes but feels helplessly unable to aid her patient, a working-class woman tied to a brutal husband by unwanted pregnancies. Just when she had decided to leave the man and begin a new life, the woman is told by the doctor she is pregnant yet again. "You must make the best of it," the doctor tells her patient, "for the children."

> The woman stared, her face wrinkling slightly, as if fanned by a hot wind.
> "The children?" Her lips moved over the words. Then she relaxed, slumping into a heap, her face in the angle of her arm. "Oh, the children: the children." ("Till Death. . . ," Jan. 1917: 6)

If Hull's story may seem to modern taste to tremble too nearly on the brink of melodrama, it remains of sociohistorical interest for one detail of its dialogue. Speaking of her longing to be rid of the dread of unwanted pregnancy, "There's ways," the woman in the story says, "but I don't know 'em" (6). It is a sentiment which an inner-city teenager deprived of adequate sex education or birth control counseling might well echo today.

Whether the fictional doctor's apologetic words to her patient, "If I had seen you a few months ago—I might have been of some use," refer to the possibility of an early abortion or to giving advice on contraception is not made clear. For a doctor to advocate either measure to a patient in January 1917, when Hull's story was published, was, in any case, illegal.[14]

The problem lay, in fact, not with the individual physician but with the restrictions laid upon doctors under the laws which made the giving of birth control information a crime. This is why, in the birth control education controversy with which a number of *Masses* contributors of both sexes were vitally concerned throughout almost the whole period of Max Eastman's editorship, the chief villain as far as *The Masses* was concerned

"WHAT'S YOUR NAME?" ELIZABETH GRIEG.
Clinic Doctor: *"What's Your Name?"*
Patient: *"Now Doctor, I've Had This Trouble for Two Years and—"*
Doctor: *"WHAT'S YOUR NAME?"*
(Courtesy General Research Division, The New York Public Library, Astor, Lenox and Tilden Foundations.)

was Anthony Comstock, special agent (later Inspector) of the Postmaster General, chief architect and zealous enforcer of a law of 1873 whereby all "obscene, lewd, lascivious, filthy and indecent" material—including medical information on the prevention of conception—was barred from the U.S. mails. A crusading Christian fundamentalist whose enthusiasm for the cause of moral purity was so intense that he would go out in person to make arrests of moral offenders, Comstock at the end of his life could boast of having secured the conviction of 3,760 such offenders and of having destroyed 160 tons of "obscene" material.[15]

In February 1914—only one month before the first major clash between Comstock and birth control educator Margaret Sanger was to develop—Gertrude Marvin interviewed Anthony Comstock for *The Masses.* "He seemed like a harmless old gentleman," Marvin reports, with a "gentle, almost furtive manner." Comstock's views, which Marvin quotes almost without comment, were another matter. "When a link is formed," Comstock told Marvin concerning sex education for school students, "from the reproductive faculties of the mind and imagination to the sensual nature, one might as well throw a loop around the child's neck and hand the other end of it to the Devil" (16). Having given Comstock rope enough to hang himself with, so to speak, Marvin took her leave and, thanking Comstock for the interview, hastened out into what she describes as the "wholesome mud" of the street.

Powerful social pressure groups other than the lobby of conservative moralists favored continuing the ban on birth control education, particularly after the outbreak of the First World War in Europe. Proponents of female fertility argued that for women to limit the number of children they bore was to court the risk of race suicide. In November 1914 *The Masses* reported that European governments were encouraging soldiers to marry," "in order that the ranks of posterity may be filled" (7). The British government had reduced the price of marriage licenses—but not, the *Masses* editors pointed out, "the cost of raising a baby." The cartoon by Cornelia Barns which accompanied this editorial comment is entitled "Patriotism for Women." It shows two shawled and scarved women, one nursing a baby, with a despondent-looking male figure in the background.[16]

North American society, like that of much of Europe, was already beginning to experience a conflict, however, between the traditional notion of the female as contented breeder of cannon fodder and newer, more diverse conceptions of women's roles. Elsie Clews Parsons, in her essay "Facing Race Suicide" in *The Masses* of June 1915, pointed out that advocates of fecundity could hardly encourage middle-class women to seek education and to practice self-expression while at the same time attempting to impose upon them the obligation of unrestricted childbearing. This attitude Parsons identified as typical not only of Boards of Education that rejected the idea of "the teacher-mother" and required women to resign from teaching as soon as they married, but also of those state legislatures (and, she might have added, of the federal legislature) which had made teaching about the control of conception an illegal act.

The most outrageous aspect of the federal and state obscenity laws which made illegal the circulation of family planning information and which forbade the sending of contraceptives through the mails was that, in the words of a *Masses* editorial of July 1916, they were "laws applying only to the poor," easily circumventable by those with money and education (Max Eastman, "Birth-Control," 27). Perhaps no one expressed this point more forcefully than did Emma Goldman when she was arrested in 1916 under Section 1142 of the New York Penal Code—which forbade distribution of contraceptives or of contraceptive information—in her speech to the court, reproduced in the June 1916 issue of *The Masses*. "The question of birth control," Goldman told the court, was "largely a working-

"PATRIOTISM FOR WOMEN," CORNELIA BARNS.
"The European Governments are encouraging all soldiers to marry before they enlist, in order that the ranks of posterity may be filled. They have reduced the cost of a marriage license in England, but not, so far as we know, the cost of raising a baby."
(Courtesy General Research Division, The New York Public Library, Astor, Lenox and Tilden Foundations.)

man's question, above all a workingwoman's question." In a country where 300,000 children died annually of malnutrition owing to their parents' inability to support them, parents—unlike the entrepreneur or the politician, who might require quantities of factory or cannon fodder—clearly had no vested interest in producing large families for their own sake. Goldman cited instances drawn from her own observations as a health worker and social activist, such as the case of a woman with a husband suffering from tuberculosis, six of whose eight children also had the disease, and who had been unable to prevent the birth of a ninth, and the case of a mother of twelve who had died in giving birth to her thirteenth child. These, said Goldman, "are but very few of the victims of our economic grinding mill, which sets a premium upon poverty, and our puritanic law which maintains a conspiracy of silence." As workers, particularly women workers, began to realize the possibility of choice in the size of their families, they would, Goldman predicted, "absolutely refuse to go on like cattle breeding more and more."[17] The judge was, unsurprisingly, not swayed by Goldman's feminist-anarchist logic (which was probably intended mainly for sympathizers and possible converts among the two hundred members of the public present in court); he sentenced her to fifteen days in jail.

For Goldman, the fight for free availability of birth control information was only one battle in the "great modern social war" of "the oppressed and disinherited of the earth against their enemies," capitalism and the state. It was "a war for a seat at the table of life" (21). The double oppression suffered by working-class women in a class society—the fight for free access to birth control information as a blow struck for the working class—is a theme which runs through much of the *Masses* commentary on the issue.

The involvement of *The Masses* with birth control education cases began in 1914, when Margaret Sanger was charged with "circulating obscene literature" on birth control. Sanger, who, like Goldman, was a trained nurse, had visited patients on New York's East Side, had seen the dozens of shawled women waiting outside the backstreet abortionist's office, had heard from her patients "the story told a thousand times of death from abortion and children going into institutions"; had seen a sick patient killed by childbearing, while the only advice her doctor could give was to tell her husband "to sleep on the roof" (*Autobiography*, 89). She became convinced that the sole solution to the misery of working-class families was to make birth control available to the mothers. In March 1914 Sanger published the first issue of *The Woman Rebel*, the magazine whose distribution led to her indictment in August of that year under Section 211 of the federal Comstock Act (*Autobiography*, 115).

While Sanger, anticipating interruption of her work by a possible jail sentence, had left for Europe after making arrangements for the publication of her pamphlet *Family Limitation,* her husband William was indicted on the same charge and sentenced to thirty days' imprisonment. "If you and your like would marry decent women," the sentencing judge reportedly told William Sanger, "you would not have time to think of such worthless projects" (Dell, "Criminals All," Oct./Nov. 1915: 21).

The *Masses* was active in this first defense of Margaret Sanger from early in 1915. A spate of editorials by Floyd Dell and Max Eastman began in April of that year and continued into 1916, when public support helped bring about dismissal of Sanger's case.[18] *Masses* contributing editor Mary Heaton Vorse helped organize a "Women's Emergency Committee" for Margaret Sanger when the case finally came to trial in January 1916 (*Footnote to Folly,* 130). Vorse was present at the pretrial dinner at the Brevoort Hotel, as were fellow *Masses* contributors Rose Pastor Stokes and Elsie Clews Parsons. Parsons proposed that twenty-five women who had used contraceptives should stand up in court with Margaret Sanger and declare themselves guilty of breaking the law. However, according to Margaret Sanger, "only one volunteered" (*Autobiography,* 189). A number of *Masses* women attended the post-trial celebrations at the Bandbox Theatre: Vorse, Parsons, and fiction writer and playwright Susan Glaspell. *The Masses* also established a Sanger legal defense fund, and acted as a contact address for the recently formed Birth Control League.

As a result of its campaigns on behalf of birth control activists—of the first Sanger case in particular—*The Masses* received thousands of readers' letters. The April 1915 issue included some of these letters, with a drawing by Elizabeth Grieg, which shows a young woman absorbed in conversation with a motherly looking older one, under a sign reading "Women's Clinic." The rest of the sign is written in European languages other than English—a not-so-subtle reminder that birth control information was freely available in much of Northern Europe. The caption under the drawing reads "What Every Young Woman Ought to Have Known" (23).

The letters came in from people in all walks of life—from an attorney, from a "Government scientific worker," from Upton Sinclair, from a self-styled "stodgy bourgeois" who deplored *The Masses'* radical views but sent a check for the Sanger defense, from a "disembodied spirit," as *The Masses* editors cruelly dubbed him, who declared that sexual abstinence alone was the answer to unwanted pregnancies.[19] Many, not surprisingly, were from women. A woman doctor voiced her enthusiastic support for Sanger: "I am familiar with what Margaret Sanger has been trying to do and believe her successful vindication would save millions of women remorse and guilt." The writer offered, in the event of any organized support for the Sanger defense, to "do her share" (April 1915: 24). Miriam Oatman, who identified herself as "an experienced campaign speaker for equal suffrage,"

Drawn by Elizabeth Grieg.

"WHAT EVERY YOUNG WOMAN OUGHT TO HAVE KNOWN," ELIZABETH GRIEG. (Courtesy General Research Division, The New York Public Library, Astor, Lenox and Tilden Foundations.)

offered, "if public speaking will do any good," to employ her skills in the case. Like the *Masses* editors, she recognized that the law against birth control education had its harshest effect "upon those who most need such information" (20). Oatman proposed the signing by a thousand women of a statement setting forth the case for legal reform and pledging themselves to fight for it. The sixth clause of Oatman's proposed statement, "That we will repeat these statements in court and take the consequences," indicates her unawareness that agitation for legalization of birth control education was not itself subject to legal penalties; only the giving of contraceptive advice was illegal. Her evident—if unfounded—concern about possible prosecution suggests, though, the atmosphere of repression with which Comstock and the Comstock Act had surrounded the whole family limitation issue.

Two of the letters published in *The Masses* were requests for information. One reads:

> As being a poor workingwoman I could not have any more children than I have at the present time. Now could you furnish me with information pertaining to family limitations, or direct me to where I could get the desired information? I am interested in the Margaret Sanger case and am prompted to write hoping you might enlighten me. (April 1915: 20)

This letter (if not a police ploy designed to entrap the editors) indicates the reach of *The Masses* beyond a liberal and radical middle-class readership.

When Sanger's newly opened birth control clinic was closed down by the police in October 1916—after only ten days of operation—Sanger, her sister Ethel Byrne, and a third worker, Fania Mindell, were all charged under Section 1142 of the New York Penal Code with distributing obscene material. Sanger was charged in addition with "maintaining a public nuisance" in the form of a birth control clinic. As they had done earlier in the year, women of *The Masses* rallied to the defense. Vorse and Parsons were members of the Committee of One Hundred which secured a governor's pardon for Ethel Byrne when, after being sentenced to thirty days in jail, she became seriously ill from a hunger strike. On January 29, 1917, the day after Sanger's trial, a letter appeared in the *New York Times* protesting the disparity in attitude of New York City's administration to two more or less unpopular laws. Since the city's Sunday drinking laws had been declared unenforceable for lack of public support, the letter argued, a similar principle might well apply to the anti–birth control laws. The Sunday closing issue was, after all, a trivial matter, the writers pointed out, in comparison with that of the eight thousand women's lives lost in 1916 in New York State alone, "largely because birth control information was not available." The letter was signed by Parsons and Vorse, along with more than sixty others.[20]

The first Sanger case, involving *The Woman Rebel,* had been dismissed, the presiding judge having expressed the view that Sanger was not "a disorderly person." In the 1917 case, however, Sanger, like her sister Ethel Byrne, upon refusal to promise future compliance with the Comstock Act, received a sentence of thirty days. It was not until 1937, in fact, that a Circuit Court of Appeals finally ruled that the Comstock Act had never been intended to prevent "the importation, sale or carriage by mail of things which might intelligently be employed [by doctors] for the . . . well-being of their patients."[21] Clearly, on this issue as on so many others which

brought them into conflict with patriarchal attitudes, Sanger and her supporters still had a long fight ahead.

"The greatest change that will have come to the world in our day is the
liberation of the genius and energies . . . of woman," predicted Max Eastman in a *Masses* obituary tribute to the suffragist and feminist Inez Milholland. "It is not a date in history, but an epoch in evolution when one
half of the race, which had been inhibited to the sole function of bearing
and rearing wakes up to the joy of being and becoming." Eastman went
on to argue that the realization of women's full potential would accom-
plish not only the cultural emancipation of a single generation, but "a
change in heredity, a change in the very kind of descendants we generate."
This is a conception he might have derived from the evolutionist feminism
of Charlotte Perkins Gilman in *Herland* (1915/1979) [22] or quite possibly from
another, less known work of feminist science fiction published by *Masses*
fiction editor Inez Irwin the previous year. Irwin's *Angel Island* (1914/1988)
offers a symbolic representation of the processes whereby women in her
time were attaining the liberation of their intellectual and creative potential, but it also embodies, albeit in fantastic form, an interest in feminist
progress as a function of evolutionary change.

The basic idea of *Angel Island* is a simple one. A group of travelers, all
men, shipwrecked on a desert island, discover that the island is visited
intermittently by strange flying creatures, which at first they take for large
birds. Only gradually does it dawn on the castaways that the visitors are a
winged evolutionary variation on the human model—and that all of them
are female. (The rest of the race to which these women belong migrated
to the Arctic, where, presumably, they became extinct.)

Discovering that these beautiful flying creatures are irresistibly attracted
to them, the men set out to capture them, cut off their wings, and reedu-
cate them into becoming housewives and mothers within a patriarchal domestic system. Naturally, the women protest this brutal curtailment of their
freedom. But, as one of their new husbands explains, the domestication
is really all for their own good: "God never intended women to fly" (268).

At first, the women seem to resign themselves to their new roles. They
sit at home while their husbands go off to plan and build elsewhere on the
island and, predictably, become the bored, complaining housewives of
male chauvinist folklore. [23] Then the unexpected happens. One of their girl
children is born with wings, an event which generates a crisis for all the
women. An anguished discussion ensues. Are they going to allow their
daughters' wings to be sheared as theirs have been? Julia, the most serious,
intelligent, and capable of the women, reaches a decision. They will teach
the little girl both to fly and to walk—and develop their own underdevel-
oped walking capacities in the bargain. Only in this way can they exist
successfully in a male-dominated world. As Julia understands, even shorn

of their wings the adult women remain "strong, full-bodied, teeming with various efficiencies and abilities." If women of the future can walk *and* fly, they will realize their fullest potential. When, at the novel's close, a male child is born with the power of flight, the women have passed on their enhanced potential to the entire human race.

As Ursula Le Guin has pointed out in her introduction to the 1988 edition of *Angel Island,* the novel can be read in terms of a wealth of allegorical references—to the suffrage movement, or to the struggles being waged at both an ideological and a practical level for women's liberation from patriarchal domination. Part of its fascination, though, certainly lies in the bold scope of its most daring speculation: by social or biological evolution, or both, the brand of feminism Irwin espouses is envisaged as extending its benefits to the entire human race.

The well-to-do feminists of *The Masses* were deeply concerned with their personal liberation; but many of them were also concerned about, and actively involved with, issues such as those of gender roles and identity, sexual repression, and marriage, which affected women of all classes; and with others, like prostitution and birth control education, which primarily concerned women of the working class. Their analyses of women's roles in society necessarily included a response to patriarchal attitudes as they affected upper-class women, as well as in relation to the working-class majority; but if feminism for them began at home, it certainly did not end there. Had it done so, their writings might have been less interesting. The importance of what they had to say to their age, and to ours, would have been very much diminished.

3

Labor

WHEN *MASSES* WOMEN WROTE on labor issues, they did so for the most part as middle-class outsiders. Their direct experience of the day-to-day life of manual workers was in most cases strictly limited—which is not to claim that the onlooker necessarily understands nothing of the game. Their poems, fiction, and articles about factories, about domestic service, and about labor unions raise a repeated question, which resounds in the debates of feminists and economic radicals in the 1990s as it did in the early 1900s: can women's personal and political liberation be achieved independently of a democratization of economic relations, a change in ownership and control of the workplace? The answer of one early *Masses* contributor, the socialist feminist Josephine Conger-Kaneko, was unambiguous. Of the "double slavery" of women, as she called it—their political disenfranchisement and their economic powerlessness—she wrote: "When the woman of the working class (for she is the vast majority, as is the man of the working class) has learned the necessity of *economic freedom* as well as political freedom, then shall we see the beginning of the end of human slavery."[1] In their fictional and nonfictional studies of workplace exploitation, later women contributors to *The Masses* seem implicitly to concur with Conger-Kaneko.

The majority of female-authored contributions to *The Masses* on labor issues were poems or short stories, many of which, in the absence of the authors' direct experience of paid manual labor, draw upon existing literary and radical traditions. Many poems, in particular, evoke a sentimental tradition of mid–nineteenth-century protest literature, which deplores the exploitative conditions of wage earners with more rhetorical pathos than circumstantial detail.[2] Elizabeth Waddell's "For Lyric Labor," (Sept. 1917: 39) falls squarely into this category. Inspired by a statement attributed to a young Italian garment worker, "It wouldn't be so bad if they would only let us sing at our work," the poem hails the factory girl as "Child of the Renaissance" and "little sister of Ariosto and of Raphael," proclaiming, "If any hush the song within your bosom, / By all your lyric land, he does not well!" The speaker laments that the U.S., when compared with Italy, is "a songless land." It calls for a day when North America will be "reborn in Beauty's image," and "every harvest brought with singing home."

Eloise Robinson's "Sweat-Shop Flowers" (Sept. 1917: 37) shows an even greater debt to Victorian pathos than Waddell's poem, owing something to Dante Gabriel Rossetti as well as to Thomas Hood.[3] In "Sweat-Shop Flowers," a factory child who has died and gone to heaven is pictured as doing there exactly what she did on earth: mass-producing ornamental flowers. For "Twenty rosebuds fashioned neatly," the child knows, "They will give a copper penny." The poem implicitly deplores the waste of the child's potential by presenting her as incapable of doing anything other than making sweatshop flowers: "Daisies have a hundred petals, primroses have five, / It was all they taught her, when she was alive." While other children run by, calling on her to join them in play, the child continues her obsessive, monotonous labor. Unfortunately, the effect of this conception is to present heaven itself as purgatory—as being, in effect, a sweatshop.

More successful, perhaps, in credibly evoking pathos is Hortense Flexner's "The Winds of Spring." Imprisoned in a basement textile factory, a woman hears with longing the call of the outside world in the gusts of wind that find their way into her prison:

> I know for all the whirr of wheels,
> And the clack of the loom's gaunt frame,
> That the winds are calling, calling away
> From the factory's gray-faced shame,
> And tugging like tiny hands at my skirt,
> And singing in tears my name.
>
> (May 1915: 18)

Particularly effective is the speaker's projection of her own frustration onto the wind, which she endows with an articulate voice.

Another poem which may be said to succeed insofar as it evokes a mood for the reader concerns not workers in the workplace, but workers en route to the New World. Published shortly after the 1917 Immigration Law finally put an end to virtually all movement of Asians to the United States, Elizabeth J. Coatsworth's "The Coolie Ship" (Nov./Dec. 1917: 43) sketches images of the dimly lit, crowded decks of an immigrant ship, "fetid with close-packed life," where "huddled" figures lie with their blankets and scanty possessions. As the ship rocks in the waves, "The stars swing and sway as though fastened to strings," the "tired" ship's engines "gasp and strain" to make headway. They "beat quick and uneven like the heart of a

"WHERE IGNORANCE IS BLISS," CORNELIA BARNS.
(Courtesy General Research Division, The New York Public Library, Astor, Lenox and Tilden Foundations.)

dying man / Across the troubled decks. . . ." In a haunted, troubled sleep, invaded by the "broken song" of a fellow passenger's flute, the new immigrants drift toward the uncertain fate awaiting them in America.

Occasionally, *Masses* poets sought to address a perceived discrepancy between their own class position and that of the wage earners whose conditions they protested—including the commercial exploitation of the worker's plight to which literary treatment might insidiously lend itself:

> She has such feeling for the wretched poor!
> —Yes—that's her limousine!—
> She writes those tales about the working girls
> In———Magazine.[4]

In "The Dream Bearer," Mary Carolyn Davies recognizes and criticizes another kind of class assertiveness—that of the well-to-do social activist. The poem's narrator went "Where weary folk toil, black with smoke," to "carry a dream" to seemingly benighted workers. What the dream was, she does not say—only that she was humbled to realize that the objects of her patronage were imaginatively richer than she was: "They had more dreams than I" (July 1916: 23).

The narrator in Margaret Sangster's "Proportionately" (Nov./Dec. 1917: 3) is, like the speaker in "The Dream-Bearer," aware of how little she knows of the economic conditions of workers. An economist friend has assured her that, since "The price of labor always advances / Proportionately, / With the price of food," there is no reason why people should go hungry for lack of adequate wages. The narrator, lacking, as she says, the advantage of a college education, "listened to him prayerfully, (More or less)." Yet she remains unable to dismiss from her memory the image of a child she has seen recently, "thin and joyless, / And old of face . . . crying for bread." In Florence Ripley Mastin's "The Dream," awareness of economic exploitation comes to the speaker in the form of a "ghostly crowd" of young female garment workers, whose drained, pale looks contrast dramatically with the gorgeous materials they cut and sew. One of the young women,

> . . . with hair as bright as corn,
> Who flashed her slender needle in a dream,
> Looked up at me. Her eyes were dark with pain.
> Then I awoke and it was sunny morn—
> But in the dawn there was for me no gleam,
> And I can never wear the dress again.
>   (June 1916: 16)

In other poems, workers are presented as demanding an improvement in their conditions. "We seek but the chance to live humbly with toil / On a wage that will pay for our needs" is the modest claim of the factory workers in Edith Smith's "The Mills of the Rich" (July 1912: 8). If not exactly revolutionary, it seems to correspond fairly closely to the position of the majority of U.S. women workers, who took part in no organized workplace agitation, either revolutionary or reformist.[5] Another group of poems urges or celebrates some form of active resistance to the employing class. Babette Deutsch, who celebrated the Russian Revolution in her poem "Banners"—"Now breaks the noise of people roused to war, / Who take their own like fire"[6]—in June 1917 published "Ironic" in *The Masses*. This poem addresses "the fireless poor"—"fireless," one may surmise, in a metaphorical as well as a literal sense—who "stare" blankly before them, envisaging no future except "bleak toil, / Hard and unsure." The poem assures victims of exploitation that life gives them "one thing only: / War":

> Your weapons are despair
> And hate,
> And the irons you wore so long,
> And famine to share.
> You are strong with all that you bore.
> You can strike. Strike!
> What do you ask for more?
>
> (48)

Lydia Gibson's "Children of Kings," about child labor, sounds a similar call to rebellion. In a sustained metaphor, the poem represents the sweatshop children as meekly subdued acolytes in Mammon's temple:

> The children learning prayers at Mammon's knees,
> Whose small starved bodies and whose weary feet
> A million and a million times repeat
> The same short way that the machine decrees . . .
> Weavers of cushions for old Mammon's seat.
>
> (May 1914: 21)

Gibson calls for the breaking of the spell which makes this subservience possible—which causes even exploited children to endorse the worship of Mammon, which perpetuates their slavery. "Why wait ye," her poem demands of the parents of these factory children, "to burn down his throne?"

Other poems do not exhort quite so glibly, but rather foretell, in prophetic vein, the coming of a liberating revolution conceived of as inevitable and which, in the violent conflicts between labor and capital of the years before World War I, sometimes appeared very close indeed. In "What of the Night," Elizabeth Waddell, recalling the 1914 massacre of twenty-six striking coal miners and their family members at Ludlow, Colorado,[7] derides the apparent blindness of those who permitted the Colorado National Guard to commit such atrocities, and yet who still "*will* not know it is war!" The anticipated revolution will come with "strife and blood," but will lead inevitably to "The Day, to seers and singers of old made known" (Mar. 1917: 6).

Rose Pastor Stokes, one of the few *Masses* poets with firsthand experience of factory work,[8] writes her prophecy of revolution, "Paterson," in the wake of the heroically sustained but finally abortive Paterson silk workers' strike of 1913. After a five-month struggle to end the recently adopted, inhuman system in the silk mills (under which a single operator might be required to work four looms simultaneously), the strikers were starved back to work by lack of funds. In Stokes' poem, although the atmosphere of the reopened mills is calm, it is also "ominous." Unknown to the mill owners, the workers at their looms weave for them "a shroud of . . . black," and the very rhythms of the mill machinery repeat the word "Beware!" (Nov. 1913: 11).

Sarah N. Cleghorn's "Comrade Jesus," while it belongs to the group of "revolutionary" poems on labor issues, is distinctive in its appropriation of Christian teaching to the cause of revolutionary organized labor. It thus lies within a tradition which seems to have been not without influence on the 1920s polemical fiction of Upton Sinclair:[9]

Thanks to Saint Matthew, who had been
At mass-meetings in Palestine,
We know whose side was spoken for
When Comrade Jesus had the floor.
(Apr. 1914: 14)

The life of Jesus, a dangerous "ignorant demagogue" in the eyes of the Pharisees, is narrated in a context of labor exploitation. Jesus will be found wherever "sore they toil and hard they lie." He identifies with the world's despised poor: "The tramp, the convict, I am he; / Cold-shoulder him, cold-shoulder me." He prophesies the exclusion of the rich, not from a heavenly afterlife, but from a future kingdom of peace and justice on earth.

The poem concludes with an account of Jesus' heroic solidarity with his "fellow-felon" during the agony on the cross (but with no hint of any supernatural resurrection) and with the identification of Jesus as a true member of the Industrial Workers of the World:

> Ah, let no Local him refuse;
> Comrade Jesus hath paid his dues.
> Whatever other be debarred,
> Comrade Jesus hath his red card.
>
> (14)

The implied question here is not whether a Wobbly may be admitted to the Kingdom of Heaven, but whether Jesus would be accepted in the company of Wobblies—a question which is answered satisfactorily in the affirmative. In *The Masses* the poem is printed framed by a group of satiric prose pieces which present the arrest, trial, and execution of Jesus as it might have been written up by a bribed popular press in first-century Palestine. "I poured the burning joy of my new-found Socialism into the poem," wrote Cleghorn more than twenty years later, in her autobiography.[10]

Not surprisingly, given the data available on the hardships of the workplace for the majority of workers—particularly for women and immigrants, who in the early 1900s (as in the 1990s) supplied much of society's cheapest labor—one finds almost no depiction in the pages of *The Masses* of work as a satisfying or pleasurable activity. The securing of work, however, as representing escape from the fear of unemployment, may be presented as offering cause for celebration, as in Elizabeth Waddell's "The Job." As a young couple hear of the reopening of the "Works" at the end of winter, they hug each other, "heedless of onlookers," in their joyful relief. The wife is "too pale for beauty," but "the dawn rose in her face" at hearing the good news. The couple snatch their one-month-old baby from the cradle and swing him "in his little blue blanket merrily to a hummed dance-tune." The observer of the scene has never witnessed "more beautiful joy" than this of "the boy and girl over the good news of a job" (Feb. 1916: 18).

Amy Lowell's "In The Grocery" presents the subject of unemployment in more complex terms. The young man in the poem, who courts the grocer's daughter and seems unable to find work, may be a feckless, work-shy character or may be, as he protests, simply one more victim of an unfavorable labor market: "Yer ain't fair to me, Alice, 'deed yer ain't / I work when anythin's doin.'" There is a satisfying ambiguity in the dialogue's development:

"Hev yer forgot the time I went expressin'
In the American office, down there?"
"And come back two weeks later!
No I ain't."
". . . I'm a sight too light fer all that liftin'. . . ."
(June 1916: 17)

Regardless of his excuses, the young woman rejects the young man.

If a good number of *Masses* poems which deal with labor issues seem rather remote from detailed representations of the workplace, and even at times a trifle simplistic in their portrayals of labor exploitation, *Masses* fiction and reportage present a good deal more complexity. Ethel Lloyd Patterson's "Things for Dolls" (Jan. 1912: 12–13) is a case in point. Patterson's story describes with powerful irony the psychological pressures imposed upon the saleswomen in a fashionable toy store. These pressures, although not as threatening to physical health as factory conditions, still exert their own kind of oppression. Mamie Tuttle, the story's central character, is an unsuccessful saleswoman: "She had not just the right attitude toward customers . . . at first she could not seem to manage the mixture of servility and tender interest and understanding that best pleases a very rich mamma about to buy a doll with real eyelashes and cords that may be pulled to make it say things" (12). Mamie has difficulty coping with a customer who has her undress every single doll, then leaves without buying, promising to "come back in the afternoon." Although the saleswoman is supposed to "handle a doll as though she loved it," Mamie, after this particular (apparently not untypical) incident, is said to have returned to her counter and "straightened a shelf of baby dolls viciously." The greatest insult to Mamie's feelings, however, turns out to be the dolls themselves, with their hand-embroidered garments adorned with real lace, their exquisitely fashioned accessories of gold and ivory. After finally managing to complete a large sale, Mamie destroys the dolls in a rebellious rage. She explains to the baffled manager that she was maddened by the thought of how the money squandered by the wealthy customer "for all them brushes and combs and dresses" would have paid for her mother's and sister's medical treatment: "And I got to hating them something awful all of a sudden" (13). The story's conclusion, with its stilted pathos and the offer to Mamie by the understanding store manager of a full-time job after she has destroyed over $340 worth of merchandise, is the story's

"SHOP TALK," CORNELIA BARNS.
"Then the red-headed feller sez ter me, he sez ter me, he sez—"
(Courtesy General Research Division, The New York Public Library, As-
tor, Lenox and Tilden Foundations.)

weakest moment. Before this point is reached, however, "Things for Dolls" has given a convincing depiction of the trials of the saleswoman, of her vulnerability to the demands of employers, of customers, and of economic need.

Even in a brief sketch, like Phyllis Wyatt's one-page narrative "The Checked Trousers" (June 1917: 17), relative complexity is apparent. The story gives a detailed description of the family-owned tailor shop where the action takes place—of its green baize curtains and artificial plants, of the tailor's helper in the fitting closet, "a gifted human cushion who was able by a slight chewing movement to emit on demand countless pins," of the customers standing with patterns pinned on their hips "while a little demoniacal chalk-marking machine ran in a circle round their unhemmed skirts." Somewhat surprisingly, in the socialist *Masses,* the story's main character is the tailor shop proprietor's wife, Mrs. Joblanska. The shop's employees are merely sketched, in an allusion to a "melée of twenty workers" in the "long, dark, tarnlike" cutting and sewing department. The central focus is upon the fellow feeling that develops between Mrs. Joblanska and one of her customers, as Mrs. Joblanska tells of her husband's illness, brought on by overwork. As the customer, herself a breadwinner with dependents, listens, and watches "the Polish woman's prehensile, quick, nervous fingers" working on her dress, "the texture of their lives, their responsibilities and fears and hopes, seemed suddenly the same." By the story's conclusion, when Mrs. Joblanska reports joyfully that her husband has made such a good recovery at the tuberculosis clinic that the checkered pants made for him at his departure have had to be let out four inches, the bond of sympathy between the two women is firmly established. The story's sympathetic treatment of a member of the employing class is fairly unusual in *The Masses,* and is perhaps rendered acceptable to readers by the narrator's insistence on Mrs. Joblanska's double burden, as a businesswoman and as a woman obliged to shoulder the responsibilities of "cumbering children" and a household. The Joblanska family's profits from the labors of the workers in the cutting room go unmentioned.

Adriana Spadoni's article "Foreladies," on the other hand, gives a firsthand account of the garment industry—in this case a large clothing factory—from the perspective of the employee. Spadoni gives a powerful description of the factory floor as viewed by a newcomer to the scene:

Giant wheels tore round. Belts whirred through mysterious holes in the floor and ceiling. The floors trembled and the walls shook. The huge loft stretched on and on across the earth. Small boys ran about with great crates of white stuff on little trucks. And the air was filled with fine gray dust. It was all alive, quivering. (Mar. 1917: 5)

All, that is, except for the dozens of motionless women at their sewing machines, "all bent forward at the same angle, each feeding the Thing before her. . . . Like the dead kings of Egypt, rigid on their stone thrones, they sat before the living machines."[11]

In particular, Spadoni gives an amusing account of the newcomer's relationship with the sewing room's supercilious forelady: "God made Heaven and earth in seven days. On the eighth day he made foreladies. They are a special creation." Awed by the woman's grand manner, the narrator follows the forelady to her new station in the sewing room, where "with her eyelids she indicated a place on the wall for my hat." The forelady has "a special peg" for her own hat and coat, which hang there "as if the entire factory had been designed for this particular nail." With "insulting patience," the forelady initiates the novice into the mysteries of stitching cuffs: "'You'll get used to it. . . .' With that articulate eyelid she consigned me to an eternity of pressing treadles" (6). Spadoni describes the torments of a novice unused to spending nine hours seated at a machine:

> Iron bands closed about my head. A sharp knife buried itself just below my shoulder blades. My wooden wrists guided the supply of cuffs. My eyes came to the very edge of their sockets. Once I shut off the power and pressed them back again. The only living, conscious, thinking things were my fingers. (5)

As she grows accustomed to the work, the narrator finds her body adjusting to the psychological and physical strains of her task: "The knife had gone from under my shoulder blades." She no longer breathes the dusty air with difficulty, and finds herself sharing the "silent rigidity" of her fellow workers, their blank unconsciousness of everything but the task in hand. She even finds herself wondering whether, had she continued working in the sewing room, she might "by some miracle" herself have become a forelady: "Would I, too, then have walked among my stone women and seen no tragedy in their patient eagerness? Found nothing to pity in their willing speed?" These questions remain purely hypothetical, however. In a slump in the garment trade—which, although the narrator makes light of its consequences for herself, points to the constant insecurity of the wage worker in an unrestrictedly laissez-faire economy—she loses her job. "I was saved. . . . The rush season was over and, with ten others, I went. The Forelady had never liked me and so I went" (6).

That the fierce competition for mere survival in the labor market could lead to ambivalent attitudes toward one's fellows is the idea implicitly explored in Spadoni's story "A Rift of Silence." Michael Pavlov, a young Russian immigrant, lives with his family in a crowded tenement house where, on hot summer nights, the "sucking beat" of others' breathing in the thick air keeps him sleepless all night, so that he longs for "one little spot of silence in that even, rhythmic beat." At the same time, Michael's father looks forward eagerly to the day when a fellow employee in the slaughterhouse will be dismissed, so that the younger man may take his place: "'He is getting old. Last week he made twice the same mistake. The company cannot afford to keep him.' There was a faint note of pride in Fedor Pavlov's voice as if he and the company were now responsible together." As the father is telling this to Michael, Michael's beloved younger brother, who has been sick with fever, dies in the adjoining room. It is then, between the sobs of the grieving family, that Michael Pavlov hears what he had longed for, and is now ironically granted: "a little rift of silence" (Feb. 1913: 13).

A number of the most effective stories by women contributors to *The Masses* deal with the relationship of a middle-class housewife to a domestic servant. Their success may not necessarily be directly attributable to the greater familiarity of the authors with the milieu they describe, but these stories certainly exhibit an astute understanding of the manner in which labor, race, and class issues and patriarchal attitudes closely intertwine within the world of domestic service in ways which interrogate the various forms of oppression both of the employee and of her middle-class female employer. The stories of domestic service published in *The Masses* are remarkable for their almost exclusive focus on the relations between a female employer and an employee pregnant and unmarried. It would be easy to level a charge of stereotyping against these stories if it were not for the central relevance of this situation to a number of interrelated issues.

What strikes the reader most forcefully about a number of the stories dealing with the relationship of servants and employers in the stories of domestic service is the degree of self-righteous moral judgment exercised by the fictional employers. On the whole, the stories present such attitudes with considerable irony. In Helen Forbes' "The Hunky Woman," the reader is supplied with information about the tragic experience of a stolid Hungarian washerwoman, to which her well-meaning but self-righteous and complacent employer has no access. Although a "kind" mistress, who has dispensed advice "and the very tangible assistance that never failed to accompany it" to "many a Bridget and Maggie," Mrs. Atwood finds herself repelled by the uncommunicative manner of Annie Szorza. Unable to patronize Annie with her generosity (and to receive, no doubt, the expected soothing words of gratitude), Mrs. Atwood only observes how her employee "snatches" her pay without thanks and without meeting her eye, and that her movements seem "sullenly abrupt": "There was something stolid, something typical of the woman's race, in the very way her dingy skirt drabbled over the rain-soaked grass." She would do better, Mrs. Atwood concludes, "to try to be nice to the ironingboard. I'd get exactly the same response." Her husband explains that "Hunkies" are indeed "only half human . . . as much emotion in a Hunky as there is in a bump on a log" (May 1917: 12).

The reader is privileged to learn that the Atwoods' estimation of Annie is gravely mistaken. Arrested and detained upon her return home from Mrs. Atwood's, upon suspicion of complicity in the crime of bigamy committed by her absent husband, Annie sits awake all night in jail, "swaying back and forth," in the knowledge that her baby, left unfed, is starving: "'Oh, my babies, my babies!' sobbed the mother over and over again." Annie does indeed return home to find that her younger child has starved to death in her absence. She goes to see Mrs. Atwood, and tries in vain to explain why she had missed work during the previous days. The employer's indignant reaction, even when she has heard Annie's garbled version of her story, is one of accusation—"You left the clothes all damp. They might have been ruined"—mingled with horror at the washerwoman's blunt statement that she has been in jail, and that her baby is dead. "You killed your baby?" Mrs. Atwood concludes. Still unsure, even when she has grasped it more fully, whether Annie's tale of her arbitrary arrest and its tragic result is true or not—"Things like that don't happen in this country"—and still half-convinced her employee is a murderess, Mrs. Atwood dismisses Annie from her service. She reluctantly concludes what her husband had maintained all along: "Those Hunkies are just animals" (13). The story, besides offering a study in class and labor relations, is also a study in racial bigotry and ideological complacency. It invites a largely middle-class readership to consider alternative responses to those of the Atwoods. Would readers, in Mrs. Atwood's position, have reacted with equal incomprehension?

An intensely intrusive concern for her employee's "moral" well-being is shown as informing the behavior of the elderly spinster Miss Cora in Helen Hull's "Usury." The employer struggles to fit her narrow conception of moral propriety to the dilemma of Lizzie, her young servant and protégée, whom, against the advice of her pious friends, Miss Cora has taken into her home after Lizzie's failed pregnancy and desertion by her lover. When the man returns to claim Lizzie, who is by now happily engaged to someone else, Miss Cora tries to convince her that it is her moral duty to marry the former lover, whom Lizzie now detests. Lizzie, for her part, is ready to yield to Miss Cora's insistence, against her better judgment, out of a sense of obligation to her employer: "The girl would heed her, then, as she had heeded her ever since Miss Cora had started to help her struggle up from the abyss of despair" (Sept. 1916: 7). "Usury" is typical of much of Helen Hull's work (first published in *The Masses*) in its exploration of two basic themes—the subjection of women of all classes to internalized patriarchal ethical codes, and the ties of obligation and exploitation that bind wives and husbands, employers and employees. The story's title alludes to debts with interest incurred, or regarded as incurred, within a complex economy of sexual, class, and material relations.

The character of Miss Cora is presented with a good deal of sympathy. Her conviction that "marriage was the way in which such mistakes as Lizzie's were remedied" is evidently sincere—and so are her underlying, and very human, doubts, her "cold little fear" that she might after all be giving Lizzie wrong advice. At last, confronted with the vision of the deep love between Lizzie and her new fiancé, she hesitantly admits to having no monopoly on moral truth: "I can't be sure. I can't tell you what to do" (8). Miss Cora's very uncertainty deconstructs not only the individual's right to pass judgment in this particular case, but the quasi-feudal assumption of the right of moral judgment of employer over servant.

In "A New Woman?" by Dorothy Weil, the part played by patriarchal attitudes, and a woman's resistance to them, are even more prominent. The tone is set by the story's opening, in which a conservative husband, learning of the recently announced pregnancy of the Irish Catholic cleaning woman, Mrs. Knox, embarks on a denunciation of "the senseless follies of the working classes." The story's narrator, his wife, dismisses her husband's class prejudice as self-righteous:

'See here, Henry Bullock,' I said, 'who're you and I, I'd like to know, that we should set up as the Lord Almighty to judge his creatures? I've an idea that we criticise a woman who slaves every day cleaning people's houses and every night scrubbing out office buildings, to feed her family. It appears to me that most anything she does after that deserves forgiveness.' (Jan. 1916: 17)

However, the temporary cleaning woman who takes the place of Mrs. Knox, while the latter is away giving birth, presents a new challenge to the narrator's confident moral certainties. Unlike the "respectable" Mrs. Knox, the newcomer is not only a mother, but unmarried—potentially, in fact, the "New Woman" of the story's title. Her single state—which, as she later explains, was a choice freely made, to give the child's father a better chance of succeeding in life unencumbered—has caused her dismissal from a series of jobs: ". . . as soon as they find out about the child, off I go" (17). In fact, the title of "New Woman" is cruelly ironic, since Jennie's situation brings with it none of the freedom which upper-class women typically associated with the term, but rather drudgery and economic insecurity.

The narrator's initial reaction to Jennie's story is to call in a minister for spiritual and practical advice on this disturbing question, but she is restrained by Jennie's plea that the involvement of social workers will lead to

"TWELVE-THIRTY," CORNELIA BARNS.
(Courtesy General Research Division, The New York Public Library, Astor, Lenox and Tilden Foundations.)

her being treated as a tubercular "case" and separated from her child. The narrator, moved by the younger woman's tears to listen sympathetically to her story, temporarily forgets all about her husband and his stern patriarchal values: "I don't suppose I would have dared to ask . . . if I had been a real good woman, and remembered the whole thing was taking place in Henry Bullock's bedroom; but I never gave Henry or his strict opinions one single thought!" (17). Jennie, for her part, forestalls any self-righteous impulses from the narrator: "It ain't folks like you in your comfort that can judge me." If the narrator shows herself somewhat disposed to sympathy with Jenny, perhaps her own relatively humble class position is offered as part-explanation. Certainly, in the narrator's homely, garrulous, sometimes ungrammatical speech—"I think you'd ought to tell me a bit more so's that I'd see clearer"—an unsnobbish, unpretentious class outlook is suggested. The narrator moves from pitying tolerance to genuine admiration for the frail yet determined younger woman: "She looked such a person, somehow. . . . I envied her knowing her own mind like that" (18). The narrator ends by paying Jennie a day's wages, even though the latter has not actually worked—although with the admission, indicative of a conflict between stinginess and generosity, that her economic dependence on the male of the household may have its uses: "I was glad Henry keeps me kind of close so I hadn't enough to give her more, like I first thought I would." However, it is Jennie's fellow worker, the initially contemptuous and disapproving Mrs. Knox, who gives Jennie help of lasting value by offering to find her night work in an office building, "if you'll keep quiet about the kid." Still, the narrator cannot relinquish the sense that she, as a middle-class employer, ought to take responsibility for the well-being of her employees. When the narrator promises not to tell her minister about Jennie and her child, Jennie points out that Mrs. Bullock could not do so, in any case: "You don't know where I live . . ." (18). The narrator comments, "The girl had me there. I didn't even know where Mrs. Knox lived, for all she'd been working for me these six years and more." The unspoken assumption on the narrator's part is that she *should* have known more about the private lives of her servants.

If *Masses* stories of domestic service offer fictional representations of oppression and liberation in the context of class relations at an interpersonal level, labor reportage by the women of *The Masses* investigates and celebrates the possibilities of liberation for employees via the trade union movement. A study of representations of labor and the workplace in the pages of *The Masses* would be incomplete without mention of the nonfictional writings of three labor reporters—Mary Heaton Vorse, Helen Marot, and Inez Irwin.

Vorse, besides being a contributing editor of *The Masses,* a successful popular fiction writer, and a suffrage activist, was among the most dedicated and gifted labor reporters of the century, and was by the mid-1930s "the acknowledged veteran of American labor journalism."[12] She covered the 1912 Lawrence textile strike, the Pennsylvania steel strikes of 1919, and the 1929 textile workers' strike in Gastonia. She wrote the history of the great organizing movement of the Congress of Industrial Organizations (CIO) during the 1930s which formed the subject of her book *Labor's New Millions* (1938). Her great gift, as Max Eastman's sister Crystal succinctly expressed it, in an invitation to cover a strike for the *Liberator,* was for the "vivid human story" of a situation, based on sharp personal observation.[13]

The impulse behind Vorse's labor journalism, as she defined it in her 1935 autobiography *A Footnote to Folly,* was to further the cause of workers by raising public awareness. She wanted others "to see what I had seen, feel what I had felt." She wanted "to see wages go up and the babies' death rate go down" (21). Her concern about such issues, however, seems to have been not unmixed with a simple thirst for excitement, if one takes as autobiographical a passage in her novel *Strike!* (1930), describing a character evidently modeled on Vorse: "Hoskins was an old-time labor reporter. . . . He made a good living as a special writer for popular magazines, and would have been well off if he could have left the labor movement alone. . . . He'd swear off, but let a strike come along . . . and there he'd be" (15).

In *A Footnote to Folly,* Vorse writes that she regarded the union movement as "a college for the workers," in which, through their active participation in a strike or a labor protest, they might learn history and economics "translated into the terms of their own lives." Moreover, through such experiences they might develop hitherto unsuspected skills as public speakers, writers or composers of songs: "Like new blood these new talents flow through the masses of the workers" (12). The students in this "college" might include both women workers and workers' wives, who in Vorse's accounts of labor conflicts spanning fifty years are often represented as playing crucial roles. Vorse tells of the support of women for their striking husbands during the Pennsylvania steel strike of 1919: ". . . if the strike was kept alive by the individual courage of the men, it was also being won by the endurance of women" (295). In *Labor's New Millions,* her account of the great CIO organizing drive, she describes the Women's Auxiliary of the 1937 Flint Chevrolet strike returning undaunted to the picket line, after having been tear-gassed (77). In *Strike!* she draws a fictional portrait of the legendary labor songwriter Ella May Wiggins ("Mamie Lewis" in the novel), who was a moving force in the Gastonia textile strike of 1929, and was killed by a deputy's gun.[14]

Ironically, at a time when Vorse was producing some of her best labor reportage for *Harper's Magazine* and *Outlook* on the Lawrence textile strike of 1912, the labor conflicts on Minnesota's Mesaba Range, and the plight of the homeless unemployed in New York City,[15] she wrote short fiction regularly for *The Masses,* but only a single labor article. "Accessories before the Fact" remains worth discussing here, however, as representative, in its concern with ordinary workers' legal rights and with the role played by women in labor protests, of Vorse's labor journalism in general. "Accessories before the Fact" deals with the outcome of an attempt by the Industrial Workers of the World to organize striking iron ore miners on Minnesota's Mesaba Range. The strike had begun spontaneously among the 16,000 non-unionized workers in June 1916. The miners' demands included an eight-hour day and abolition of a subcontracted piecework system. To the employers, the presence of IWW organizers—"outside agitators," the mine bosses preferred to call them—was most unwelcome. Vorse, summoned to report on the strike by appeals from labor organizer Elizabeth Gurley Flynn, was struck, upon her arrival on the range, by the presence everywhere of company-hired gunmen.[16] "At first you smile at them," Vorse writes; "many of them are such caricatures." They looked to her "like motion-picture plug-uglies . . . bloated, unshaven, toddy blossoms on noses . . . too exaggerated to be real." Later, she adds, "You do not feel like smiling when you have seen the bruises on the bodies of women caused by their hands and clubs, or after you have heard the excited women in the little bleak villages tell in broken English stories of fights for water, of arrests and abuse" (Nov. 1916: 6).

The article's main focus, though, is on the case of a miner's wife, Militza Masonovitch, accused, with her husband, three of her lodgers, and three IWW organizers (one of them Flynn's lover Carlo Tresca) of the shooting of a deputy. None of the accused who witnessed the shooting actually possessed a gun—an inconvenient detail that did not prevent the authorities from charging eight people, including three who had not even seen the killing. Vorse concentrates on Mrs. Masonovitch, arrested with her baby, as representative of the bewildered victims of the campaign of repression launched against the workers: "Mrs. Masonovitch is in jail accused of murder. Just why she's there is hard for anyone to understand. It's not much wonder that she cries and cries . . ." (7). It may have been partly due to the extensive press coverage of the case—to which Vorse contributed with articles in *Harper's, The Outlook,* and *The Globe,* as well as *The Masses*—that, although Phillip Masonovitch and two of the other miners received prison sentences, Mrs. Masonovitch and the three union organizers were acquitted.[17]

For Vorse, the line betweeen journalistic coverage of a strike and active involvement in it was fluid. In the Lawrence strike of 1912, for instance, she had been less a neutral reporter than "a sort of assistant" to the strike leaders. Even in later strikes, where she maintained a more detached stance, she donated to strikers' relief funds, and made no secret, in her reports, of her active sympathy for the cause of labor.[18]

Helen Marot, in her writings for *The Masses* as in her books, was the most detached of labor reporters, less a commentator and recorder of specific events than an analyst of movements and trends. She was a member of the executive board of the Women's Trade Union League (WTUL) of New York, in which capacity she did take part in organizing the great strike of New York's women textile workers in 1909–1910. She was also a contributing editor of the socialist *New Review,* a founding member of the National Labor Defense Counsel, and a cooperative shareholder in *The Masses.*[19] Her work on the New York Child Labor Committee led to the passing in New York State of the Compulsory Education Act of 1903. Marot wrote numerous articles on labor issues and two books, *American Labor Unions* (1914) and *The Creative Impulse in Industry* (1918).

American Labor Unions surveys the various branches of the U.S. union movement, interpreting policies and methods to the general reader from "the labor union point of view." In the book Marot comments perceptively on the successes and difficulties of women within the labor movement. As the executive secretary of a WTUL chapter, whose main function was to assist women in their efforts to unionize, Marot was well qualified to comment on the psychological and economic obstacles to women's organization. Not only do women work in occupations with a high employee turnover, Marot points out, but they bear a double burden of domestic and "outside" labor, which, according to her observations, often makes meeting attendance difficult. Male prejudice presents a further barrier to women's advancement in the union. While Marot, not without a certain complacency, claims that it is "practically impossible" in 1914 to find instances of sex discrimination in the admittance of women to rank-and-file membership of a union representing their trade, she views women as actively excluded from serving on union executive boards by prejudiced male executives.[20] Moreover, women themselves, in Marot's view, often lack "the courage and determination" to overcome "the prevailing attitude that women are unfit to assume executive responsibility" (68). Marot anticipates that such attitudes will alter over time. She also considers that union women already have a great deal to be proud of: "It is now a generally accepted fact among all unionists that women make the best strikers," in their tenacity and their opposition to premature compromise during strike negotiations. Not only does "the quality of the revolutionist" become apparent in women on strike, according to Marot, but this quality has the potential, when women rise in the labor movement, to reshape it radically: "There are women who have served their unions for a decade or more

who have never lost the militant spirit which characterized them as strikers" (74).

In *The Creative Impulse in Industry,* Marot argues the importance of
job satisfaction to manual workers, and advocates a holistic approach
to craft education—involving trainees in every phase of production and
marketing—which is still regarded as experimental and progressive today.[21] Her articles for *The Masses* included "Railroads and Revolution"
(Nov. 1916) on the Railroad Brotherhoods, "Revolution and the Garment
Trade" (Aug. 1916), and "Immigration and Militarism" (Apr. 1916). "Revolution and the Garment Trade" discusses the administrative politics of the
New York garment workers' unions. "Immigration and Militarism," written one year before the U.S. entry into World War I, addresses the question of U.S. manufacturers' employment of cheap labor overseas, and pre-
sciently foresees an extension of U.S. military power to protect U.S.
economic interests, a movement that was then still in its beginnings.[22]

As a commentator on union affairs, Marot regarded trade unionism as offering training in civic participation. Not only was improvement of workers' economic situation a precondition for the securing of real political
power, but union organization itself represented a form of political empowerment. Marot, who was a Fabian democratic socialist, somewhat dis-
ingenuously claimed to "hold no brief" for the conservative American
Federation of Labor (AF of L) over the much smaller—and of course far
more radical—Industrial Workers of the World (IWW), which called for
workers' ownership of the means of production. Yet she makes clear a
preference for industrial unionism (organization according to industry,
regardless of skill or training) over the craft unionism of the American
Federation of Labor. This preference aligns her more closely with the
IWW and the socialist minority in the AF of L than with the majority of
AF of L members. Clearly, her hopes for the development of the U.S.
labor movement extended beyond the mere betterment of workers' material conditions. In a *Masses* article "The Revolutionary Spirit at Seattle,"
on the AF of L convention of 1914, Marot expressed her disappointment
at the reluctance of the socialist minority within the AF of L to fight for
the class-conscious industrial unionism they professed theoretically. She
saw "hope even at Seattle," however, in the fight for industrial unionism
among West Coast unionists in the same year. The West Coast leaders,
although they "were never called Socialists," showed, in Marot's view, a
powerful inter-union solidarity which promised well for the democratic
expansion of the labor movement as a whole (Jan. 1914: 16).

The theme of democratic political empowerment recurs in "Actors and
Teachers" (June 1916), Marot's article for *The Masses* on a recent, nearly
unanimous decision of a meeting of New York vaudeville actors to join

the AF of L. Marot remarks that actors, however they may insist upon their special status as artists, must nonetheless, in order to deal with the low pay, physical hardships, and economic insecurity imposed upon them by employers, "fight for their rights as workingmen" (16). The advantages to the labor movement of the unionization of professionals go beyond the material benefits to the new professional members, however. Such movements among middle-class employees offer, according to Marot, "an indication that some breaches are being made in the social barriers which have so long kept apart those who make their living in slightly different ways." (It happened, coincidentally, that on the evening of the actors' vote, two thousand New York public school teachers also voted to lobby among their colleagues for the formation of a union, further establishing the right of professionals to unionize.)

Marot also understands the limits to the dissolving of social barriers represented by professional unionization, particularly those set by class distinctions. Solidarity among professionals within their profession does not necessarily by any means imply social egalitarianism. Just as the actors, in Marot's slightly sarcastic words, were relieved to learn that AF of L affiliation would not commit them to "invite teamsters and longshoremen to tea," so, at the teachers' meeting, "nothing was said about the value of solidarity between teachers and janitors of school buildings." Marot warns that anyone who naively hopes for the emergence of solidarity across class lines as an immediate result of the unionization of professionals "is likely to be disappointed a little later on." Yet Marot does believe that, in the long run, such unionization is conducive to greater democracy within the profession. The "aristocrats of labor" are, she believes, "extremely unlikely to use their new-found strength solely in a fight for a few hours a day less or a few dollars a week more." She predicts (perhaps overconfidently) that unionized professionals will also strive for greater control over the institutions they serve: "The organizing of the teachers will mean a fight to relegate board of education meddling with their business to the dust-heap. The organizing of actors will mean a struggle to convert managers into elected and paid servants of the actors' union." The consequences of these developments *would* be truly radical: "Any measure of success they may achieve will establish in the minds of the people the revolutionary significance of trade union organization, inspire labor with a new desire for power, and initiate an era of real industrial democracy" (16).

Inez Haynes Irwin was better known for her popular fiction than for her labor journalism, but she did write several pieces on labor issues for *The Masses*. While her fiction for *The Masses* deals mostly with the social relations of a leisured upper class, her labor articles record impressions of investigative hearings and trade union conventions—events which her sometimes hyperbolic style imbues with a sense of urgency and drama.

Although solidly middle class in her own social status, Irwin could claim to be the daughter of a millworker. Her mother, before her marriage to actor and penal reformer Gideon Haynes, had worked in the Massachusetts mills in the years when such work was still considered respectable premarital employment for New England women. But it was the legends of her ancestors' heroism during the American Revolution, and the living example of her feminist aunt, that explained why Irwin, "the most timid of created beings," as she called herself, was "always in one civic fight at least; often in two; sometimes in more" ("Adventures", 553).

Her actions certainly seem to belie her claim of timidity. Before moving to New York and joining the staff of *The Masses,* Irwin worked as a reporter and speaker on labor issues in California. Her chief involvement there was with the Ford and Suhr case, on which she wrote in 1914 for *Harper's Weekly.* IWW organizers Richard Ford and Herman Suhr were charged with murdering District Attorney Ed Manwell, shot dead during a hop pickers' strike. Neither Ford nor Suhr had taken any part in the fight in which Manwell had died. They were, as Irwin explains, "found guilty of being the *leaders of a strike which resulted in violence*" (319).

Both men were found guilty and sentenced to life imprisonment. Irwin and her friend Maud Younger toured California's union locals, speaking and fundraising on the jailed men's behalf: "In all, we addressed ninety-one unions; sometimes as many as three in a night" (320).

This activity earned her both praise and opprobrium. When she attended the hearings of the Walsh Commission on Industrial Relations, she remembers, "strange young I.W.W.'s would make themselves known to me, and would express their thanks to Maud and me for our efforts on behalf of Ford and Suhr" (320). She was also vilified in the conservative press, and referred to as "the Gillmore woman," which "was, of course, the time-honored way in which . . . the public prints referred to a prostitute" (321). For six months, as she learned later through her second husband's contacts, she was followed by a federal detective (324). It must have been a source of considerable personal satisfaction when in 1925 and 1926, respectively, Ford and Suhr were paroled (Foner, *Labor Movement,* 278).

In 1915 Irwin attended a hearing of the Federal Commission on Industrial Relations, convened to investigate the causes of labor disputes, including the violence of the previous spring against miners and their families in Colorado. To observe the "rows of eyes" of the motionless spectators as they listened tensely to the retelling of the events of the Ludlow Massacre was, she wrote, "like looking into the barrels of rows of guns" ("At the Industrial Hearing," March 1915: 8).

In the light of such events, Irwin's vision is one of labor and capital locked in an implacable combat. Although capitalism is, in her (no doubt overly sanguine) view, imminently "doomed," yet the battle must still be fought "to the death." If the mine-owning Rockefellers, with their hypo-critical professions of concern for their Colorado employees, are the villains of Irwin's article, she sees in the most well-intentioned type of capitalist employer—in Henry Ford, for example, with his model factories and employee housing—"only another phase of the charity he deprecates" (8).

Unlike other labor reporters for *The Masses*—and although she later included a substantial section on women in unions in her book *Angels and Amazons*[23]—Irwin wrote surprisingly little on women's issues in her short articles on labor. A notable exception is her portrait of the legendary labor organizer Mary Harris ("Mother") Jones in the *Masses* article "Shadows of Revolt" (July 1915). Jones, then eighty-six years old, gave a government commission *her* version of the events in Colorado—and of much else besides. In the course of her digressive testimony, Mother Jones, a "little, trim, tight-waisted old lady," with "kind blue eyes" and "close-set lips," told the tale of her fifty years of "wandering and organizing." She told of the time when she organized a singing protest of strikers' wives and their babies, to get them released from jail, and of numerous occasions on which she challenged armed strikebreakers, or befriended those who had arrested her: "I pitied those poor kids carrying guns to kill people. I used to wonder what their mothers thought of them" (8). To Irwin, Jones was "mother to a working people of an entire country . . . the first lady of the land in every moral and spiritual meaning."[24]

Irwin reported for *The Masses* on the AF of L convention of 1916, and was struck by the erudition of the convention delegates: "The thing that struck me most forcibly . . . was *how much they knew*. Working conditions you would expect, and Parliamentary law. But they knew living conditions; the economic laws behind them; world-movements. . . . 'Here are citizens,' I said to myself again and again. . . ." Where the schools taught only a "war-begetting patriotism," and the colleges produced "high-brows," the only institution in the country to offer "a training in citizenship," according to Irwin, was the trade union. She saw, in the ethnically diverse and union-educated convention membership, "the kind of Americanism that we have all hoped would emerge from this experiment in the government of the people by the people—that Americanism which is another word for democracy." For Irwin, "a real citizenship" implied "the end of politics."[25]

This agenda sounds radical indeed. Yet, paradoxically, Irwin retained respect for the individual leaders of the AF of L despite their conservatism. For example, she expressed fervent admiration, in her report on the AF of L convention, for "the great brain and the overpowering personality" of the conservative craft unionist and President of the AF of L, Samuel Gompers.

Despite differences in ideological perspective, the three labor reporters associated with *The Masses*—Vorse, Marot, and Irwin—shared very similar conceptions of the union as an avenue for workers' attainment to real democratic participation in society. For Vorse, the union movement offered a "college" for striking workers. For Marot, the entry of middle-class professionals into the movement offered the potential for creation of a new model of power sharing between employees and management. For Irwin, the union was a training ground in citizenship, whose graduates would find their places in a society transformed by the struggles of organized labor. Each of these conceptions represents utopian hopes for the future of the labor movement—some of them more easily realized than others.

The last word on the labor movement as represented in the pages of *The Masses* properly belongs, however, not to the professional labor reporters, but to a woman worker—one of the anonymous millions of the magazine's title, whose words only found their way into print through the mediation of others. In 1913, Inis Weed and Louise Carey conducted an interview for *The Masses* with Teresa, an Italian silk weaver in the Bamford mill in Paterson, New Jersey. The historic and bitterly contested strike had just ended in overall defeat, but with minor concessions to some of the 25,000 workers involved. Teresa tells her interviewers of her work in the mills since the age of thirteen, where until the strike she tended two ribbon looms, "a task too heavy for a strong man." Predictably, she fell ill from the pressures of her working day: "The doctor said it was because I hurry so." She tells of the system of fines and deductions—"Maybe a girl wastes a little silk. If they do not know who did it, they fine everyone." She tells of being cheated of a year's pay through a legal loophole in her contract, of the unpaid Saturday afternoons spent cleaning up the mill, of the screaming and bullying of the bosses.[26]

The strike, in which as an IWW member Teresa took an active part, brought about minor improvements in pay and conditions at Bamford's. The union is to her a source of hope and encouragement in an otherwise bleak existence. She explains: "Since the strike I am more happy here. . . . We are all together. We stand solid." Teresa's hope for the future is one breathtaking in its simplicity and its daring. Her father, she explains, dislikes her membership in the union, and thinks it foolish to challenge the employers: "My father he says there will always be bosses." Teresa's answer is equally to the point: "I say 'Yes? Then we shall be the bosses . . .'" (Nov. 1913: 7).

4

The War and Suffrage

BEGINNING IN 1914, a new topic grows ever more insistently present in the pages of *The Masses:* that of the war declared in Europe. Long before the United States entered the war in 1917 (an event which was to lead to the closing down of the magazine, and the trial of its editors, under the Espionage Act), every issue carried antiwar cartoons, reports from the European fronts, and pacifist poetry. A significant proportion of these antiwar gestures were the work of women.

Even before the administration of Woodrow Wilson committed U.S. citizens to direct involvement in the war, it had become an issue which divided the nation between isolationists and advocates of intervention. With direct entry into the war, these divisions were intensified. They imposed on reformers and radicals alike the necessity of taking stands on U.S. participation, whether on grounds of principle or of political expediency. Conflicts generated by the position to be taken on the war all but destroyed the U.S. Socialist Party, for instance. It suffered from the jailing of its leaders and the anti-Left hysteria of the war years and after. The party itself became split between its antiwar majority and a minority faction which supported the Allies against "German militarism."[1]

The U.S. suffrage movement found itself torn by similar divisions. The leaders of the mainstream National American Woman Suffrage Association (NAWSA) (less militant in tactics than its more radical offspring, the splinter-group National Woman's Party, formed to pursue an aggressive strategy of demonstrating and picketing against the Wilson administration), saw in women's involvement in all kinds of "war work" an opportunity to prove women's patriotism and their practical capability as citizens.[2] The Woman's Party, while its leaders took no official stand on the war, included among its supporters a number of convinced opponents of U.S. involvement in the war.[3] Among these were *Masses* contributors Louise Bryant and Dorothy Day.

The great majority of contributors to *The Masses,* whether or not they were members of the Woman's Party, were both strongly opposed to U.S.

involvement in the war and, it goes without saying, energetically support-ive of women's right to vote. However, two questions seem to invite closer examination: the very diverse arguments different contributors used in support of both positions, and their attitudes to women who did not share their views on either of these questions. I will first consider the reflections of *Masses* women on war in general, and the War in particular. I will then examine their prosuffrage arguments, some of which are closely connected with their pacifism. Their attitudes to both are in many cases, I will argue, related to their hopes as reformers or radicals for the development of a more peaceful, more harmonious, and more socially just world.

Women's antiwar statements in *The Masses* took the forms of verse, prose, and satirical drawings. At their most simple and direct, they repre-sent cries of outrage. Typical of this type of statement is Irene McKeehan's short piece "Adieu, Plaisant Pays de France." Printed in 1917, three years after the outbreak of the World War in Europe, it is a meditation on a visitor's memories of a peaceful France, idealized in recollection—a place of genial, smiling natives. McKeehan's narrator recalls them one by one: a cheerful "blond fisherman" seen at Le Havre; a café waiter, "a handsome, black-eyed boy . . . laughing saucily at a group of girls"; and (in an omi-nous intimation of the coming war) a "little red-legged soldier with his hands in his pockets, smiling in a comfortable and friendly way at the whole . . . world." After each of these vignettes, the narrator imagines a grim contrast, in the possible fate of each of these men. The fisherman, perhaps, is a drowned war victim who "swings gently to and fro" in the sway of the tides. The former waiter may be fatally wounded in a trench in Flanders, his hands "frantic," his eyes "blind with blood." Perhaps the smiling soldier now smiles "in a new way," his teeth grinning out of a bare skull, where he lies in what, in the "old dream-like, forgotten days of peace," was a flourishing wheatfield and now is a muddy wasteland. This meditation ends with a prayer, for France: "Let not war devour her!" (June 1917: 45).

Protest against the reduction of a human being to a thing is made more tellingly, perhaps—certainly with greater economy—in a drawing, "Re-quiem," by Cornelia Barns (Feb. 1916: 20). In Barns' drawing of a dead soldier, the corpse lies prone, its head touching the very edge of the draw-ing's foreground frame, its legs raised by the thick grass in which it lies half-buried, causing the lifeless weight to seem to slide forward towards the beholder. Above it perches a small songbird, very much alert and alive, in contrast with the corpse below. It is the bird which is the witness of this futile tragedy, and which gives the drawing its ironic title.

Unlike McKeehan's prose poem or Barns' drawing, Elizabeth Waddell's satiric poem "The Dear Little Bullet" makes its antiwar protest with sar-donic detachment. The bullet of the title is one approved by international

"REQUIEM," CORNELIA BARNS.
(Courtesy General Research Division, The New York Public Library, Astor, Lenox and Tilden Foundations.)

agreement as being "clean-wounding" and hence more "humane" than other, presumably outlawed, types of bullets. The poem's persona, while admitting that her notions of combat and of combat injuries are "rather vague," nonetheless claims to believe it would give her "most exquisite pleasure" to be wounded by the highly recommended bullet of the title: "The neat little bullet, the clean-wounding bullet, / Humane little bullet approved by the Hague" (Apr. 1915: 24). Through this playful, even facetious eulogy, Waddell exposes the absurd paradox of the very idea of a "humane" instrument of death. The bullet in turn becomes a symbol of the absurdity and folly of the war being waged in Europe.

In May 1915, Rosika Schwimmer, an internationally known peace activist and feminist, wrote an article for *The Masses*. Although "News from the Front" was her only contribution to the magazine, it is worth mentioning here because of the major role Schwimmer played in the peace and feminist movements, in the United States and in her native Hungary. Co-leader of the Hungarian feminist and pacifist organization *Feministák Egyesülete* (Feminists' Union), she was also a journalist and editor, and translator into Hungarian of Charlotte Perkins Gilman's socialist/feminist classic *Women and Economics* (1898/1970). In 1914, Schwimmer was a London-based press secretary for the International Woman Suffrage Alliance. In August of that year she joined the American suffrage leader Carrie Chapman Catt in presenting Woodrow Wilson with a million-signature petition from European suffragists, urging the (then neutral) United States to mediate between the warring European nations. Schwimmer was instrumental in inspiring the setting up of a number of U.S. peace groups, which in turn joined to form the Woman's Peace Party. After the war, she was briefly appointed Hungarian ambassador to Switzerland.

Schwimmer was, apparently, a stirring orator. Reading her article for *The Masses,* one can well believe the declaration of one biographer: ". . . her vivid descriptions of war's devastation were deeply affecting . . . her appeal in 1914 before the Chicago Association of Commerce was so moving that the speaker scheduled to follow her declined to do so."[4] Even in cold print, Schwimmer's account of the individual tragedies of the war is powerful in its utter simplicity. For the most part, she quotes personal experiences and eyewitness accounts, allowing people to tell their own stories. She quotes a letter from the front, from a man tortured by guilt at his inability to shoot a wounded comrade. From the man's abdomen the entrails flowed "like the train of a woman's dress," and he begged to be put out of his misery. She recalls the words of an American war correspondent who saw women in flight from their devastated homes, "overcome with pains giving birth to children on the road, taking the newborn babes in handkerchiefs and running on as if they had stopped for nothing more important than to blow their noses." After relating a number of such accounts, Schwimmer contrasts with them the dry detachment of most newspaper accounts of the war. In the daily press, in the pretelevision age in which Schwimmer writes, the war is presented as a matter of

> . . . careful information about the number of men and guns captured back and forth. Figures, neat and businesslike as in the ledger of a re-spectable merchant's office. Then, as a pleasant break in the tiresome statistics, comes some interesting information about Victoria and Iron Crosses bestowed upon heroes. Regularly five or six ships, dread-noughts, submarines, go to the bottom of the sea, ornamenting the military reports like the brass buttons on the coats of the generals. (May 1915: 10)

For Schwimmer, such reports, which stand "like a screen" between the reader and "the real happenings," serve to obscure, not vicariously clarify, the experience of war. The newspaper of the very correspondent who told her the story of the women giving birth by the roadside "is registering every cannon and every inch of soil conquered and reconquered by the opposing forces. . . ." Yet this paper, according to Schwimmer, printed not "a single word about this human, or, shall I say, inhuman, side of the war" (10).

Mary Heaton Vorse did not write on the war for *The Masses*, but since she was at once a central figure on the magazine's editorial board, and active in both the prewar peace movement and the suffrage movement, some mention of her firsthand reporting seems due in the present con-text. Vorse traveled extensively in wartime France, Germany, Holland, and Switzerland, and after the war in Eastern Europe and the newly estab-lished Soviet Union, witnessing the human devastation everywhere.

Before the war, Vorse had been active in the suffrage movement and in the women's peace movement. For the suffrage cause she contributed a chapter to *The Sturdy Oak* (1917), a prosuffrage novel written collectively by fourteen authors and edited by Elizabeth Jordan, the proceeds from which went to suffrage campaign funds. In 1915 Vorse was chosen by the New York Woman Suffrage Party as a delegate to the 1915 International Women's Peace Conference in Amsterdam. There and then, she came to a conviction of the futility of all efforts to prevent the war:

> In the midst of her speech Rosika Schwimmer paused and requested the audience to rise to its feet, and standing, spend a minute of silent thought on the dead of all Europe and on Europe's stricken women. . . . I do not know how long we stood there in that terrible quiet. . . . Tears streamed down the faces of the women. . . . An awful, silent, hopeless frozen grief swept over this audience. . . . These women

could only suffer. They hated war, but could not make a significant, arresting protest against it. (*Footnote to Folly,* 87)

Nearly thirty years later, her perceptions no doubt influenced by the recent U.S. entry into World War II, Vorse would express a certain sympathy with supporters of the first war. They were "fighting for something great," she wrote in *Time and the Town* (1942). Still, as a journalist during World War I, she continued to record her agonized sense of the cruelties of war, above all its effects on women and children, in articles like "Les Evacuées" (*Outlook,* 10 Nov. 1915) and "The Sinistrées of France" (*Century,* 1917).

"Milorad" appeared in the January 1920 issue of *Harper's Magazine.* It tells of a meeting in Serbia with a war orphan, a ragged twelve-year-old boy, the Milorad of the title. This boy attached himself to Vorse, and begged her repeatedly to "adopt" him and take him back with her to America. Vorse, a busy reporter awaiting reassignment to Greece or Rumania,[5] tells of her distress at leaving the child behind. Milorad had seemed to her a "symbol of the lost children" of Europe, "crawling miserably over the roadways of the world, sleeping, as he had recently done, in the mud of ditches" (262). Even when the Red Cross clothed him and found him a Serbian foster mother, Milorad continues to epitomize for Vorse the emotional, as opposed to the physical, devastation wrought by the war:

He is safe; he does not walk the highways of the earth, nor sleep in ditches. He is not chased, hungry, from door to door. The woman from Mladnavo is good to him—but she is not his mother. Once by chance he encountered her . . . and for a happy moment our love flowed together. But when I look out over the implacable silence that divides us, I wonder if it would not have been better if we had not met. (262)

The majority of *Masses* contributors were not unconditional pacifists. Although they denounced the horrors and miseries of what they perceived as an imperialist war serving ruling-class capitalist interests, they did not necessarily express a comparable abhorrence where popular revolutions were concerned. Elizabeth Waddell, for instance, at a time of violent repression of labor protest in the United States, wrote hopefully, seeing in the intensified conflict a possible sign of an impending revolution. This revolution, although it might be accompanied by "more or less of strife and blood," would usher in a more equitable social order.[6] Sarah Cleghorn, like Waddell, was strongly opposed to U.S. intervention in World War I. She took part in demonstrations against the war and wrote pacifist verse on the subject, and her novel *The Spinster* (1916) had a heroine who became a socialist and a pacifist. Yet, as she recalls in her autobiography, at the news of the workers' uprisings of 1917 and 1918 in Russia, in Austria, and in Hungary, she rejoiced (*Threescore*, 186, 214–215). Miriam Allen de Ford, in a tribute to the executed labor leader Joe Hill, writes of proletarian revolution as "sacred wrath"—and this in 1916, when the European conflict had been raging for two years.[7]

Similarly, Louise Bryant, in an article written in collaboration with John Reed, deplores the folly of the war in Europe, the suffering it imposes upon ordinary people ("News from France," Oct. 1917). Yet, in a *Masses* article on the 1916 "Easter Rising" of the Irish against the British occupiers of their country, she contrasts the latter conflict with World War I. The former, unlike the latter, she regards as fully deserving of support by believers in "the Brotherhood of Man":

> With horror we have beheld so many champions of the Brotherhood of Man go down before the scorching flame of hatred—though we all know that the present struggle is merely a commercial war without the shadow of an ideal to inspire anyone. ("The Poets' Revolution," July 1916: 29)

The abortive Irish revolution, on the other hand, Bryant points out, has more in common with the anticolonial struggles being waged in India and elsewhere. The rising was led, moreover, by poets and scholars, a fact which in and of itself, Bryant considers, has given "a depressed and bewildered" world "a new faith in mankind." The rebellion is hailed for its rootedness in Irish working-class radicalism, on the one hand, and in the Celtic literary revival on the other; also for its perceived affinities with America's own revolt against British hegemony one hundred and forty years earlier. Above all, Bryant seems to welcome it for its effect in shaking the unthinking complacency of American editorial writers and generating a more critical attitude concerning U.S. support for Britain in the World War:

> [Americans] have discovered with great surprise that England would have shot every one of the signers of our own Declaration of Independence if she could have laid hands on them at the time. Horrified editors of unimpeachable conventionality have announced that Sir Roger Casement did no more in going to Germany for assistance than Benjamin Franklin did in going to France during our Revolution. . . . This turning inward of the eyes of the American people cannot help but be of some benefit and may possibly help to counteract the hysterical Pre-

paredness propaganda so fostered by England in her desire to drag us into war against "the Hun." (29)

Like other supporters of popular uprising, whether class-based or national in origin, Bryant regarded killing and bloodshed as necessary in pursuit of a particular end, while remaining deeply opposed to nationalist militarism and to her country's entry into World War I.[8]

Not surprisingly, a number of *Masses* women dissociated themselves from support for the war on gender grounds. For example, Frances Anderson's review of Mishael Artzibashef's play, "War," praises the play for its sensitive treatment of the "psychological horrors" of war's aftermath. The play depicts the effect on a wife of seeing her much-loved husband come back from the war a cripple. "How," Anderson asks, "do young and vital women respond to the pathetically maimed, often unrecognizable victims who return in the place of husbands and lovers?" (June 1914: 35). As Rosika Schwimmer likewise perceived, this was a war in which, whatever political gains some of the survivors might reap later, many women seemed likely to attain nothing but suffering. This point is made graphically clear in her account of a Russian general's retort to the accusation that a group of his soldiers had raped a local woman in territory occupied by them. "Serves you right!" the commander shouted at the woman's husband, who came to make the accusation. "Why did the women of this place flee when we settled? Why didn't you leave women enough for my soldiers?" (May 1915: 10).

In her verses, Alice Duer Miller draws attention to ways in which male interests in wartime operate—if less brutally than in Schwimmer's narrative, even more pervasively at women's expense—in the social arrangements of her own country. Miller was associated with the more conservative NAWSA, rather than with the Woman's Party. (In 1916 she chaired the NAWSA Committee on Resolutions.) *Masses* poetry editor Floyd Dell called Miller's *Are Women People?* (1915) "the most delightful book of the year so far." Subtitled *A Book of Rhymes for Suffrage Times,* the collection (and its sequel, *Women Are People!* [1917]) includes a number of pieces dealing with women's roles in wartime. "Women," a parody of Kipling's poem "Tommy Atkins" (on the British public's attitude towards the private soldier), draws attention to the treatment of women as convenient tools of a male-managed economy, whether in peace or in wartime:

I went into a factory to earn my daily bread;
Men said: "The home is woman's sphere."
    "I have no home," I said.
But when the men all marched to war, they
    cried to wife and maid,

"Oh, never mind about the home, but save
    the export trade."
For it's women this and women that, and
    home's the place for you,
But it's patriotic angels when there's outside
                        work to do. . . . (74–75)

Equally sardonic, in this case about both genders, is an Elsie Clews Parsons essay, "On the Loose," published in *The New Republic* in February 1915. The essay's central thesis deals with war's emotional appeal to bored and frustrated citizens:

> . . . war is the "bust" par excellence—alike for those who go and for those who stay at home. It is the greatest of gregarious forms of excitement. It sweeps people off their feet; it carries them along; it gives them something to think about, or rather feel about; it makes them forget themselves. (101)

The "more monotonous" an individual's life, Parsons continues, the stronger the appeal of wartime patriotic emotions will be, and "the duller the nature, the more welcome the appeal." Parsons finds women to be, if only relatively speaking, "less warlike" than men. Her explanations for this alleged lack of aggressiveness are unflattering, however,—and, as the opinions of a lifelong feminist, come as something of a surprise:

> Another reason for their comparative pacifism lies in their disinclination in general for periodic debauch. Women do not go on "busts" like men—perhaps because they are comparatively incapable of or unused to, steady, protracted effort; scatter-brained and volatile, they feel no need of breaking bounds. (101)

In her essay "The Secret of War," based on firsthand observations made in France and England in 1914, Mabel Dodge argues explicitly in favor of the withdrawal of women from the war effort. Unlike men, who are excited by fighting and come from the battlefront with their eyes "full of light" from the experience of killing, women, Dodge contends categorically, "don't like war." While it may be true that European women are to be found "urging their men into the field," in Dodge's view this is only a temporary reaction to a superficial ideological appeal. Women have been duped for the time being into helping "to maintain the illusion of Empire." However, Dodge expresses the hope that, in the long run, women's "instinct against war—aroused and conscious," may prevail over militarism: "The only hope of a permanent peace lies in a woman's war against war."[9]

This hope on Dodge's part may well be unfounded. It certainly does not represent the view of a number of other *Masses* contributors, as will shortly become apparent. However, it also receives its fair share of corroboration in two other pieces of writing by women in *The Masses*. One of them, published under the title "A Wife's Troubles," is a letter from "the wife of a man who came out for militarism" (Dec. 1916: 38). The writer complains that her husband has opted to support the Allies in the war. She reports her futile efforts to harass the erring spouse into changing his views. However, she has finally concluded that her husband is only another of "that numerous species" of "irrational, immature, destructive adult male" creatures, "whom women have made the mistake all these centuries of treating as if they were mature, rational contemporaries." The writer has further concluded that "the world will never know anything approaching sanity and civilization until the above species is exterminated and matriarchal dominance re-inaugurated." However, since in the contemporary conflict men "seem to be attending to the job of wholesale self-destruction for themselves," she has decided to "wash her hands" of "the whole outfit of them." The lightness of the letter's tone may be accounted for by the fact that the wayward husband ("after all these years") is apparently an older man, not himself subject to drafting into the military, and also that the United States was not at that time directly involved in the war. Despite its flippancy, however, the letter expresses a strong underlying hope that women—"my own rational sex"—or at least those women, the writer adds ominously, "who did not take part in the Preparedness Parade"—may yet show superior judgment to men in taking a stand against U.S. entry into the war. But then men, unlike the women of the day, had votes.

Sarah Cleghorn's poem "The Masquerader" deconstructs the phallic ideal supportive of militarism:

Who is this tall Incognito
   Bravely attended?
Singing boys before him go,
And fifes and trumpets blare and blow
   Loud, proud and splendid.
Before his helmet richly bossed
   Folk kneel in honor;—
Beneath his feather brightly tossed
   And gold-fringed banner.
              (Jan. 1914 : 19)

In Cleghorn's extended personification, war itself is depicted as an armed knight, the very embodiment of machismo. To this glittering figure, every woman, "Mother by mother," sacrifices her children. At last, however, the spell is broken. The "revel master" (the poet? the social activist with a pacifist conscience? history?) calls for the unmasking of the splendid knight. The knight resists such demystification, "Vain respite asking." The revel master is relentless. At last, naked, stripped of his trappings of banners and trumpets, war is seen by men and women in a new light. Its futility and folly appear exposed to the public gaze: "His poor blank, idiot face / And dead illusion."

"The Poltroon," published in Cleghorn's verse collection *Portraits and Protests* (1917), may be read as offering an alternative (and highly controversial) version of the masculine ideal to that presented in "The Masquerader." Cleghorn's ideal in "The Poltroon" is that of a man who, although his country "cowered under the mailed fist" of military occupation, refused to volunteer to join the resistance. Instead, "He talked in ill-timed, ill-judged platitudes / Urging a most unpatriotic peace," and called for turning of the other cheek. The poem's narrator, ironically presented as subscribing to more traditional notions of manhood, expresses contempt for the man's attitudes—but a grudging acknowledgment that, "milksop as he was / He was at least consistent," in that he

> . . . let himself
> Be knocked about the streets and spit upon,
> And never had the manhood to hit back.
> Of course he had no sense at all of honor.

Even without prior knowledge of Cleghorn's political and religious beliefs, the reader is likely to guess very quickly the identity of the hero of "The Poltroon." The poem's last line reads: "Contemptible poltroon! His name was Jesus" (65).

It is not only on gender, on humanitarian, or on religious grounds that *Masses* women dissociated themselves from support for the war. Another prominent strain in their writings is one of opposition to national chauvinism—of a conception of the individual as a citizen, not of the United States, nor of any other nation-state, but of the human race. Accompanying such views, there often went a sense that the nation's leaders had betrayed the nation's own professed ideals. As the military budget mounted in the years before United States entry into the war, and tensions mounted over Germany's use of submarine warfare against U.S. vessels carrying war matériel to Britain, this sense, for some writers, became a conviction that had to be shared with their fellow citizens.

The internationalist convictions of the *Masses* women also had important implications for the ways in which a number of them viewed the fight for the vote—a point which will be addressed in due course.

In 1916, when the Preparedness campaign in the United States was at its height, *The Masses* published the results of a survey in which American writers and thinkers—the majority of them liberals—responded to the question "Do You Believe in Patriotism?" Martha Gruening replied with "Prepared," a satiric dramatic monologue, in which the patriot's intolerance toward ethnic minorities, dissenters, and "deviants" in his own country is viewed as lending support to a blind will to defend his privileges, as a property-owning conservative white male, against perceived threats both from abroad and at home:

As long as I can hang a Jew or burn a nigger,
Or ride the labor agitator on a rail;
As long as I can put any man I don't like
In jail, and keep him there
On the flimsiest pretext or none,
And shut the mouth of the fool
Who cries for free speech and assembly—
When for chastity's sake, I jail the prostitute
After I'm through with her; when, revering motherhood,
I snatch the bread from the lips of the working mother . . .
When American life is kept cheap, and American profits sacred
Why shouldn't I stand prepared to defend American freedom?
Why shouldn't I shed my blood as well as the blood of my neighbor
To guard these inherited rights against any alien invader?

(Mar. 1916: 13)

In her poem "When the Seventeen Came Home," about the Americans killed in the 1914 intervention of the U.S. military in Mexico,[10] Mary Carolyn Davies, unlike Gruening, considers the phenomenon of nationalism and its tragic consequences, not from the point of view of its beneficiaries, but from that of its dupes, the soldiers who die at the behest of hypocritical politicians and profiteers. Davies takes as her occasion the solemn pomp of a military funeral. "Nobody laughed when the seventeen came home," the poem relates,

But perhaps, under the flags, the seventeen laughed
when they saw the people who had sent them out to
die, standing in rows with their hats off, being sorry.

(July 1914: 17)

A number of *Masses* writers find an alternative to nationalistic militarism only in a new spirit of internationalism, which will transcend the old
chauvinism and xenophobia. "*People* are going to make peace," Rosika
Schwimmer declared. Inez Irwin, responding in *The Masses* to the question
"Do You Believe in Patriotism?" called for an extension of the love of
country, which she viewed as analogous to "love of family," into a more
inclusive attachment to the human race: "I believe that we should use love
of country as a unit to teach children to look upon all countries as their
country. . . . An earth-family—a world-country. I believe in that kind of
patriotism" (Mar. 1916: 12).

Other writers make a case for opposing U.S. intervention in the war by
pointing to the disparity between America's declared ideals and the intervention proposed by the Wilson administration. The speaker in Elizabeth
Waddell's poem "The First Gun" reflects on her struggles to understand
her own feelings about the war and her continuing resistance to any sense
of involvement in these events. She is "Weary of the wrangle: It is his war,
it is their war. / It is no war of mine! . . ." As she is thus "Sitting down to
think it over," one realization dawns upon her "in a flash." The original
breaker of the world's peace, according to this revelation, was none other
than that self-proclaimed "serene Arbitress," that nation "from a pedestal
giving light to the world," her own country of peace-loving democrats. It
was the United States that was responsible for initiating a new age of
warfare, by the military intervention in Mexico: "You it was that broke
the peace of the World Powers, / Yonder at Vera Cruz" (Sept. 1915: 8).

In "And Thou, Too, America?" Sarah Cleghorn writes in a similar vein,
critically examining the denunciations made by American congressmen of
German "militarism" while they continue to vote increased appropriations
for the U.S. military budget, in disregard of American citizens' social
needs: [11] "While poor men's children still in gutters play, / And poor men's
lungs still rot for want of sun!" Does her country really prefer to "invest
in tools for killing men" rather than to "save the little children of her
poor?" Apparently, the answer is yes, in which case the only possible conclusion to be drawn is that the democratic American nation does not "so
much condemn / These German lords of war, as envy them" (June 1916: 8).

Opposition to the war by *Masses* women contributors is sometimes
premised on declared allegiance to the working class, or at least on sympathy with the economically exploited. The socialist labor leader Elizabeth
Gurley Flynn, asked by *The Masses* editors whether she believes in patriotism, grounds her response in an ideal of international solidarity. If she
has fellow feeling for other American citizens, it is for America's workers,
for the murdered and jailed strikers and organizers, and for other "victims
of the class war." As for a nationalism that requires citizens to fight, Flynn
decisively rejects such a notion, as long as America remains a class-divided

society: "This country is not 'our' country. Then why should the toilers love it or fight for it. . . . Let those who own the country, who are howling for and profiting by preparedness, fight to defend their property." Flynn sees great hope in America's ethnic diversity as counteractive of national chauvinsim, moreover: "Internationalism becomes the logical patriotism of a heterogeneous population." Flynn's ideal America is a "giant loom," weaving a "beautiful human fabric" of diverse races and cultures. But she will not affirm patriotism to an America in which "murder instruments are made for gold," and where, in the black smoke of factory chimneys, she is haunted by visions of dead workers, "our poor, deluded slain brothers" who let themselves be worked to death to profit the capitalists. Flynn concludes with the ringing assertion: "I re-affirm my faith, 'It is better to be a traitor to your country than a traitor to your class'" (Mar. 1916: 12).

The veteran suffrage leader Sara Bard Field comments upon patriotism along very similar lines. In 1916, she had written an article for *The Masses* on the use by San Francisco politicians and property owners of the anti-radical hysteria following a bomb attack at a Preparedness parade in the city to suppress the very effective labor movement there.[12] Her response to the question "Do You Believe in Patriotism?" shows a kindred awareness of the relationship between nationalism and class interest, although with a different emphasis. It is perfectly logical, Field contends, for a Rockefeller to feel patriotic toward the country which has enabled him to grow wealthy at others' expense. Such patriotism is only "a practical and natural gratitude to the country for value received—a sort of scented note of thanks." On the other hand, the patriotism of the exploited, to whom the country "has yielded nothing but the chance to be fuel for the fires of the rich," is "an idiotic gratitude for something less than no value received . . . it is grace said at a bare table" (Mar. 1916: 12).

Elizabeth Waddell's poem "The Tenant Farmer" dramatizes such patriotism of the economically exploited in the image of a ruined sharecropper, who dreams of military glory as a flight from his wretched existence. The farmer works thirteen hours a day, only to give two-fifths of his crop to the landlord. The prices of food and clothing are soaring, and his farm is going to ruin. As he reads the paper by lamplight in the evening, the farmer entertains a fantasy of himself as a war hero, taking "a hundred yards of enemy trenches," and coming home wounded to receive a medal. The poem concludes ironically, ". . . he is peeved considerable because he cannot tell and no one will tell him / Whether it is the Victoria Cross, the Iron Cross or the Cross of the Legion of Honor" (Aug. 1916: 8).

A Margaret Widdemer poem explores the possible consequences for the ruling class of a nation's actual involvement in the miseries of a prolonged war. "War-March" opens with an account of a feudal rather than a capitalist world order, but one which has clear implicit application to the contemporary situation and the contemporary war—particularly, one might add with hindsight, to conditions in a still-feudal society like that of Russia. In the poem, the King explains his conception of his people's social function, which is

"To be sent to death
For the sake of Our thrones:
For this shall your women breed
Fighting-men to our need,
For this ye shall drudge, to mold
Toil into guarding gold—
For we build our thrones
Of gold and slain men's bones,
     And this is of God," the King saith.
                    (Aug. 1915: 17)

At the start of the war, the oppressed people are too frightened of the ruling power to question the King's decree: "'Ay,' said the Folk, 'we know. Great are God and the King. We go.'" As the horrors and miseries of the war prolong themselves, however, they start to awaken:

And the sullen murmur broke
Like waves when the storm is near;
"The Kings," they said, "are but dust—
Who hath made God's world for Kings?"

Widdemer's poem seems to invite comparison with a poem by Elizabeth Waddell, "Making a Safe." (The poem's title, of course, is a play on Woodrow Wilson's phrase, often quoted in connection with the First World War, "making the world safe for democracy.") Waddell converts the adjective into a noun—the safe in which democracy is "preserved" by the rulers, by locking it up. The safe's combination is known only to the "Powers that Be," the privileged few, who in their wisdom are alone qualified to "benignly decide" when "It is safe to unlock it at last." As in Widdemer's poem, liberation from an intolerable situation is presented as depending upon the revolt of the masses: "The people must blow up the safe by and by." [13]

"News From France," briefly referred to earlier, is an article written by Louise Bryant and John Reed in 1917, based partly on Bryant's observations during a visit to France. The article describes the war-weariness of the French people after three years of hostilities, and sets this observation of the popular mood in the context of the Czar's overthrow in Russia, and of the previous history of France's own revolutionary struggles: "Alone among the belligerent peoples the French can be depended upon to meet the truth magnificently, as they did in 1789, in 1815, 1830, and 1871." Despite press censorship, Bryant and Reed find expressed in the French newspapers "a low, bitter growl against diplomats, financiers, statesmen, and all the respectable powers which plunge people into war on false pretences" (Oct. 1917: 5). This is certainly a very different description of the popular mood from that given by Mabel Dodge in "The Secret of War" three years earlier (Nov. 1914). Bryant and Reed's article predicts—over-optimistically, as subsequent events proved—that proletarian revolution might be imminent: "When the French are defeated they look searchingly into themselves, then they proceed to remove the cankers" (Oct. 1917: 5).

Elsie Clews Parsons was more realistic than either Bryant or Reed about the power over many people's minds of patriotic or other crowd emotions, and about the enthusiastic participation of individuals in support for war. In "A Pacifist Patriot" she analyzes the limitations of the beliefs of her friend Randolph Bourne that war was primarily an "upper-class sport" into which the masses were passively or reluctantly driven, "with no more enthusiasm than into industry." In this review for *The Dial* of Bourne's *Untimely Papers* (published in 1920, two years after the war ended), Parsons contends that Bourne simply failed to grasp that workers' readiness to fight fellow workers in a rival nation state is grounded in something more dynamic than mere apathy: "How meagre a part thought plays in social life he came in a measure to understand; but of the emotions that take the place of thought he had little grasp, nor of the emotional gratifications that are brought by war to the irrational" (1920: 368).

As indicated by even this brief sampling of the contributions of women to *The Masses* on the subject of war, they found more-than-sufficient reason to denounce what they viewed as the war's criminal folly—as humanitarians, as feminists, as "world citizens," or as sympathizers with the working class. Needless to say, the majority of American women did not share these opinions. The widespread loyal support of American women—if not for military adventures per se, at least for their own government and its decision to join the Allies in fighting "the Hun"—was not without implications for the U.S. suffrage movement (a point which remains to be addressed in greater detail). Even so astute and critical a social observer as Inez Irwin eventually declared her support for U.S. intervention. As she recalled in her autobiography, her sympathies, during a stay in wartime France, became "profoundly Ally . . . we developed the sympathy which inevitably comes to those who dwell in an invaded country. . . . When in 1917, Germany declared an unlimited submarine warfare, we knew that Wilson must declare war" ("Adventures," 358).

Yet Irwin never fell into the psychological trap of demonizing the enemy. An acquaintance, a socially conservative American army officer, told Irwin that French and German workers and radicals still trusted one another, "just as they had done before the war." The officer "seemed to think that indicated a horrible condition of things," Irwin explains, "but it brought the tears to *my* eyes" (243).

More wholeheartedly pacifist *Masses* contributors attacked what they regarded as the ideological complicity of conservative women in support for an evil cause. In "It Costs," a short feature essay for *The Masses,* Elsie Clews Parsons writes of the circumstances surrounding an accident to a small boy injured in a fall from the roof of his home, where he had been trying to set up an American flag. The article implies that the child had been indoctrinated by his schoolteacher, who had asked her students if they liked "The Star Spangled Banner." Parsons quotes the child: "We all said we did, 'cep' Marjorie." The teacher had said "she didn't want anybody 'round what didn't like 'the Star Spangled Banner.' She said if a soldier said he didn't like it he'd be sent out of the army . . ." (Oct. 1917: 35). Parsons seems to imply (although she does not explicitly say so) that in this kind of repeated indoctrination lies the key to Jim's attempt to set up the flag on the roof, and his broken arm. The arm has set badly, and will probably never be quite straight again. "It costs to make a patriot," Parsons concludes.

Other *Masses* contributors portray women as quite as culpable as the schoolteacher in Parsons' narrative. Mary Carolyn Davies' poem "To the Women of England," is bitter in its accusation. The poem considers the reluctance of Americans to donate money for the Allied victims of the war in Europe. The English women, their eyes "dull with tears," are imagined to "peer across the sea / In wonder at our callousness." According to Davies' poem, such "callousness" on the part of American women is—so long as Americans remain neutral in the war—fully justified:

> We women have a right to dance and shop
> And to refuse you pennies,
> We have never—
> Yet—
> Pinned a feather on a boy and killed him.
> (Apr. 1916: 7)

(The poem's final line refers to the custom of British women during World War I of publicly presenting any man not in military uniform with a white feather, with the aim of shaming him into enlisting.)

A somewhat less coercive tactic employed in the U.S. recruiting effort is illustrated in Cornelia Barns' cartoon of August 1917, "To-night Will Be

"TO-NIGHT WILL BE ARMY AND NAVY NIGHT," CORNELIA BARNS.
"To-night will be Army and Navy night. Any man who will sign a pledge at a desk inside the tent of the Alley Theatre to go to a recruiting office and make a sincere effort to enlist in the army, navy, or marine corps, will be formally kissed by one of 'a number of society girls,' whose names are being withheld. Additional police protection will be provided to keep the waiting crowds from breaking out of line."
(Courtesy General Research Division, The New York Public Library, Astor, Lenox, and Tilden Foundations.)

Army and Navy Night" (11). The drawing is based on a report in *The New York Times* that "a number of society girls" would volunteer their services in a recruiting drive, by "formally kissing" any man who would "sign a pledge . . . to . . . make a sincere effort to enlist in the army, navy or marine corps." The drawing has the playful Barns touch; the awkward, unhandsome men with their glumly resigned faces look as if they were indeed lining up to be shot, rather than to be kissed. They submit clumsily and with embarrassment to the embraces of the women, whose faces—perhaps in keeping with the statement in the *Times* report that the women's names are being withheld—are completely hidden from sight. At the back of the line one volunteer, who apparently has lost his nerve (whether at the sight

"THE FLIGHT OF THE INNOCENTS," CORNELIA BARNS.
"An alarmed patriotess has appealed to the ladies of the Boston Auxiliary of the National Security League to 'register their automobiles for the purpose of carrying the virgins inland in case of invasion.'"
(Courtesy General Research Division, The New York Public Library, Astor, Lenox and Tilden Foundations.)

of the women or at the prospect of facing the Hun is hard to tell), is being thrust back into line by one of a row of policemen, whose dark looming silhouettes fence in both sides of the scene. With all the playfulness of its humor, the cartoon makes its serious point: however clumsily conceived on the part of the organizers the gimmick may be, its ultimate purpose is to use the women's misguided patriotism to persuade men to throw away their lives.

Barns also has a "Preparedness" cartoon, more than a little satirical of women who succumb to war hysteria even before war has actually broken out. "The Flight of the Innocents" illustrates a news item which reads, "An alarmed patriotess has appealed to the ladies of the Boston Auxiliary of the National Security League to 'register their automobiles for the purpose of carrying the virgins inland in case of invasion'" (July 1916: 13). The drawing depicts this exodus—a group of women, huddled together in a car, a variety of comic expressions of alarm on their faces—except for the stern-faced spinster who rides on the car's hood, a banner held rigidly aloft. On the banner, the words "Safety First."

If some women are criticized for contributing to an atmosphere of war hysteria, *Masses* contributors also satirize those who are merely complacent or unaware. Pauline B. Barrington's "Toy Guns" considers the responsibility of parents who help raise a new generation of militarists by allowing their children to play war games. The poem addresses a mother:

> The rain is slipping, dripping down the street,
> The day is gray as ashes on the hearth,
> The children play with soldiers made of tin,
>   While you sew
> Row after row. . . .
>
>   (May 1916: 13)

The children's "mimic battle" ends in tears, after one of them "has shot and wounded his small brother." But this mimic battle merely reenacts in symbolic form the grim reality of the conflict in Europe, where not rain but blood is "slipping, dripping" in the mud of trenches, where "the bullets search the quick among the dead." In the living room, the quietly sewing mother is unaware that her children, so innocently playing, may in fact unconsciously be training themselves for an adulthood in which they will act out their games in earnest: [14]

> If the child is father of the man . . .
> Is the toy gun father of the Krupps?
>   For Christ's sake think!
>   While you sew
> Row after row.
>
>   (13)

"The Game," by Marie Louise Van Saanen, a short story published in *The Masses* for May 1916, develops in prose a theme very similar to that of Barrington's poem. The setting of "The Game" is a village in wartime France. Little Philippe's mother, embittered at the death of Philippe's older brother in the battle of the Marne, has forbidden her surviving child to join in the other children's war games. Philippe is thus marked out by the others as a scapegoat, and treated in their games as the symbolic enemy: "Sentries were posted at his door. . . . Scouts reconnoitered stealthily beneath his window. . . ." When one boy's father, home on leave from the front, tells the excited boys his war tales, he further inflames their imaginations. He shows off his weapons. "Virgile wanted to know how a revolver was loaded. His father showed him. The boy followed every detail of the lesson . . ." (9). Predictably, the story ends in tragedy when Virgile, having learned where the gun is kept, takes it out, loads it, and uses it to shoot the "enemy," Philippe—all in childish fun.

A significant detail of the story is the war fervor of the children's mothers, no different from that of the men: "The Leroux boy strutted, jigging his wooden sword. . . . The women looked on approvingly. 'The little dears! If their fathers could only see them!'" (9)

Among *Masses* women who demonstrated strong opposition to the war were a number who were also active in the woman suffrage movement. Women with this dual commitment included Louise Bryant, Dorothy Day, Miriam Allen de Ford, Alice Duer Miller, and (in the early years of the war) Inez Irwin. Their deeply held internationalist or socialist convictions caused some of them to entertain perhaps unrealistic hopes and expectations as to what woman suffrage could achieve in helping to bring about a more peaceful and just world order.

By 1914 the idea of "votes for women" enjoyed widespread support in U.S. society, with an estimated 54 percent of "prominent" women favoring suffrage, according to surveys of the period.[15] Ten Western states had already granted women full voting rights. Yet women's admission to the voting booth was by no means regarded as an automatic right by all sections of American society. Even among educated women, an estimated 9.5 percent were still, in principle, opposed to it. President Wilson, although expressing himself as in theory supportive of voting rights for women, in practice continued to stall on supporting a suffrage amendment then under discussion in Congress. Writers and speakers on behalf of suffrage brought all their ingenuity to bear on winning converts in Congress and among the general public, and in attempting to put pressure on the President and the Democratic Party to modify their attitude. Before considering the relationship between the pacifism of some *Masses* women and their support for the suffrage movement, it seems useful to consider the terms in which *Masses* women expressed their suffrage ideals—in particular, the awareness their work demonstrates of the social forces in favor of or presenting obstacles to women's attainment of suffrage.

The well-known journalist and suffragist Rheta Childe Dorr edited the Woman's Party magazine *The Suffragist* and in June 1914 was the principal figure in a short verbal dispute with Woodrow Wilson over the suffrage issue, which gained the party front-page publicity in the national press.[16] In July 1913 Dorr wrote a short news item for *The Masses*. The story ("Adv.") suggests the ambivalence felt toward the suffrage movement by more conservative elements in society. A New York store, which had sold hundreds of "parade hats" to be worn in one of the annual suffrage parades which had become a custom in New York and other cities, had given its employees permission to march in the parade if they were willing to forfeit half a day's pay. However, an employee who took this offer seriously was later questioned by her supervisor as to whether she had marched. When she answered in the affirmative, the young woman was summarily dismissed. "So now Christine is jobless as well as voteless," Dorr remarks drily (15).

While suffrage parades attracted thousands of marchers and supporters,[17] more militant actions provoked hostility, from the authorities and from the public alike.

It was Inez Irwin who first suggested that the National Woman's Party picket the White House. A member of the party's National Advisory Council, Irwin had been a convinced suffragist from the age of thirteen, when a school teacher had assigned her the composition topic "Should Women Vote?" "The question converted me," Irwin was later to claim. While a special student at Radcliffe, she joined with Maud Wood Park to found the National College Equal Suffrage League, thereby beginning a twenty-year involvement in work for the suffrage cause ("Adventures" 450–460).

Irwin recalls how she first conceived of the picketing idea during a visit to her home from Alice Paul, leader and founder of the National Woman's Party:

> Alice said, "Mrs. Irwin, can you think of any method by which, every time the President of the United States appears in public, we can draw attention to the suffrage fight?" Fresh from California and the labor fights I saw there, I said instantly, "Why don't you picket him?" Less than a week later, as we sat down to breakfast, Bill took up his newspaper, exclaimed, "Alice Paul has taken your advice, Inez." The first four pickets in the long campaign of picketing had appeared at the gates of the White House. (460)

Almost as soon as the picketing began, picketers were jeered at by angry bystanders, who regarded such behavior not only as inappropriate for women, but as unpatriotic in wartime. As a Woman's Party member, Irwin was denied a passport by the State Department when she applied for one to visit wartime France—a further indication of the suspicion in which the authorities held the Party.

In June 1917, arrests of picketers began. Altogether, two hundred and eighteen women were arrested, and ninety-seven sentenced to jail terms. The women were roughly handled, held incommunicado, and served food full of worms. A group of them went on a ten-day hunger strike. Among these was Dorothy Day, for whom the strike was a harrowing ordeal. She gives a graphic account of the experience in her autobiography, *The Long Loneliness*.[18]

In her *Story of Alice Paul and the National Woman's Party* (1921), Inez Irwin gives a dramatic account of the women's battles on the picket line with police who tore suffrage banners from their hands, and of the pressures to which their opponents subjected landlords, donors to the party,

PICKETING SUFFRAGIST, BOARDMAN ROBINSON.
"This is one of the banners for which the suffragists were jailed. —[Ed.]"
(Courtesy General Research Division, The New York Public Library, Astor, Lenox and Tilden Foundations.)

and newspaper editors in efforts to reduce their organization's power base. As Irwin recalls in her autobiography,

> Our pickets were mobbed, man-handled by mobs, knocked down, injured. They were arrested and sent to jail where they were badly treated and where they hunger-struck. Alice Paul was taken to a hospital and her sanity investigated. But all the time, more and more women came forward to march on the picket lines. ("Adventures," 460)

Picketing and hunger striking were the heroic tactics of a minority. But even the great majority of suffrage supporters, who did not find themselves involved in such dramatic actions, could hardly fail to be aware of more pervasive intolerance in society at large. It is this type of conservative resistance to suffrage, an opposition which endorsed a number of stereo-types, with which contributions to *The Masses* mainly deal.[19]

The perception of women as psychologically and physically inferior to men naturally played a major role in suffrage propaganda. As the suffragist and socialist Lena Morrow Lewis is quoted as arguing in an early *Masses* interview with Ethel Lloyd Patterson, male gestures of deference towards women could in themselves represent veiled manifestations of contempt: "Why should men rise to give me a seat in a car and refuse to give me a vote upon the laws which govern me? If there is anything of real reverence in their attitude, certainly it is not for my mentality" (July 1911: 13). In her satirical article "As Mars Sees Us," Inez Irwin lists some of the qualities traditionally attributed by men to women. "The decorative sex," the "toy sex," the "codeless [amoral] sex," the "inarticulate sex," are some of the epithets applied. Moreover, women, excluded from participation in politi-cal life, are doubly subject to male caprice under two codes of rules, legal and social:

The Earth-laws are made entirely by men. They are inadequate to pro-tect the weaker sex. And so, for the further protection of women, men have developed a supplementary system called "the man's code." As the law neither compels the man to adopt this code nor punishes him if he offend against it, the women find it a highly unsatisfactory arrangement. (Aug. 1912: 12)

In their challenging of the notion that woman's place was in the home and man's in the political sphere—in their insistence that the polling booth and the public platform were proper places for women to be seen—suffragists attracted accusations of moral depravity. (Ironically, they also attracted the hostility of saloon keepers and liquor manufacturers, who for historical reasons associated feminism with the temperance movement, and regarded suffragists as too "moral" for the good of their business.) In his review of Miller's *Are Women People?* Floyd Dell quotes lines from the book which parody these assumptions of immorality. A conservative woman warns her son, who has recently attained the age of majority, against the corrupting influence of the suffragist:

They smirch, degrade and coarsen.
Terrible things they do
To quiet, elderly women—
What would they do to you!
("Last But Not Least," July 1915: 22)

"LOOK AT THAT SUFFRAGETTE, MADGE," ELIZABETH GRIEG.
"Look at that suffragette, Madge—right out in the streets—wouldn't you think she'd die of shame?"
"Yeh—you bet."
(Courtesy General Research Division, The New York Public Library, Astor, Lenox and Tilden Foundations.)

It is in this context of perceived immorality that one needs to understand news items like that cited in *The Masses* for November 1913, which deals with the accusation of a prominent female antisuffragist that suffragists were "responsible for the present vogue of indecency in dancing, literature, plays and dress." The *Masses* columnist counters by pointing to the efforts of San Francisco's recently enfranchised women to close down the bars and brothels of the city's notorious "Barbary Coast." Apparently, the writer concludes, "these provincial ladies way out West" have been "too busy with their housecleaning" to pay much attention to denunciations of their involvement in public life.[20] The perception of suffragists as "immoral" also supplies the key to Elizabeth Grieg's cartoon of two women, evidently prostitutes, seated near a sign reading "Votes Women

1915," around which some kind of public appeal for woman suffrage, with women speakers, is apparently going on. One "shameless" prostitute says to the other, "Look at that suffragette, Madge—right out in the street— wouldn't you think she'd die of shame?" (Oct./Nov. 1915: 19). Ad hoc "soapboxing" in the cause of suffrage was a very common practice in the early twentieth century,[21] but women's engagement in it was frowned upon by more conservative members of society.

In response to the charge of female inferiority to men (and hence incompetence to vote), some *Masses* suffrage advocates counterattacked, turning the tables to present the male sex in an unfavorable light. A number of Cornelia Barns' cartoons employ this strategy. The drawing entitled "Voters" (Dec. 1915: 4) shows a group of loutish-looking men hanging out on a street corner. "Anti-Suffrage Argument No. 187" (which runs, "Women are too frivolous. They think of nothing but styles and fashions") shows three men, themselves dressed in the height of fashion, gathered admiringly round a tailor's window (Mar. 1913: 12). Alice Duer Miller's "Unauthorised Interview" between the Statue of Liberty and a group of suffragist women implicitly indicts male conservatism and hypocrisy, which have supplanted the liberty for which the statue supposedly stands. In fact, the statue herself firmly disclaims having anything to do with such aspirations: "Be not deceived, my daughters, I'm not she— / The winged Goddess, who sets nations free." She represents, rather, the liberty which "when men win / They think that others' seeking is a sin." Men therefore made the statue "out of bronze, and hollow, / Immovable, for fear that I might follow / Some fresh rebellion," and welded her torch "securely" in her hand, "Lest I should pass it on. . . ." She is, she concludes, "a milestone, / Not an inspiration." Only in the spirit of the suffragists does liberty still "flicker faintly" in America (*Women Are People,* 87).

Grace Potter directly attacks male refusal to grant women the vote. She goes beyond Barns and Miller (who merely attack male foolishness, frivolity, and hypocrisy) to an assertion that men actually need illusions of superiority. In "Breaking Up the Home," Potter makes the ironic (but not perhaps wholly ironic) argument that the male monopoly of the vote represents the last defense of man's illusion of superiority over women. If the male were really to understand the weight of scientific and historical evidence in favor of woman suffrage, let alone the evidence of the states in the Union "where women have voted for years," his confidence would be irreparably shattered. Even worse, women's ability to manipulate the male by playing on his complacent assumption of superiority would be lost for ever.[22]

In more serious vein, Lida Parce, writing in an early issue of *The Masses,* actually argues that women possess "special traits," different from those of men, that they are, in their possession of these traits, in some respects ac-

"ANTI-SUFFRAGE ARGUMENT NO. 187," CORNELIA BARNS.
"Women are too frivolous. They think about nothing but styles and fashions."
(Courtesy General Research Division, The New York Public Library, Astor, Lenox and Tilden Foundations.)

tually the superior of the male. In "Woman Suffrage: Why?" (Dec. 1911: 12) she contends not only that women possess a broader capacity to sympathize with the needs of others than men do, but that "woman psychology" is thus "by nature" inclined to resist the ruthless, individualistic competitiveness of the capitalist system. In Parce's view, if these allegedly distinct female traits were allowed to influence political life through women's securing of the vote, society could only become more harmonious, more cooperative, and more just.

Most *Masses* contributors who were active in the suffrage movement beyond their contributions to *The Masses*—in the sense that they spoke in public, marched, picketed, or wrote suffrage articles for other publications—were also active opponents of nationalist militarism in general and of U.S. involvement in the First World War in particular. Louise Bryant, who was active in the Woman's Party, was arrested during the 1917 picketing while taking part in a burning of the President in effigy, and went on hunger strike. She was a strong opponent of national militarism. Dorothy Day was among the suffragist hunger strikers imprisoned in the Occoquan workhouse, but had also taken part earlier in the year in a speaking tour on behalf of the Anti-Conscription League.[23] Miriam Allen de Ford had worked for the suffrage cause from the age of fourteen. She was also an antimilitarist socialist, who joined the Industrial Workers of the World as a gesture of protest against the war.[24] Alice Duer Miller was known as a writer and speaker on the suffrage issue, but her collections of verse also contain a number of pacifist pieces.[25] Inez Irwin, who wrote and spoke widely for the suffrage movement, came to hope for an Allied victory, but at the start of the war had wanted the United States to maintain neutrality. Mary Heaton Vorse took part in organizing suffrage campaigning, and before the war began was involved in the international women's peace movement of which Rosika Schwimmer was a leader; she attended the abortive peace conference of women in 1917. Only Rheta Childe Dorr, of suffragists who at some point in their careers contributed to *The Masses*, whole-heartedly and unreservedly supported her country's entry into the war.[26] Most women more closely connected with the work of *The Masses* were suffragists for the same reason they were antimilitarists: both, for them, were subsumed under a broader utopian program that saw women's participation in politics as only one necessary step toward the creation of a more harmonious, more peaceful, and more just society.

Inez Irwin might, with hindsight, view the political gains of women in wartime as "the silver lining to a sinister cloud" (*Angels and Amazons,* 278). Very few *Masses* women viewed the matter in that light in 1917. Most of them were ideologically closest to the antimilitarist element in the Woman's Party, and least in sympathy with the two million members of the more conservative National American Woman Suffrage Association. NAWSA's president, Carrie Chapman Catt, seeing the political gains to be reaped from suffragists' active participation in the war effort, persuaded the government to form the Women's Committee of the Council of National Defense, of which Anna Howard Shaw was appointed chair.[27] *Masses* editors denounced this compromise of NAWSA women with the military bureaucracy. In an editorial praising the women of the Woman's Party for their courage in courting arrest by picketing the White House, and their refusal to "succumb to the temptation of bargaining with militarism for the vote," the editors add that the spectacle of NAWSA women

anxious to assist a military bureaucracy in depriving others of their liberties, as signified by their offer to help in the work of conscription

registration, in order to gain a political privilege, has been viewed
with intense chagrin by those who regard the political emancipation
of women as part and parcel of human emancipation.

("Suffrage and Sedition," Aug. 1917: 42)

The more radical suffragists found themselves at odds with their conservative sisters not only over the issue of support for the war effort, but also
over their broader social hopes for what women's participation in political
life might achieve. In "The Married Woman Speaks," Jane Snow imagines
an angry suffragist denouncing the complacency of wealthy housewives:
"Millions of women are being exploited by their employers. . . . / But what
do you care? (Aug. 1917: 47).

Some suffragists with a radical social agenda clearly expected too much
of women's entry into electoral politics. In "The Mother Follows," Sarah
Cleghorn outlines a broad social agenda in which women, as mothers,
would have a special interest. In the world of the unenfranchised woman,
as Cleghorn's poem points out, the mother who concerns herself with the
problems of prostitution or of alcoholism, or with her children's safety in
the factories full of "fenceless cogs" and polluted air in which they work,
or with "Amendments to the Tenement Bill," is called a "meddlesome
woman" for her pains by male politicians, who tell her her place is in the
home. The response to such treatment by the heroine of Cleghorn's poem
is to become a suffragist—her way of demanding of the world, "Let me
take care of my children!"[28]

In her book *What Eight Million Women Want* (1910), written during the
years when she was still concerned with labor issues and ideologically close
to the Socialist Party, Rheta Childe Dorr makes the case for women's supposed power to change the world through their entry into politics. Like
Sarah Cleghorn, Dorr takes the idea that woman's place is in the home and
reinscribes "home" as synonymous with the human community. Thanks
to women's future involvement in political life, the community of the future will be "like a great, well-ordered, comfortable sanitary household":

> Everything will be as clean as in a good home. Every one, as in a
> family, will have enough to eat. . . . There will be no slums, no sweat
> shops . . . no babies dying because of an impure milk supply. . . . All
> the family will be taken care of. . . . (328)

For Dorr, "woman's work" includes "race preservation, race improvement." Whoever opposes woman's mission thus to shape society "simply
fights nature" (330). Dorr further believes that the evils of society result
from the monopoly of power by "half the human race," which in her view
does not possess "even half the moral power contained in the race." She

"VOTERS," CORNELIA BARNS.
(Courtesy General Research Division, The New York Public Library, Astor, Lenox and Tilden Foundations.)

further contends (an ironic point, in view of her later conservative militarism), that, unlike men, whose "government rests on force, on violence," women "will not tolerate violence. They loathe waste" (329).

In her article "Woman Suffrage: Why?" from which I quoted earlier, Lida Parce (who approvingly cites Dorr's *What Eight Million Women Want*) sees in the interest taken in social welfare by middle-class women a beginning made in "the steps which must lead" in the end to socialism. As mentioned earlier, Parce expresses the greatest optimism concerning "the contribution to civilization which woman has to make when she shall be liberated from political and social restrictions" (Dec. 1911: 12).

Unlike Cleghorn, Dorr, and Parce, some *Masses* women were never very sanguine about the possibility that the entry of women into electoral politics would, in and of itself, transform society. Emma Goldman might complain, in a *Mother Earth* editorial quoted in *The Masses*, that even the enlightened editors of the magazine seem to have become infected with what she calls "the suffrage disease."[29] (Goldman, as an anarchist, viewed all political activity within the framework of existing institutions as a distraction and a delusion.) However, not all *Masses* women who fought for the vote really expected too much from it. In an interview about her suffrage activities published in 1975, Miriam Allen de Ford claims that she never assumed, for example, that women legislators would necessarily be less corruptible than men. For de Ford, woman suffrage is, quite simply, a matter of principle: ". . . we're human beings and citizens and we have a right to vote" (Gluck, *Parlor to Prison*, 175).

As for the antiwar movement, more than fifteen years after the First World War had ended, and almost fifteen years after the vote had been won, two prominent *Masses* women expressed diametrically opposite opinions as to what the achievement of suffrage for women had accomplished in the cause of peace. In her *Angels and Amazons* (1934), Inez Irwin contends that women have more than proved themselves as pacifists, thus exerting a positive influence on society: "Statistics, wherever available, show how much more our women incline toward peace than our men. For example, there are five major national women's organizations concerned with peace and nothing else." In peace groups open to both sexes, women are observed to "outnumber men in their membership, and stand high in their leadership" (420). Mary Heaton Vorse, on the other hand, expresses deep disillusionment concerning women's alleged achievements—or lack of them—since women's winning of the vote. In *A Footnote to Folly* (1935), she writes, "I was confident that Anglo-Saxon women, having got the vote, would go on from there. That was one of the cherished illusions of those days. Women had come into politics. We would fight the battle of children. We would prevent war."[30] Vorse concedes that women can hardly be held to blame for the adverse circumstances of the Depression during which she writes. Yet she does hold them responsible for not having pursued the political advantage gained by the vote—and for not having brought the same determination required to win it, to bear on new causes:

> If the women protested against war and the traffic in munitions with the furious concentration with which they demanded their enfranchisement, what would happen? At least they would advertise the cause of peace. It has always seemed strange that they should get worked up enough to overthrow all the old conventions, go singing to jail, undergo the torture of a hunger strike for the franchise—for what? Why, unless they had a further imperative objective—the protection of all children, for instance, or an equal passion for peace? (169)

This chapter ends with a question, for the dichotomy posed by the disparate conclusions of Irwin and Vorse remains with us today. If we consider the involvement in militarism of female politicians within living memory, whether they have waged war against the alleged "aggression" of other nations or merely served on an Armed Services Committee in Congress, we may incline to agree with Vorse that women have thrown away an opportunity to make of the attainment of the vote something that could have changed the course of history. On the other hand, in support of Irwin's claim, there are the women activists of the world's various "Green" parties, and—outside the electoral process—the various anti-nuclear organizations that receive support from women. There are also still the women relief workers of many nations. Recently I heard a representative of such workers in the war in Cambodia speak in a late-night television panel discussion. She angrily condemned the hesitations of male politicians to come to the conference table and end the fighting as the deliberations of "a lot of men," endlessly talking while the children she worked for continued to die. And that, too, sadly, is a situation Vorse would have recognized.

The verdict remains open.

5

Ethnicity

FEMINISTS AND LEFTISTS, rebels in a conformist society, *Masses* women yet share with white Anglo-Saxon Protestant contemporaries of similar class backgrounds a concern with the situation of the ethnic "other"—the newly arrived immigrant or the even more despised Native American or native-born African-American. For *Masses* women this concern is more often than not imbued with guilt for the exploitation and oppression these others endure, but it may also evince the fears and hopes of members of the white majority culture about the possible future shape, and racial composition, of the United States. In no sphere of discourse are this interest and anxiety more apparent than in *Masses* women contributors' writings on ethnic minorities among society's working-class majority.

However, *Masses* women do not address ethnic issues with a single voice, although the overwhelming majority of their works present ethnic minorities in stereotypical terms. (These stereotypes may be positive idealizations of a given race or culture, or—in a few instances—negatively racist.) A second, substantial body of work protests various forms of prejudice, discrimination, and persecution to which members of ethnic minority groups are subjected. A third category of writings celebrates mutual respect and harmony between members of different races. In each of these categories one finds works which attempt to engage the intricate relationship between ethnicity, social class, and gender, within the framework of white, capitalist, patriarchal society.

The sociocultural atmosphere in which *Masses* contributors discussed ethnicity was a charged one. The years 1911 to 1917 were the years of the notorious Dillingham Congressional Commission whose findings, in the words of one account, "gave credence to the popular belief that Northwestern European immigrants were more desirable as future U.S. citizens than their counterparts from Southern and Eastern Europe"; of a Supreme Court decision which removed from aliens part of the Fifth and Sixth Amendment protections afforded in criminal cases; of the exclusion from the United States of most remaining Asian groups not already denied entry by earlier legislation.[1] During the previous five years, in which ten million newcomers had arrived, politicians like Theodore Roosevelt and racist anthropologists like W. Z. Ripley had expressed concern about the declining birthrate among white, native-born members of the upper classes, and espoused dubious biological and ethnological theories which, in offering "proof" of the superiority of some races over others, supplied rationalizations for deep-seated anxieties about ethnic difference. *Masses* contributors could hardly be unaware of racist rhetoric, as enunciated by the most impeccably respectable of social commentators. "That the Mediterranean peoples are morally below the races of northern Europe is as certain as any social fact," wrote Edward A. Ross in *Century* magazine in 1914. "Without likening immigrants to negroes, one may point out how the latter-day employer resembles the old-time planter in his blindness to the effects of his labor policies upon the blood of the nation. . . ."[2] According to one erudite congressman quoted by Mary Katharine Reely, "Unblushing lying is so universal among the Japanese as to be one of the leading national traits. . . . The vast majority of the Japanese people do not understand the meaning of the word 'morality'. . . ."[3] For W. Z. Ripley, in a 1908 article for the *Atlantic Monthly,* the United States, in permitting the entry of Greeks, Armenians, and Syrians, had "tapped the political sinks of Europe."[4] In comparison with such diatribes, the commentator in the *Journal of Education* who merely complains that immigrants tend to import "their own standards of living, their own social customs" along with "ingrained suspicions of government" sounds positively enlightened.[5]

One possible response to such negative stereotyping, as indicated by much writing by *Masses* women, is to create reverse images—positive stereotypes. If racist opponents of immigration portray immigrants as crass, ignorant, idle, immoral, and lacking in civic awareness, writers like Mary Isabelle Henke, Mary Heaton Vorse, and Adriana Spadoni, among others, counter by depicting them as sensitive, hungry for education, hard-working, morally upright, and socially responsible.

The persona of Mary Isabelle Henke's poem "Brother of Poets" is an immigrant factory worker who, contrary to the popular view of the immigrant "son of peasants" as indifferent to literary values, possesses "the mind and soul of a poet." It is the hardships of the life of a worker in "a mill where they grind out the hearts and the souls of men" which prevent the poet from realizing his vocation, as he falls asleep from exhaustion, "head on the table," at the day's end. When, at work, he pauses to try to recall "the beautiful thing" he wants to set down in writing, "the foreman swears at me. . . /I think I shall never get it written" (Nov./Dec. 1917: 41).

A common figure having affinities with Henke's millworker poet is that of a foreign woman, refined and sensitive, transplanted to ugly, forbidding surroundings in the United States. The child worker of Elizabeth Waddell's poem "For Lyric Labor" (discussed in chapter 3) fits this stereo-type—but so do Elizabeth Gurley Flynn's and Mary Heaton Vorse's non-fictional portraits of Militza Masonovitch, a Montenegrin woman whose plight became a cause célèbre after her wrongful arrest during a shooting incident in the Mesaba Range mining strike of 1916. Flynn published an article in *The Masses* to appeal for legal defense funds for the strikers and their family members accused as "accessories before the act" on a trumped-up murder charge. In the appeal, Mrs. Masonovitch features as "a particu-larly pathetic and appealing figure, a young and beautiful Montenegrin woman . . ." Flynn's article plays upon the theme of a sensitive, bewildered being ("She speaks little English") entrapped in an alien environment in which, if the mother were to be convicted, her five children would be orphaned. Mary Heaton Vorse also wrote for *The Masses* of Mrs. Maso-novitch's plight. Like Flynn, she emphasizes the pathos of the victim's situation—her innocence and above all her sense of alienation. Even that "comfortable body," the sheriff's wife, who tries to comfort her, is not to be relied on.[6]

The image of a sensitive woman forced by socioeconomic pressures to dwell in squalid surroundings recurs in Vorse's work. In *A Footnote to Folly*, writing of her memories of the Lawrence textile strike of 1912, she recalls a visit to the home of a "beautiful wide-faced Syrian girl who looked like someone out of the *Arabian Nights*" as she stood in the dark, bare room overlooking a courtyard filled with garbage and said, "in what a tone of yearning homesickness, 'How I wish we had never come away from Da-mascus!'"(11). In an earlier piece of writing, a January 1920 article on the Youngstown, Ohio, steel strike, Vorse portrays the wives of Slovak steel strikers as compelled to raise their children in darned and patched cloth-ing amid dreary surroundings, but as training them to be "sound, good-tempered and good-mannered." Despite their loving, conscientious care for their families, their own dreams are denied; their "bright treasure of hope" for a new and better life in America lies "buried . . . under the garbage of the streets . . ."[7]

It would be an oversimplification to overlook the other predominant motif in Vorse's writings about immigrant women—her celebration of their bold toughness in dealing with strike vigilantes, or in demonstrations like the one Vorse covered in Southern Kansas in 1923, in which four to six thousand women of many different national origins marched to sup-port striking menfolk.[8] Whether she writes of the pathos of the immi-grants' lot or praises their heroism, however, Vorse is unequivocal in cele-brating as a cultural enrichment what others in her society viewed as a nuisance or even a threat. In the Massachusetts community of Province-town where Vorse made her home for part of the year, the Portuguese population greatly expanded between 1911 and 1940. While, as Vorse explains in *Time and the Town,* in the early twentieth century "half of the school children were of New England blood and half were Portuguese," by the early 1940s "ninety per cent of Provincetown school children are Portuguese" (166). Vorse recalls the burning by the Klan of a fiery cross in front of the local Catholic church in the racist hysteria that followed the First World War. She also writes with appreciation of the role played by the Portuguese in the fishing industry: "They, like other foreigners, have taken up the dangerous and difficult tasks which those of American blood have laid down . . ." (162). She views the Portuguese as having brought to Provincetown a "Latin warmth and gaiety" formerly lacking in the New England setting: "Dark faces on the streets, beautiful dark-eyed girls who love color and who make the streets gay with their bright dresses and their laughter. The daring of Portuguese fishermen is part of Provincetown's legend . . ." (76). Vorse's proudest boast in connection with the newcomers is that her neighbors have accepted her as one of their own: "I know there is nothing makes me prouder than when one of my other family calls me Mother Vorse" (109).

Adriana Spadoni is one of very few *Masses* contributors not of white Protestant descent. However, in her fiction she deals very little with ethnic minority culture, most of her characters being middle-class White Anglo-Saxon Protestants (WASPs). When she does write of an Italian family, Spadoni outdoes even Mary Heaton Vorse in her idealization of a community to which both the author and her characters appear to be outsiders. In Spadoni's novel *Mrs. Phelps' Husband* (1924), Elinor and Stuart visit a hotel run by an Italian family. The family's daily life is characterized via "the heavy warmth of rich spicy food," the "chattering" of the children "in another tongue," the "intimacy of this small *strange* room" (emphasis mine). The setting "throbs" with "heavy fruitful living"; it presents "a folk-poem of abundance." The visitors agree that the atmosphere of the hotel is most unmercenary, "as if they were friends, and happened to be serving us through some chance. It's not their business in life to serve, but their preference, and they never serve against it." (Tell that to the Italian factory worker!) Stuart's response to these remarks of Elinor's seems worth quoting in full:

> It's in the race, just as their exuberant living is. It's all or nothing. And no matter how commercial and sophisticated they become or seem to become, it's always there, a deep swift emotionalism, like a hidden mountain spring, ready to carry them forward in a torrent of joy, or drown them in despair. The very earth of Italy feels that way. . . .
> (118–119)

As if to illustrate this alleged sense of contact with the Italian earth, the family's oldest daughter is bountifully pregnant (119).

It is not unusual to find *Masses* women alleging the cultural superiority of members of ethnic minorities over Anglo-Saxons. In "I Make Cheap Silk," a documentary account of the life of a young Italian millworker, the Italian gardens of the mill district are praised for the welcome contrast they provide to the "dreary" backyards of "so many American workers' houses." The authors, Inis Weed and Louise Carey, find that the love of the Italians for their grape arbors and vegetable patches makes "a definite contribution to the civic life of Paterson" (Nov. 1913: 7). An article by Helen Marot on the organization of the New York garment industry makes the perhaps questionable assertion that Russian workers lack a well-developed democratic sense and prefer to follow a leader. But Marot praises the Italian garment workers for what she perceives as their appreciation of democratic ideals. Indeed, the final sentence of "Revolution and the Garment Trade" suggests slyly that the Italian democratic sense may even be more highly developed than the American: "The Italian conception of revolution and democracy is not the conception of the Russian Jews; it is more nearly ours—or, I would rather say, ours is more nearly Italian" (Aug. 1916: 29). While such broad claims are, inevitably, intrinsically suspect, Marot's generalizations clearly not only echo Vorse's praise of the immigrant family or Spadoni's of Italian *joie de vivre,* but take the positive stereotyping a step further, in the assertion of cultural superiority over the Anglo-Saxon.

In *Masses* writers' impressions of the culture of at least one group of native Americans, one finds a preference expressed for Indian culture over Anglo-Saxon. Mabel Dodge, Elsie Clews Parsons, and Mary Heaton Vorse all write of the Pueblo Indians in highly positive terms. Above all, they emphasize the instinctive sense of community in Pueblo society, which, for these writers, the white world clearly lacks.

Mabel Dodge lived in Taos, New Mexico, for only five months before she decided to settle there. Five years later, she married Antonio Lujan, a member of the local Pueblo community. The marriage was not without its strains, as might be expected in the relationship of two very strong-willed people from very different cultures, but endured until Mabel Dodge Luhan died in 1962. (Her husband died one year later.)

In Taos, Dodge felt herself to have finally discovered her true spiritual home.[9] In the final part of her autobiography, *Intimate Memories,* she writes of "the spirit of the tribe" of the Pueblo people: "a great, fiery Being without name, without heart, without sorrow or pain, but with purpose and wisdom" (*Edge of Taos Desert,* 64). Her husband educated her emotionally, Dodge claims, into a new capacity for intimacy with another:

"Tony was the first one I ever knew who broke open in me the capacity to actually share the feeling of another person" (218). But the Pueblos, in her view, have a lesson to teach white society at large: "Perhaps the only way to go free is to live as a group, and to be part and parcel of a living organism, to share everything, joy, pain, food, land, life and death, and so lose the individual anguish and hunger . . ." (109–110). Some pages earlier she addresses her "fellow mortals" along similar lines: "Until you learn how to join together once more, to fuse your sorrowful and lonely hearts in some new communion, you can never make true music" (64).

Elsie Clews Parsons conducted a number of anthropological studies among the Pueblo Indians—occasionally resorting to what may look to the uninitiated lay person like ethically somewhat dubious shifts to persuade individual tribe members to betray the religious secrets of the tribe, in the interests of science. (Parsons herself justified her information-gathering methods with claims that she recorded customs for posterity, including the Indians' descendants, and that she wrote out of admiration for the Pueblo culture.) Although she had been ceremonially adopted as the honorary "daughter" of a Pueblo tribe, her writings angered and offended some Pueblos, including Antonio Lujan, not for any pejorative comment but because the secrecy surrounding Pueblo religious rites had been violated.[10]

Still, Parsons' deep admiration for the Pueblo sense of community is evident. Like Mabel Dodge, she finds in Pueblo forms of social organization a lesson for white society, "a system not unworthy the attention of those who would unite happiness and contentment with labor." She reads in the Hopi adage "Because any time any one may need help, therefore all help one another" a philosophy of "realistic mutual helpfulness" that makes a mockery of missionaries' endeavors to "civilize" the Pueblos: "That the Missionary or Trader should feel that he has superior goods or methods to offer the people on the mesa is matter, surely, for the God of Laughter or the grimmer God of Irony."[11]

In 1922 Parsons lent her support to a campaign begun by Mabel Dodge to fight the Bursum Bill, a proposal which, if it had passed in Congress, would have legalized numerous dubious land claims of non–native Americans, depriving the Pueblos of sixty thousand acres of mostly fertile landholdings. Mabel Dodge and Antonio Lujan were already working tirelessly, lobbying government for improved medical care, education, and security of land tenure for the Pueblos. In the fight against the Bursum Bill, Dodge contacted not only Parsons, who submitted a motion condemning the Bill to the American Ethnological Society, but former *Masses* business manager Dolly Sloan, who collected signatures and campaigned among old Greenwich Village acquaintances. Dodge herself wrote reports on the Bursum Bill for the Bureau of Indian Affairs, canvassed women's clubs in New Mexico, and arranged for a demonstration by native Americans in New York City (Rudnick, *Mabel Dodge Luhan,* 325).

Although the defeated Bursum Bill was quickly replaced by the Pueblo Lands Act of 1923, the latter laid the burden of proof of claims to Indian land more squarely on the non–native American claimant, and required successful claimants to pay compensation. Thus, the efforts devoted to opposing the Bursum Bill were far from wasted. Mabel Dodge's campaign was also not without a certain historic significance, as the first national campaign to protect Indian land rights in United States history (Rudnick, 176–181).

Mary Heaton Vorse was publicity director for the Federal Indian Bureau, for just under two years, from 1935 to 1937, and a firm supporter of the policies of the bureau's director. John Collier advocated the preservation of native American culture and traditions, over the forced assimilation of native Americans into white society. It was Congressional opposition to these controversial views, coupled with a redbaiting campaign, which contributed to Vorse's eventual dismissal from her post.[12]

"Deer Dance in Taos," an article Vorse had written for *The Nation* five years previously, suggests that her views on native American culture predate her New Deal appointment. She writes of the beauty of the Hopi women's costumes, of the "exquisite rhythms" of the deer dance, and—a touch characteristic of Vorse's journalism—of the behavior of the adults toward the young children who are still learning the dance: "They dance a little stiffly, they have not yet the magnificent rhythm of the accomplished dancers. Now a child has not held the eagle feather in the prescribed manner. The father, with a gesture of unconscious tenderness, puts his arm around the little one and corrects the error . . ." (13 Aug. 1930: 178). Her conclusion is a cry for the preservation of Hopi culture in the face of a world that, if it destroys that culture, has nothing to offer in its place:

> "You may look at us," they have seemed to say, "at the calm acceptance of our women, at the vivid tranquillity of our youth, at the venerable wisdom of the aged, at the furious intensity of our anger. . . . Listen to our laughter. Have you anything to give us? . . . Then since you have nothing to add, nothing to give us, let us live. Let us alone. Let us cherish our own secret of life in the kivas. Do not try to pull us apart until we shall have become disintegrated and a people without a soul" (179).

Not all work by *Masses* contributors is unreservedly appreciative of minority culture. Even when the author's intention appears sympathetic, much of the work seems insensitive, at least from a 1990s perspective.

The treatment of the Irish is a case in point. Mary Heaton Vorse's "The Story of Michael Shea" in *The Masses* for November 1913 tells of a man tamed and demoralized by a happy marriage to the point where he loses his "natural" Irish love of fighting. Observing this sad situation, the narrator comments:

> . . . when you show me an Irishman who's fussy about his food, I'll show you an Irishman who's *fell*. Real Irishmen are too full o' fight or love or politics or sport—too full o' feelin' to know what they're eatin'. . . . They're by nature romantic an' they show it by the way they crack each others' heads open for no reason but they want a scrap. That's what I call idealism, when a man wants to fight for somethin' so bad he'll fight for nothing . . . (16)

It would be interesting to know what Vorse's second husband Joe O'Brien thought of such representations of the Irish.

Vorse is by no means the only *Masses* contributor to perpetuate the stereotype of the romantic, combative Irish. Romantic idealism forms an essential element in a story by Florence Kiper Frank, "In the Pride of His Youth," in which James O'Donnell steals a rhinestone hairband he cannot afford to buy, to adorn the hair of his young sweetheart. Though arrested for his crime, he finds comfort in an imaginative identification with the figure of Robin Hood, seen in a movie, and, recalling "the white shine and glitter of the precious gift" in the "dusky hair" of his sweetheart, considers the price worth paying (July 1912: 10). The supposed Irish combativeness is exemplified by the caption under a Cornelia Barns cartoon of two neighbors chatting over the garden fence:

> "Mrs. Callahan, the Irish seem to have forgotten the Home Rule trouble since the war began."
> "I guess they don't mind, so they do be fighting." (Nov. 1914: 24)

These stereotypes of the Irish, alienating and dehumanizing as they are, are difficult to square with, say, Louise Bryant's celebration in "The Poets' Revolution" (July 1916) of the clearheaded, principled idealism of the nationalists of Easter 1916. They exemplify an uncritical imitation and endorsement of existing racist stereotypes, none the less destructive for their evident lack of malice.

A number of writings about other minority groups by *Masses* women contributors exhibit a sense of these groups as more or less alien, in behavior, in beliefs, or even in their very biological essence, to the member of the majority culture who describes them.

"A Rift of Silence," Adriana Spadoni's story of Russian immigrants,

"MRS. CALLAHAN, THE IRISH . . . ," CORNELIA BARNS.
"Mrs. Callahan, the Irish seem to have forgotten the Home Rule trouble since the war began."
"I guess they don't mind, so they do be fighting."
(Courtesy General Research Division, The New York Public Library, Astor, Lenox and Tilden Foundations.)

betrays a sense of difference between characters and narrator in the stilted diction in which the family members (who at home would presumably address one another in Russian!) are represented as conversing. To cite a few instances: "Little mother, I think Misha is sick. In the night he talked of strange things, and now feel his face, it is like fire. . . ." "Why, thou sleepest. . . . " "It is so with us all. It is not to blush . . . " (Feb. 1913: 12). The distorted grammatical structures, the awkward *thous* and *thees* which might find their place in a representation of a foreigner addressing a native speaker, here serve only to give the reader an uneasy sense of the quaintness and otherness of an exotic race.

In a very different manner, though one perhaps not unrelated to the sense of otherness conveyed by the dialogue of Spadoni's story, a *Masses* poem by Ruth Fitch entitled "Chinese Music" powerfully suggests a sense of another culture as alien—even nonhuman:

> A white wail full of loneliness,
> Like the crying of the wind at night,
> When the bare trees shiver at his coming.
> Then, a dull throbbing
> As of many frogs
> Complaining in a marsh.
> At last, a human voice
> Harsh, discordant, impotently tragic. . . .
>
> (July 1917: 45)

The likening of the instrumental component of the music to the voices of frogs may tend to suggest to some readers that these human-made sounds are in fact subhuman. In any case, the comparison of a piece of music to the noise of croaking from a marsh can hardly serve to raise it, or its producers, in the esteem of anyone. On the other hand, unlike the instrumental sounds, which are at least endowed with animation (the frog voices, the wail of the personified wind), the human voice of the Chinese singer is distanced and dehumanized. It is "harsh" and "discordant," apparently lacking in the harmony the Western ear expects of the singing voice (and on that account also possibly less identifiably human).

"Yellow Hair," a short story by Helen Hull published in *The Masses* in February 1916, is interestingly ambiguous in its racial attitudes. Its central character is a Portuguese worker named Pedro, who is described via an array of stereotypically predictable physical traits. Pedro has a "swarthy" forehead, huge hands covered with "crisp" black hair. He produces "guttural" sounds from his throat and, though a millhand by occupation, walks with the gait of "a pirate." Somewhat unexpectedly, given this menacing description, Pedro turns out to be anything but piratical in nature. He is, in fact, the victim of an unfaithful woman who has run off and left him to return to an empty home each evening, his eyes ever averted from "the sight of the cold, smokeless chimney." When the woman returns, bringing Pedro's young son, Pedro is shown to be a caring father, tenderly covering the child as he sleeps. It is Pedro's Anglo wife who cunningly plays upon the man's sense of his own racial inferiority: "'Not many white women'd love you,' said the woman, slyly." Given this context, Pedro's "Me—I'm black—You all white—and yellow hair," might be read less as an implied assertion of white racial superiority on Hull's part than as a representation of her character's internalization of such attitudes (15). Still, the stereotypical depiction of the southern European as physically powerful, passionate, inarticulate, and above all, as capable of forming a relationship with a blonde woman only on the basis of physical attraction, remains ultimately limiting.[13]

Hull's story invites comparison with a piece of early short fiction published in the *Atlantic Monthly* by Mary Heaton Vorse. "The Madelon Viera" again deals with the relationship of a Portuguese man and an Anglo woman. However, in Vorse's story Madelon (after whom Raphael Viera names his fishing vessel) experiences a paradoxical combination of fascination and repulsion for Raphael. She marries him, against her better judgment— almost against her will—only to join "the primeval battle of the Northern white woman's inner hatred for the darker blood, and her passionate desire to keep her race pure against the Southerner who looks with longing eyes to the woman, fair-haired, whiter-skinned than his own sisters; fire and ice met there and fought . . ." (Jan. 1907: 461). In the end, Raphael allows himself to drown at sea, having realized that Madelon can never bring herself to truly love him. Raphael's perspective in this story is presented with both pathos and respect for his heroism and devotion to the woman who cannot return his love. What is ultimately racist in the story is its narrator's unquestioning assumption that it is somehow *natural* for white women to resist sexual union with darker-skinned men—that they typically experience both "horror" and "shrinking fascination" in their response to "the men of the South," and a sense of their intrinsic "strangeness" (456). The racism of this early story, published in April 1910, is probably a virtually inevitable result of Vorse's early upbringing in a well-to-do Victorian WASP family. As her experience of the world expanded her encounters with people of many different cultures and ethnic backgrounds, in the United States and abroad, such narrow attitudes were to undergo considerable modification, in ways which will shortly be examined.

The sense of otherness again shades over into outright racism in "Nigger Tilly," a group of poems published in *The Masses* by Jane Burr. These writings constitute probably the most offensive representation of a member of an ethnic minority *The Masses* ever published. The first of Burr's poems describes the family nursemaid as "Generous, insane, romantic,/An ape even to copying the jerking limp of her mistress. . . ." Burr's Tilly is a half-human being, a grotesque blend of saintly mother-figure, possessing "A heart so big it made me wonder/That one skin could house so much of goodness"; of sensuous lover, bearing a scar where "One raging Othello/Had nearly loved her to death"; and, most disturbingly, of subhuman primate with "long gorilla arms." In another poem, Tilly is said actually to regress on the evolutionary scale. She has gone insane, and the authorities are called in to restrain her. They chase Tilly up a tree: "Ten million years back she went,/Clawing her way up into an acorn tree/And there on a branch she chittered and jibbered . . ." (Apr. 1916: 6). The implication here that African-Americans are more "primitive" than members of other races, representing an earlier evolutionary stage closer to that of nonhuman primates, was one firmly enshrined in contemporary ethnological theory. Still, the "Tilly" poems remain unique in the pages of *The Masses* in the blatant quality of their racism.

It is difficult to explain how the *Masses* editors, who prided themselves on their progressive views, could have accepted Burr's poems for publication in the first place. One explanation may be that, as with the cartoons of "Negro" life drawn by Stuart Davis and others, they accepted too readily Burr's assumption that her portraits of Tilly were sympathetic. The following comment in a letter from Carlotta Russell Lowell to *The Masses* indicates what at least one contemporary reader thought (the letter concerns *Masses* cartoons in particular, but its application to Burr's verse is patent):

> If I understand *The Masses* rightly, its general policy is to inspire the weak and unfortunate with courage and self-respect and to bring home to oppressors the injustice of their ways. Your pictures of colored people would have, I should think, exactly the opposite effect. They would depress the negroes themselves and confirm the whites in their contemptuous and scornful attitude. (*"The Masses* and the Negro," May 1915: 6)

While the work of *Masses* women, like that of their male fellow contributors, may reveal insensitivity or ignorance in dealing with racial and cross-cultural issues, it also presents numerous instances of attempts to represent and protest the sufferings and injustices to which members of ethnic minorities in the United States are subject—as aliens, as workers, or as native-born descendants of slaves whose rights continue to be denied.

The poem "A Greek Coffee House" by Florence K. Mixter protests no blatant oppression, no gross inequity—but it does evoke the pathos of the lonely situation of the unmarried immigrant. It considers the surprising

"DISCRIMINATION," ALICE BEACH WINTER.
(Courtesy General Research Division, The New York Public Library, Astor, Lenox and Tilden Foundations.)

phenomenon of a group of men who, on a magnificent spring evening, choose to huddle inside a "stifling" smoke-filled cafeteria, with its "dingy walls" and "blurred windows." In the flickering arc-lights, the customers are diminished, ghost-like figures, their identities hidden under the brims of "slouch hats," whose clothing alone seems to "bind/Body and soul together." They engage in seemingly endless compulsive card-playing and coffee-drinking, while their cigarette smoke drifts "inertly on the lifeless air." Not that these men are intrinsically apathetic; in other circumstances, they might be capable of love, or "passionate hate." It is the "dense black loneliness," the "stifling heart-ache" of their homesickness and sense of isolation, which keeps them from purposeful action and which has made them close the coffee house doors against the "scent of lilacs," the poignant nostalgia aroused by the return of spring (Aug. 1917: 13).

"Immigration and Militarism," a wartime *Masses* essay by labor analyst Helen Marot, offers a reminder that American workers grappled with more immediately pressing (and material) problems than that of homesickness. Her article discusses the U.S. capitalists' perception of a wartime threat to what Marot calls "the American institution" of low wages and long hours, as a result of wartime labor shortages. She rather sardonically summarizes a 1916 address by Elihu Root to the Bar Association—a speech which warned against the menace of the "millions of immigrants," the "insidious foes from within." By this, Marot points out, Root simply means those workers who "have been in this country long enough to want higher wages and shorter hours, and . . . are trying to get them."[14]

With a remarkable consistency, *Masses* women seldom consider questions of oppression of minorities without directly or indirectly linking such oppression with the situation of women (which does not mean that they overlook those situations in which women are themselves oppressors). In this context of the oppression of ethnic minorities, Alice Beach Winter's cartoon titled "Discrimination" (Feb. 1913: 8) takes on a new significance, in that women, like members of ethnic minorities, are excluded by prejudice from full participation in society.

That the female member of an ethnic minority labors under a double burden forms the theme not only of much *Masses* labor journalism by women contributors—Mary Heaton Vorse in particular—but also of a body of *Masses* women's fiction. Babette Deutsch, for example, deals briefly with the struggles and sufferings of immigrant women in her autobiographical novel *A Brittle Heaven* (1926). Bianca, the novel's main character, a young woman from a comfortable upper-middle-class home, joins a New York union strike-relief committee and is sent to visit the wives of striking workers. In one apartment, a woman addresses her child, who is crying with hunger, "with the regularity of a metronome: 'Shut up!' she said, periodically, without anger, even with a kind of tenderness, 'Shuttup.'"

(182–183). In another home, a woman holds forth about her troubles amid the steam and smell of washing. Her husband has been jobless for nearly two months: "It would have been better if he hadn't been such a *Macher*. What use was the Union, anyway? But even when there were no strikes and no committees, there were the dull seasons. . . . How could you feed the baby when yourself you were living on bread and tea . . ." (184–185). The one thing both mothers share, despite the different ways in which they react to their poverty, is "their pity for their children" (185). Bianca wonders how women forced to live in such circumstances consent to reproduce at all. But, as she reflects, more than a little patronizingly, "They didn't know any better. It was the rich who controlled the number of children they had, not the poor" (185).

The above reflection of Deutsch's fictional character serves as a reminder that, for many turn-of-the-century social thinkers, if only because of the pervasive influence of racist phobias in white mainstream society, questions of female reproduction and questions of ethnicity could never be kept far apart.[15] In her June 1915 essay for *The Masses* entitled "Facing Race Suicide," Elsie Clews Parsons takes issue with those Americans who consider the continuing decline in "the native birthrate" a calamity of stupendous proportions—for reasons that, in Parsons' view, have little to do with logic. Prophets of race suicide, Parsons claims, "will talk to you about the high cost of living, pampered wives, nationality, or the god of an alien, ancient race, all facts, more or less . . . but none holding any relation whatsoever to the emotion of regret over the fallen birthrate which always warms up the speaker's peroration. . . ." More to the point, in Parsons' view, is the need to reform the "social conditions . . . which at present make childbearing impossible or possible only at great sacrifice" for those upper-class women whom the race suicide prophets consider the most suitable mothers. As long, Parsons continues, as the middle- or upper-class American woman is "taught to seek self-expression and then denied it because of the narrow limits within which love and maternity are open to her," the native-born American woman's critics ought "to be satisfied with having the population maintained by immigration." Or, Parsons adds more problematically, "by the birthrate among those immigrants whose peasant education is consistent with the conditions for mating and childbearing obtaining in America. . . ."[16]

A crucial area in which class- and race-based oppression intersect with gender issues is that of domestic employment. In Jean Starr Untermeyer's poem "Sonya," about a children's nursemaid, the awareness of inequality and exploitation is complicated by the fact that the poet/narrator expresses unease about her own role in it. While the latter derives pleasure from the presence of Sonya in her house, is "made happy just to look at" the kindly little woman with her pleasant features, at the same time the employer finds "a long-rebelling thought" (of guilt? of jealousy?) assails her at hearing the servant's voice "pouring love-words" on her child. Such emotional commitment to another woman's child, the narrator feels, can only be given at the giver's expense. She has accepted Sonya's devoted service, but with "almost shame," which persists even after Sonya has left employment with her:

> And you have gone,
> Passed with fierce loyalty to another home,
> And squander mother-love on strangers' children
> For twenty-seven dollars every month.
> (Sept. 1916: 17)

In Untermeyer's poem "Church Sociable," published in *The Masses'* successor *The Liberator*, it is racial prejudice rather than class exploitation which draws divisions in the ranks of sisterhood. The sight of people milling around at a village church bazaar brings back an old memory:

> I was a child again, and Mrs. Lee
> And other members of the Ladies' Aid
> At tables on the lawn . . .
> Were serving cakes. . . .
> (*Liberator*, Mar. 1918: 12)

The narrator recalls how, even as a child, she sensed the hypocrisy of "this weak pomp of charity/This pauper feast to aid the stricken poor." What the child subsequently witnessed, however, was even more instructive. She received her first lesson in the nature of racism, as she saw the "too-thin ladies" demonstrate true charity by "turning their Christian backs on Mrs. Cohn."[17]

Where "Church Sociable" illustrates the breaking of solidarity between women by racism, "Chivalry," a story by Elizabeth Hines Hanley, explores the potential for sympathy of one victim for another—of an oppressed, browbeaten wife for the scapegoat in a racially motivated lynching. In "Chivalry" a man returns to his wife from taking part in a mob killing, fairly evidently based on the Leo Frank case (in which Frank's Jewishness was at least a contributing factor in his arrest and subsequent lynching, allegedly for the murder of a child factory worker). In 1916 this case, to which Inez Irwin also alludes in an essay published in *The Masses* seven months before "Chivalry," was presumably fresh in readers' minds.[18]

The wife, in Hanley's story, is characterized as belonging to "that great array of women in the wilds of the world everywhere to whom the husband still stands as the oracle of heaven and earth." Yet so disturbed is Sally by the knowledge of her husband's crime that when he demands to know why she cannot look him in the face, she yields to the "heresy" of questioning his judgment: "'It's the lynchin'!' she cried then ringingly, facing him squarely with challenging eyes. 'You didn't know that man was guilty—nobody did. It seemed more like he was innocent'" (June 1916: 5).

The emotions aroused by the lynching move Sally to give vent to all her grievances against a patriarchal system for which "chivalry" offers a pretext: "Killin' a thousand men wouldn't do that poor little girl no good! All you men would much better have done something for her while she was livin'—seen that she got her growth an' education before she was sent up against the dangers of the world!" Sally's protest against the lynching modulates into a cry against the wretched lives endured by women as victims of patriarchy. If chivalry has any meaning, Sally charges, it would reside not in defending Southern womanhood by the lynching of a scapegoat, but in relieving women from their domestic burdens, from "cookin' an' sweeping an' dusting an' makin' beds an' tendin' children an' chickens an' dogs an' gardens, and countless other things, day in an' day out, until they drop into the grave!" Sally does not stand up to her husband for long. His threats subdue her, and she "shuffles" off to get him breakfast, "her feet once more firmly set on the treadmill of her daily slavery" (5).

Heavy-handed though Hanley's story is, it does offer an effective illustration of the specious justification of prejudice in one of its most violent manifestations, through an appeal to patriarchal attitudes in the guise of "chivalry."

Mary White Ovington is better known as one of the white founders of the National Association for the Advancement of Colored People (NAACP) than as a writer of fiction. However, besides her prolific polemical journalism in *The New Review* and *The New Republic,* and works like *Half a Man: The Status of the Negro in New York* (1911), or *The Walls Came Tumbling Down* (1947), an autobiography which focuses on the history of the NAACP, she also wrote adult fiction, plays, and short stories for children. Her novel *The Shadow* (1920) tells of the search for identity of a young woman raised as an adopted child by a loving black family, who learns that the people who abandoned her (and to whom she can feel no emotional ties whatever) are white. From then on her fate is to be torn between the two worlds engendered by white bigotry, and yet to learn in the end that "color" is indeed a cultural construct, "a state of mind" (330).

Ovington's story "The White Brute" was published in *The Masses* in November 1915. Like *The Shadow*—and a number of writings by women in *The Masses*—"The White Brute" examines the relations between oppression of an ethnic minority and the situation of women within that oppression.

Like Hanley's "Chivalry," "The White Brute" deals with the racist crimes of Southern white males. However, whereas in "Chivalry" a victimized woman is merely an onlooker at an act of violence which she finds employed as a pretext for the perpetuation of her own oppression, in Ovington's story a woman is victimized both as a woman and as a member of an ethnic group.

Sam and Melinda are a newly married couple. As they wait for a train in a dreary little lounge marked "Colored" on a hot Mississippi afternoon, they exchange loving words. Melinda reassures Sam, who wonders aloud why Melinda chose him over better-educated men: "You make me feel safe."

While taking the air on the station platform, the couple find their path barred by two young white men with "coarse, somewhat bloated faces," one of whom carries a gun. One of them refers in a bullying manner to the lighter-skinned Melinda as "a white girl," supposedly too white to be a black man's companion. Frightened, Sam pretends to laugh with his persecutors, answering their questions with uneasy laughter and a servile readiness that perfectly captures his dread: "'De train from the South, sah. Ought to be hyar by two o'clock, but it ain't comin' till fo'. Pretty po' train, to keep a bride waitin'.' He showed his white teeth again in a broad smile, but his eyes were fixed anxiously on the white man's face" (17).

The full extent of Sam and Melinda's vulnerability becomes unambiguously clear when one of the men announces his intention to "Give your girl a good time" (17). Sam contemplates putting up a fight—and then he contemplates a mental image of his own lynching that would be the likely consequence: "As he stood there, alert, tense, ready to strike, before his eyes there flashed the picture of a man tied to a post, writhing amid flames, while to his nostrils came the smell of burning flesh." Instead of fighting, Sam pleads pathetically with the men. They knock him to the ground, and drag Melinda away. Sam, "in his strength and his helplessness," is left waiting on the station platform "through the interminable hours" (18).

At last the rapists return with their victim, and bundle Sam and Melinda onto the train. The couple travel on in silence, to what Sam had intended as an idyllic home for his bride.

Melinda never explicitly blames Sam for his failure to defend her, but as she shivers, starts at every sound, and that night breaks down in tears, he finds her withdrawing from him: "'Honey,' he whispered, 'I's glad you kin cry. Let the tears come. Dey'll help you to furget.' He would have laid her head upon his breast, but she drew away" (18).

Distraught, Sam pleads that his death could in any case not have saved

Melinda; that, as matters stand, at least "You ain't alone now, Melindy . . . and I'll toil for you while I lives." Still his wife turns away, "snuggled close to the wall as if seeking protection there." Sam is left alone in the dark to face himself: "'A dead man or a live cur,' he said to himself; and he turned upon his face with a sob" (18). Clearly, the reader's sympathy is invoked not only for Melinda, but for Sam, whose tragedy, like hers, is to find himself at the mercy of a society whose dominant members are most selective in their application of the ideal of "chivalry" to women.

Ovington's powerful narrative provoked a number of letters from *Masses* readers, which were published along with a response from Ovington herself. Some readers questioned not only the "truth" of Ovington's story but also, in Ovington's own words, "my right as a Northerner to attempt to portray Southern conditions." Ovington identifies the source of her story as an incident related to her by "a Southern white woman." This woman "had no feeling of any special sympathy for the Negro" but "perhaps because I was sympathetic she began to talk freely and tell me of the difficulties the colored girl met with who tried to live a virtuous life. And then, in just a sentence, she gave me my tale" (Jan. 1916: 20).

That readers' protests to a radical magazine questioned not the right or the ability of a white person to enter imaginatively into the lives of African-Americans, but rather the credentials of Northern whites to write critically of racism in the South, suggests how sociocultural perspectives have altered over the decades. Ovington herself seems to feel obliged to answer the charge of ignorance of "Southern conditions." She explains that she has visited the South on numerous occasions, and talked with members of the black community there, adding that residence in a given area does not in itself guarantee more familiarity with the situation of people of another class (or race) than a sympathetic, open-minded stranger might acquire. In fact, a similar "ignorance of the life of workers" on the part of the employer is "common everywhere," and in the South, racial segregation compounds this ignorance:

> So your Southern woman may know where her cook lives, and as mistress may go into her cook's home, but she never enters the Negro section to take any part in its life. She never visits the schools, never goes to a colored church, and especially never meets on any terms whatever, the educated, well-to-do Negroes. . . . The ambitions, the strivings, of the growing Negro youth who is two generations removed from slavery she does not understand. . . . To her, the good Negro is still the faithful servant. . . . (20)

If some *Masses* women recognized the existing obstacles to the creation of a multiracial society on terms of equality, others sought and found, even amid the pervasive racism of the contemporary social setting, faint but hopeful signs of potential for a more harmonious society in the future. Unlike contemporary advocates of Americanization—meaning assimilation to a preexistent ideal prescription for cultural homogeneity—*Masses* contributors inclined to the celebration of (to use a 1990s catch-word) "diversity"—to an appreciation of heterogeneity and cultural difference. At their most enlightened, the contributions of *Masses* women endorsed the ideal for the American society of the future outlined by Elizabeth Gurley Flynn in "Do You Believe in Patriotism?": "America—not as a melting-pot that produces a jingoistic, mercenary, one-mold type, but as a giant loom weaving into a mighty whole the song, the poetry, the traditions and the customs of all races, until a beautiful human fabric, with each thread intact comes forth . . ." (Mar. 1916: 12).

Not surprisingly, children, representative both of innocence and of the potential of a new generation, feature largely in *Masses* contributors' explorations of racial issues. "Puzzle: Find the Race Problem," by Alice Beach Winter, a *Masses* artist who specialized in representations of children, illustrates both aspects of the childhood theme (Mar. 1914: 20). The drawing shows a little white girl cradling a black doll, and a little black boy hugging a white doll. The girl is smiling, the boy apparently deep in serious thought. The children sit nearly back to back, but close together, suggesting both children's wordless contentment in one another's company. If these ideal little citizens of the future seem a trifle too sweet, too well behaved—even too good to be true—this sense of the drawing's undoubted sentimentality may be qualified by our knowledge that the adult world in which children have to function, and which some day they will have to enter as adults themselves, will not be founded upon such innocent harmony.

A poem by Babette Deutsch, written many years after her work for *The Masses* and published in her *Collected Poems, 1919–1962* (1963), seems relevant here for its portrait of a "Small Colored Boy in the Subway." The poem describes a beautiful black child, who falls asleep on the subway train, "in the surrender of weariness still keeping dignity,/As if, a child, you honorably upheld/What was too heavy for a child to hold." Deutsch's lines suggest the African-American struggle for dignity in a white racist society. While some readers might find disquieting the poem's insistence on images of oral consumption—the child's eyes are "dark as plums" with "the aubergine's lustre," his skin like "coffee in the bean," the child "a morsel/So fine that you feed the eye"—these images may be read as serving a function other than that of (say) a tabooed expression of erotic desire. The comparison of the child to preconscious life-forms—to fruits, or to "a slight-boned animal" may also suggest his preadult innocence. On one level, he exists as spontaneously as an animal or plant. It is this very innocence which constitutes the child's unspoken, unconscious indictment of adult injustice: ". . . even in sleep,/Without defense, darkly your grace proffers/ The grave accusation of innocence" (136).

Like that of Winter's "Find the Race Problem" and of Deutsch's "Colored Boy on the Subway" the subtext of Dorothy Day's image of "Mulberry Street" may be read as follows: verbal language, the mode of the articulate consciousness of the adult world, is also the mode in which prejudices, racial epithets, and negative stereotypes are formulated and crystallized. Thus Day's Italian boy shows wordless affection to his sister: "Turns sympathetically/Wipes her nose with the end of his ragged shirt/And gives her a lick" (July 1917: 49). In Lydia Gibson's "Children Playing," it is interracial harmony that such nonverbal communication secures:

> The little blond babies and the little brown babies,
> And the Chinese babies like canary birds,
> Play in the street in the golden sleepy evening,
> And call and twitter without any words.
>
> (Apr. 1917: 42)

While young children may represent the freedom from prejudice conducive to racial harmony, women characters in *The Masses* may be portrayed as that harmony's conscious agents. While otherwise very different, "The Classmates," an early story by Inez Irwin, and Mary Heaton Vorse's "Tolerance," share this underlying idea. Like some of Vorse's fiction, too, "The Classmates" represents an earnest attempt to overcome socially inculcated racism.[19]

In "The Classmates," a young student is asked to play hostess to the grandfather of a black classmate whose very presence in the same college as herself Patty-Maud regards as an affront to her dignity.

Patty-Maud's first glimpse of the guest is unpromising. It must also be admitted that the narrator's description clearly shows the influence of contemporary racist ethnology: "His profile presented the most . . . African malformations of contours. . . ." Patty-Maud, by contrast, is notable for the "subtle modelling" of her features, for her "columnar fairness" and "the beauty of her clear gray eyes." Moreover, the old man's tufts of "grizzled" hair and baggy clothing give him a look of "premeditated eccentricity." Yet, despite the racism of the description, the old man is said to project "some kind of inherent dignity" (Mar. 1911: 13).

In spite of her indignation at being assigned what she considers a humiliating task, Patty-Maud escorts the elderly gentleman around the campus, and the afternoon passes uneventfully. Later, however, Patty-Maud

"PUZZLE: FIND THE RACE PROBLEM," ALICE BEACH WINTER.
(Courtesy General Research Division, The New York Public Library, Astor, Lenox and Tilden Foundations.)

finds herself greeted by the old man's granddaughter. Startlingly (and perhaps somewhat improbably), Mabel Johnson thanks Patty-Maud not only for accompanying her grandfather, but also for "not letting him realize certain things" (15). Apparently the poor deluded old man believes that the Emancipation Proclamation really spelled equality between the races (a belief difficult to sustain, one would have thought, for one who had spent his whole life in the postbellum South!). At any rate, Mabel Johnson knows better: "Not that I myself am deceived—that I misunderstand—" (15).

Hearing these remarks from Mabel, Patty-Maud bristles. Finally though, she is won over by Mabel's evident sincerity as Mabel talks of the bond between classmates, and goes on to generalize about class solidarity of a different kind—about "that feeling which made men and women of all religions and races fight behind the barricades at Moscow" in the abortive revolution of 1905 (18). As she listens, Patty-Maud finds herself won over, not only to a new understanding of Mabel's point of view, but to a new sense of kinship. Clearly, this kinship involves no discovery of the intrinsic worth of minority culture—Patty-Maud knows that, "in essentials, her attitude towards the race which Mabel Johnson represented, could never change"—yet she does recognize in Mabel "a girl, who, except for the infusion in the skin of a certain pigment, was her own counterpart."

In this case, it is an assimilative ideal which triumphs. The sense of sisterhood is what overrides racial prejudice. Patty-Maud sees in Mabel another woman, "subject, like herself, to all the tragedies of the woman-lot," and laboring under the "social handicaps and racial limitations" that Patty-Maud, as a white woman, will never have to deal with. The story closes with a moment in which all this understanding is expressed in wordless communication: "Patty-Maud's eyes, which had been kept fixed frostily on her companion's face, melted and filled slowly. Mabel Johnson's deep gaze filled too, and for a long instant gray eyes and brown eyes said to each other the things that could never be put into words" (18).

Contrived though Irwin's narrative may be, it may serve as a representative example of the well-meaning liberal sentiments on racial issues of *Masses* women for whom an ethnically diverse social world of equals formed no part of their immediate experience.

Mary Heaton Vorse's "Tolerance," though its characters are treated in a spirit of comedy, approaches closer to Flynn's ideal of the multicultural human fabric. Like "The Classmates," though, it portrays women both as peacemakers and as agents of social harmony.

The Irish Grogans and the German Schultzes live next door to one another in a U.S. mill town. Both families belong to the elite of the local working class, and to "the oldest emigration." The fathers, skilled workers, and contemptuous of the newly arrived, unskilled immigrants, have "come out of town since the Slavs, Pollaks, Lithuanians, Ginnies, French Canadians and what not" have "poured in" (Feb. 1914: 12).

Grogans and Schultzes have lived in friendship for years, even though the Grogans are devout Catholics and supporters of the conservative American Federation of Labor (a union which organized only skilled workers), and Mr. Schultz is a confirmed atheist and a member of the Socialist Party. But this friendship is severely tested when the younger generation quarrel. Lonnie Grogan, who is engaged to marry Elizabeth Schultz, starts an argument which begins with an attack on the family belief system, but ends with the flinging of racial epithets:

> Lonnie scalded her heart so she et the face offen him! He called her a narrow-minded Socialist an' she called him an idol-worshipping Papist and from there on they went until Lonnie was throwin' 'Dutchman' in her face and she 'Paddy' in his. (13)

The family situation grows more complicated when the town's unskilled mill hands, whom both Mr. Grogan and Mr. Schultz regard as a "disorderly, unorganized mob of inferior nations," succeed in organizing a strike under the banner, not of the AF of L, nor even of the Socialist Party, but of "them ruffeens from the west," as Mr. Grogan refers to them, the radical syndicalist Industrial Workers of the World. As if this were not bad enough in itself, Mr. Grogan learns to his outrage that Lonnie has joined the strike committee and now declares himself a syndicalist.

When the infuriated father appeals next door for the sympathy of Mr. Schultz, he runs into unexpected misunderstanding, based not on ethnic difference, but on ideology. Mr. Grogan makes a quite innocent remark, which assumes that syndicalism, a doctrine anathema to Schultz, is identical with Schultz's cherished creed of socialism, and "the battle was on. Between them they tore the tolerant friendship of years to pieces" (14).

Meanwhile, the younger generation have patched up their differences. The narrator suggests that they will be more open-minded than their elders; after all, Lonnie has found his true comrades among the despised unskilled foreign workers in the "one big union" of the IWW. It remains for the women of the two families to employ their superior feminine wisdom, and feminine negotiating skills, to reconcile the stubborn male elders:

> Mrs. Schultz shook her head again: 'Young people,' said she, gets ofer lots of dings, M's Grogan, but old mens like Schultz and Grogan gets ofer noddings maybe, und now ve poor vomens alone have got to talk dem ofer into gettin' ofer eferythings.' (15)

As in "Tolerance," an ideal which extends beyond mere tolerance to appreciation of diversity is often adumbrated in the works of *Masses* women, if not explicitly developed in any detail. If there is satire in Vorse's story—on the various creeds imported from the Old Country to which the families cling with fierce devotion—there is also appreciation of the vitality and variety those creeds bring to life, and a not so implicit criticism of the Schultz daughter when she dismisses the Junior Socialists at the local high school as "a bunch of Dutch girls" (12).

Still, it would be a mistake to overemphasize the capacity of *Masses* women explicitly to celebrate, rather than merely to tolerate, ethnic difference. They are, after all, products of the all-white middle and upper classes which enclosed so many of them, and of their time, with its racist ethnology and its lack of access to the written word for many members of ethnic minorities. The fact remains that although *The Masses* speaks *about* minorities constantly, minority-authored works hardly appear in its pages. However, celebration of ethnic differences does make its appearance in the writings of *Masses* contributors beyond the pages of *The Masses*—notably in the writings of Mabel Dodge and Elsie Clews Parsons about Pueblo culture, and in those of Mary Heaton Vorse about immigrant workers.

Socialists and internationalists, *Masses* contributors could yet reveal themselves as romantic about their nation's future potential as any jingoistic capitalist. Thus, for example, Dorothy Day in *The Long Loneliness,* recalls her youthful impressions of the ethnically diverse population of turn-of-the-century Chicago:

> There were all nationalities in Chicago and there were Socialist groups in every nationality. They had come to the United States to better their condition and they became the exploited in sweatshops, in the stockyards . . . there were Slovaks, Poles, Bohemians, Croatians, Ukrainians and Germans, Lithuanians and Estonians. The thing I felt strongly was that there were changes taking place in the world. . . . They were part of a movement, a slow upheaval . . . and they were beginning to feel within themselves a power and a possibility.[20]

A similar sense of the vibrant potential of the new society being shaped by the mingling of races and cultures in twentieth-century North America is evident in the close of Mary Heaton Vorse's novel *Second Cabin* (1928). Here the emphasis is not, as in Day's reminiscence, on worker solidarity, but on the possibility of a fresh start in the New World for a woman from the Old.[21] A young "picture bride" from northern Italy, dispatched by her family to the United States for an arranged marriage with a man she has never seen, has made up her mind not to land but to return home, after an unhappy shipboard love affair with a married man. Then the skyline of New York comes into view:

> The New York skyline appeared, tremendous and indifferent. There it stood, the gateway of America. Newcomers looked at it with amazement. The homecoming Americans were amazed, also. They had forgotten the new thing that they had builded. People crowded to the rails. . . .
>   Some emotional German-Americans were weeping. Excitement enveloped all of them. America, with New York as its question mark, interrogated the ship's company. (318)

Elsa experiences a change of heart. She will not sacrifice herself to her shipboard love affair by returning home; but neither, one suspects, will she marry the man for whom she is intended as a "picture bride." She feels the call of a different adventure. The other passengers are "pressing forward, streaming out to America, asking New York to suck them in":

> As though drawn on an unseen tide, Elsa slipped through the crowd. Lefty slid his eyes after her. "She'll land awri', awri'," he said. . . .

Mrs. Donovan peered at Lefty as though his naiveté was as deep as the towers of New York high:

"Did ye ever doubt it?" she inquired. (319)

Vorse's account of the docking of this ship full of excited immigrants brings to mind Elizabeth Gurley Flynn's image, cited earlier, of America as a many-colored human fabric. As Elsa and the others crowd forward to the landing, we know the loom is already strung, the shuttles weaving.

6

Keeping the Faith?

ELEVEN *MASSES* WOMEN may be regarded as central to the life of *The Masses* for the frequency of their contributions or for their editorial involvement, or both: Cornelia Barns, Alice Beach Winter, Helen Marot, Mabel Dodge, Elsie Clews Parsons, Inez Haynes Irwin, Helen Hull, Adriana Spadoni, Louise Bryant, Dorothy Day, Mary Heaton Vorse. Of these, the subsequent careers of the last-mentioned seven are well worth tracing, not only for the substantial literary output of most of them, or for the celebrity—and occasional notoriety—of their careers, but for their representative status as the century's first generation of feminist left-wing radicals. Their seven subsequent histories, taken together, offer one means of charting the decline (and the persistence) of left-wing radicalism and of feminism over the next forty years. As will shortly be seen, where they did persist, both the leftist allegiances and the feminist commitments underwent some surprising transmutations.

Three of these figures were to become known primarily as novelists: Irwin, Hull, and Spadoni. Both Irwin and Hull, while retaining feminist concerns in their fiction, became politically more conservative overall. Spadoni, on the other hand, seems to have rediscovered a commitment to radical fiction some twenty years after her work for *The Masses*. The other four are better known for their nonfictional prose: Parsons as a social critic and anthropologist, and Bryant, Vorse, and Day for their journalism. In varying degrees, the three journalists also engaged in other forms of social activism. All three remained politically more or less radical, but with modifications in the positions they held during the *Masses* years, in the cases of Day and Bryant.

Of the novelists, the most versatile, in terms of her facility in employing genres other than fiction, is Irwin, who practiced labor journalism and war reporting and wrote feminist essays, history, biography, and stories for children. Much of the early fiction, like the early nonfiction, expresses a strong commitment both to political radicalism and, more frequently, to feminism.

One statement of Irwin's about her own work must be viewed with critical skepticism when considered in the light of her total literary output. In her autobiography, written when she was seventy-seven, she makes the astonishing claim that she cannot recall a single sentence in any of her writing

> . . . which bore a message. And there, I think, I put a finger on my great lack. I have no message. I have never liked fiction, whether play, whether novel, whether short story, which deals—except as atmosphere—either with political or sociological conditions. ("Adventures," 519)

From a well-known suffrage activist and historian, a member of the National Advisory Council of the National Woman's Party on the eve of the suffrage victory, author of *Angel Island* and *The Story of Alice Paul and the National Woman's Party,* this assertion is startling indeed. It seems an indication of the conservatism to which Irwin succumbed in later life. The banality of novels like *Family Circle* (1931) seems to be at least in part a product of her loss of any sense of "message." One further indication of this later conservatism, as manifested in "Adventures of Yesterday," is that in writing of *Angel Island* she stresses, not the novel's militantly feminist themes, its satiric critique of patriarchy, or even its progressive evolutionism, but the pleasure she experienced in creating a fantasy setting: "Writing that novel was fun; for not only did I invent my geography, my topography, but I created my weather and my tides. Perhaps I enjoyed this bit of creative fantasy more than any other" ("Adventures," 504).

Arguably, fantasy settings of a different kind are what come to occupy the center of Irwin's later fiction. This escapist tendency was always potentially present in Irwin's fictional writing, in the early short stories and sketches, and even in a story like "Henry," published in *The Masses.* But in her later work it takes over with a vengeance, seeming to exist for its own sake. In family novels like *Family Circle,* or even in Irwin's detective fiction, the settings are the elaborately furnished, elegant homes of the wealthy, where seemingly interminable descriptions of room interiors and clothing form what many readers must have found an unwelcome distraction from development of character and plot. Still, even amid this clutter, if a reader has the patience, Irwin's novels offer some interesting moments. Three novels deserve specific mention: *The Lady of Kingdoms* (1917), *Gertrude Haviland's Divorce* (1925), and *Gideon* (1927).

The Lady of Kingdoms is interesting for its background of radical social ferment, vividly evoked from Irwin's own contemporary experience of New York's feminist and socialist movements. Her two main women characters, Southward and Hester, visit the city together, and Hester falls under the spell of John, a socialist, who opens Hester's eyes to the existence of class exploitation and takes her to a meeting of feminist socialists (223). The novel's most engaging aspect, to many modern readers, will not be the novel's leading figure, Southward Drake, the "sparklingly handsome" lady of the title who shoots her lover in a fit of jealousy (and later marries him). More compelling—certainly more controversially feminist—is the "subplot" involving Hester, in which this young woman raised in a genteel setting, who longs for children, persuades a total stranger to sleep with her. A solitary unmarried mother, she sets out to raise her child with the help of her mother, who has become reconciled to her daughter's unconventional choice. The agonizing personal struggles of Hester, alone in New York, unable to marry the man she loves, are movingly juxtaposed with the stirring collective movement of a suffrage parade—of the female sex, quite literally, on the march. The passage seems worth quoting at length:

> A company of mounted police headed this parade. Behind the parade came a band playing "The Marseillaise." Behind the band walked alone a tall beautiful young woman in white, carrying a big yellow suffrage flag. Behind her, on a white horse, rode another woman, young also, beautiful and in white, carrying a big American flag. Behind her came many women on horseback. Behind the horsewomen came women on foot. More women and more women and more women, pouring up from Washington Square. . . . Young mothers pushed perambulators, wound in yellow, holding babies who would perhaps see the fruition of this movement. . . . Then came the men, hundreds strong. Then came the socialists, men and women, hundreds strong. And then more of the striding women. Always by eights. . . . White women and black women. Nondescript women and distinguished women. Self-conscious women and unembarrassed women. Frank, free fine women. Tired, dull, sodden women. Inspired women. . . . Striding towards that goal under the shadowy Park trees as though everything that Woman desired awaited them there.
>   . . . "Did you notice that tall blond girl that we passed on the right? The tears were just *streaming* down her face."
>   "Yes. But if she's so interested, I wonder she isn't marching."
>   "Perhaps she'll fall in."
>   But Hester did not fall in. (427–429)

Gertrude Haviland's Divorce and *Gideon* also deal with feminist themes, although more indirectly than *The Lady of Kingdoms*. In *Gertrude Haviland*, the title character is a woman so absorbed in domesticity and mothering that five years pass before she notices that her husband has been having an affair with another woman. Divorced from Will Haviland, she goes with her children to live in a small New England town. At first, Gertrude feels herself a complete outsider to this setting, but gradually begins to make a new life. She becomes a pillar of the local women's club, and of the community. When the United States enters the First World War—in keeping with Irwin's support of U.S. intervention—Gertrude teaches French to soldiers about to be posted overseas, and lectures on the plight of invaded France. She becomes a businesswoman, renting out her property as a source of income. In short, she becomes an independent individual, with goals and interests of her own.

When Gertrude's husband, whose second wife has died in the meantime, arrives to suggest remarriage, he is disconcerted by the gracious self-confidence with which Gertrude turns his offer down, and by her smiling assurance that she has no need of his financial support (378). The final chapter of *Gertrude Haviland* makes clear that Gertrude will probably remarry—in this respect the novel is no less conventional than Irwin's other novels—not her former husband, however, but a man more suited to her new conception of feminine independence. The chapter's concluding sentences suggest that if Gertrude marries the man of her choice, it will be on her own terms. In the words of the narrator, Gertrude "held out her arms. And when he reached her side, she took him into them" (389).

Gideon is a study of an adolescent's maturation, the discovery of his identity in relation to the adult members of his family. But it is also a moral fable about two contrasting models of femininity, as represented by Bella, Gideon's biological mother, and Laurel Hallam, his father's second wife.

During a summer visit to his father's new home, Gideon has the chance to compare the two women. At first he is fiercely loyal to Bella, deeply resentful of the woman he regards as having "stolen" his father from her. Gradually, however, Gideon's perceptions begin to change, as it dawns on him that Bella is mercenary. (Her principal aim in sending Gideon to stay with his father is to extract money from her ex-husband.) She is sly, and has directed her son to spy on the new Mrs. Hallam. She is vain, affected, frivolous, manipulative of men in traditional feminine ways, yet ultimately dominated and victimized by her parasitic male companions. By contrast, Laurel Hallam is fairly indifferent both to conspicuous consumption and to an opulent social life. She and her husband live in a remote rural area by choice. She is both shrewd in a worldly sense, understanding perfectly that Gideon has been sent to spy on her, and too well mannered and self-assured to allude to her knowledge. She is intellectually serious. In contrast to Bella's drunken, gossipy cocktail parties, her dinners provide an opportunity for talk about psychoanalysis, international politics, and the Woman's Party. Unlike Bella, who has spent her whole life in a "feminine" world, as traditionally constituted, Laurel is both adventurous and well traveled, having been on safari in Africa. Her bold resourcefulness and her idealism are represented by her smuggling over the state line of an ex-convict persecuted by the authorities (217–219).

In Irwin's contrastive study, house interiors and clothing are employed as indices of definitions of femininity judged as appropriate or inappropriate. Thus, Gideon, who at first had been repelled by the austere simplicity of Laurel Hallam's house, on returning to Bella's home experiences something of a counter–culture shock: "What had happened to the room? It was smaller than Gideon remembered it . . . lower—closer, somehow. What a jarring jumble of colors and things. . . . For a curious moment it seemed to Gideon that he was finding it hard to breathe" (256). Where Laurel, with her sleek, short black hair, subtle makeup, and pale skin, has the appearance of "a marble head in cameo," Bella appears to the returning Gideon "appalling" in her make-up, her cheeks "horribly pink" under "smeared" eye hollows, her lips a "blood-wet scarlet" (145, 195, 254).

Though filled with a desperate pity for Bella in her emotionally and materially impoverished existence, Gideon finally recognizes that Bella's conception of femininity is a spent ideal, while to the reader it becomes clear that Laurel Hallam (who appears in many ways to be an idealized portrait of Irwin herself) represents the New Woman, come of age. When at last he learns that his father did not, in fact, desert Bella as she had alleged, but left her because of her cynical desertions of him for other men, Gideon adopts Laurel Hallam as a second mother.

It is regrettable that, after *Gideon,* Irwin produced so little of interest. After 1951 she ceased publishing completely. Still, if only for their often very astute feminist insights, at least three of Irwin's novels of the 1920s repay reading today.

In the intervals of teaching creative writing at Wellesley and then at Columbia, Helen Hull wrote seventeen novels, over sixty short stories, four books about writing, and a biography of Mayling Soong Chiang, Hull's former student at Wellesley, who married Chiang Kai-shek. Her short fiction was published in *Harper's, Collier's, The Saturday Evening Post, Cosmopolitan,* and the *Ladies Home Journal.* Her entire fictional output is marked by an abiding feminist commitment, especially her work during the period that begins with her first stories in *The Masses* and extends through the early novels *Quest* (1922), *Labyrinth* (1923), and *The Surrey Family* (1925). Each of these novels deals with a woman's challenge to patriarchally defined conceptions of feminine roles. The culmination of this series comes with *Islanders* (1927), a novel justly praised at its publication, and republished in 1988 with a perceptive and sympathetic Afterword by Patricia McClelland Miller.

The main character in *Islanders,* Ellen Dacey, like other women of her generation, is an "islander," a single woman cut off by her lack of power and status from the mainland of the wider, male-dominated world.

Cheated out of her inheritance by her menfolk, who squander the proceeds from the sale of her land, Ellen is forced to live a stale, unfruitful life as a household drudge, taken for granted as the resident (and powerless) "maiden aunt," first in her brother's household, then with her nephew and his wife.

The one source of solace in Ellen's life lies in her hopes for the new generation, as represented by her great-niece Anne:

> Slowly she lifted one finger and laid it delicately against the soft tiny head, with its astonishing tuft of dark hair, against the soft, rapid pulsation of the skull. With that beating at her finger tip, a kind of ecstasy crept into Ellen, as if life and growth entered her, as if her emptiness shrivelled at the touch of this new thing. (180)

Ellen vows to "forge some armor for Anne, from the steel of her own hard years" (182). But Anne's mother wants her raised to be a young lady. Anne returns from boarding school a charming, decorative creature, full of self-consciousness and affectation, and now confined to the genteel occupations considered proper to her gender:

> Later, when the boys clattered downstairs, to pedal off madly on their bicycles, to swim, Anne shrugged. Deep within her an old self tugged faintly; but it was a kite, flat on the ground, and she no longer flung it into the air, letting out string as she ran, trying to sail it higher than the world. This new self was a stranger, holding her to unfamiliar language, fluttering at her eyelids, a thing of wiles and enticing humilities that Anne had never before felt. (256)

Ellen perseveres, however—Anne must understand that life contains richer, more challenging possibilities than "fancy work and fellows," and must not yield to the notion that only males are "expected to do things" (264). She must learn to leave her island and merge with society.

The seed takes root. Anne, graduated from college and restless, recalls Ellen's words, and finally understands: "I have to do it myself. Me, Anne Dacey" (277). There follows a series of abortive attempts to find her place in life—to avoid, as Anne puts it to herself, "the pattern that is supposed to fit me" (277). She tries voluntary social work, secretarial training, and a job with the woman suffrage campaign. In a conclusion which at least one reviewer has thought a capitulation to conventional ideals of the feminine role,[1] Anne finds a sense of fulfillment in marriage. Even though she rejects the rich young ne'er-do-well her family had expected her to marry in favor of a young journalist who can offer her a more active life, the novel's last sentence remains powerfully ambiguous. Ellen, now on her deathbed, is

Inez Haynes Irwin. (H. W. Wilson Company.)

unable to cling to life until Anne can bring her lover to meet Ellen at the bedside. Anne hurries towards the sickroom, calling her aunt's name—and "Ellen heard her, remotely. But she had at last to let go of Anne" (312).

Although Hull's later novels continue to express feminist ideals, the radicalism of that feminism diminishes somewhat. *Heat Lightning,* a novel palatable enough to mainstream taste to be a Book-of-the-Month Club selection in 1932 when it was published, portrays a number of strong female characters in a rural family setting. The central character, Amy, goes to her family home in the country for a visit, in order to reevaluate her troubled relationship with her estranged husband. Perhaps through a new understanding of her family she can gain a fresh understanding of herself, and so reexamine her marriage.

The "heat lightning" of the title refers to the emotions unleashed by the clash of interests over the sharing of Grandma's property when the family matriarch dies intestate. This conflict provides rich opportunities for character study. Felice, who is French and has "married into" Amy's family, is

Helen Hull. (H. W. Wilson Company.)

presented as one possible feminine ideal, notably in her level-headed ratio-nality: "Ideas for Felice were never thin disguises for her own prejudices, they were on another level where emotion did not penetrate. She had no desire to coerce another to her way of thinking" (85). This paragon of rationality is contrasted with the placidly unreflecting Emma, while Amy herself reflects that she must "stand somewhere between" these two ex-tremes. Then there is Grandma herself, benevolent and maternalistic, a protector of weaker members of the community and, until her death, the family peacemaker.

Hull's theoretical social conservatism is particularly apparent in *Heat Lightning* in her portrayal of Harriet, a character involved in an unhappy love affair with another woman. Harriet is treated very differently from Hull's characters in her early short stories or in *Labyrinth* who form gay relationships. In these earlier works the characters and relationships are explored sympathetically or even—in *Labyrinth*—celebrated. In view of Hull's own lifelong, happy lesbian relationship with Mabel Louise Rob-inson, it seems particularly ironic that the lesbian character Harriet in *Heat Lightning* should be portrayed as lazy, resentful, a self-pitying whiner (111), "soft as wet putty," as Amy says of her (106). Even more surprisingly, Harriet's sexual orientation is treated as a perverse reaction to her family upbringing. Harriet's mother is spoiled, nagging, her living-room furni-ture "loaded down" with bric-a-brac: "Small wonder Harriet slicked back her hair and went in for tweeds" (109).

Heat Lightning is indicative of Hull's intensified social conservatism in another respect, one that invites comparison with Hull's early stories in *The Masses* about the sexual exploitation of women in domestic service. In *Heat Lightning* the servant girl Lulu, seduced and made pregnant by a male member of the household, is not, as in the *Masses* stories, a central character, but a minor one, whose seduction seems introduced mainly to illustrate the foolishness, fecklessness, and general lack of maturity of the seducer, young Tom. The narrator's attitude to the family's solution to this problem is interesting, too. Grandma offers to rescue Tom by buying Lulu off—"If that girl has money for a dowry, some man of her own class would be glad to marry her"—a sentiment which the reader is invited to view with approval. To Lulu's credit, she has too much respect to accept the family's payoff, and decamps before they can implement their plans for her (207).

Despite the muting of Hull's earlier, bolder feminism, feminist themes do persist in one form or another in her later fiction. *A Circle in the Water* (1932) invites parallels with Inez Irwin's *Gertrude Haviland's Divorce*—although the resolution of Hull's novel is far more tentative and ambigu-ous than that of Irwin's novel. *A Circle in the Water* examines the disinte-gration, over a period of years, of Vera's relationship with her husband

Hilary, a novelist. Hilary's public personae, as college teacher, artist, and delinquent son who defiantly chose a writing career over inheritance of the family farm, conceal "profound uncertainty and insecurity about himself" (99). Paradoxically, as Hilary becomes more successful as a writer, these self-doubts increase, under the strain of forging his career. Hilary complains of feeling trapped by his marriage to Vera, and by what he imagines are her expectations of him: "I've felt like a trick bear, a squirrel in a cage, you outside the door . . . waiting for me to do my tricks. You'd invested in me, hadn't you?" Vera is appalled at this paranoid outburst: "He made her sound like a dreadful kind of leech" (264).

Hilary's insecurity, his resentments, and his infidelities pull the marriage apart. Vera and Hilary both remarry—Vera more successfully than Hilary. Hilary's second wife bullies and dominates him, while reveling in her role as the wife of the Hollywood writer Hilary has become. Hilary, now dependent on ghostwriters to devise material for him, has effectively ceased to produce as an artist. The novel's conclusion, in contrast to the triumphant close of *Gertrude Haviland's Divorce,* is full of implied denunciation of the destruction of a relationship by male narcissism.

Even the more conventional later novels indicate Hull's continuing preoccupation, not simply with the weaknesses and obsessions of middle- and upper-class women, but with the social context which shapes (or warps) their personalities. In one of her radio talks about writing, Hull explains this conception of the purpose of family fiction. The family, she contends, is "the microcosm of the world," since the family is "the smallest unit of society in which people have to deal with the problem which is life itself, the problem of learning how to live with other human beings. . . . There are no problems of life which do not exist within family walls. Birth is there, as a problem in emotion or in economics. . . ."[2]

Hawk's Flight (1946) is a study of four marriages—in particular, of the four wives. Ellen Hunter is a working wife with a career in advertising who craves social success, both in her career and in her marriage. Her ambitions force her into the pursuit of achievement as society defines it. Adelaide Burchall, on the other hand, almost totally effaces her own personality in slavish devotion to her career-minded husband and her sons. Genevieve Willett, who bears some resemblance to the neurasthenic Grace and the hypochondriac Mary in *Islanders,* is another character who has succumbed entirely to identification with the traditional feminine domestic role, but who, like those characters, has found ways to use "feminine weakness" for her own purposes, dominating her husband by playing on his guilt feelings about her ill health. Only the fourth wife, Carey Moore—despite her difficulties in overcoming her fear of human relatedness as a possible obstacle to her ambitions—possesses the necessary detachment, the "hard and brilliant eye" of the dispassionate observer, which enables her to review all these lives, including her own, with insight. Despite its conventional form, *Hawk's Flight* offers an implicit critique (although far more muted than in earlier, more overtly polemical work) of the strains imposed by bourgeois marriage on its adherents.

Hull's last novel, *Close Her Pale Blue Eyes* (1963), was published as a mystery novel in the Dodd, Mead "Red Badge Detective" series. The book is written in the bald, clichéd style of hard-boiled crime fiction—another indication, perhaps, that Hull, whose work became unfashionable in the 1950s, dismissed as "women's fiction," was driven to produce work according to a commercial formula. In fact, *Close Her Pale Blue Eyes* both conforms to and contests the mystery format. The reader knows early on who the killer is—Hank, the husband of the dying Delilah, who has engineered the death of his already gravely sick wife, not by any complicated murder plot, but by the simple expedient of causing her enough emotional distress at intervals to bring on the seizures he knows will eventually prove fatal: "Nothing there that any autopsy, any jury could fasten on him. He was free . . ." (210).

Hank *does* become a murderer in the legally prosecutable sense only in the novel's final pages as, overwrought and guilty at his wife's death, he rounds on his blackmailing mistress and strangles her. Even when this second killing is discovered, Hank is haunted only by the vision of the accusing stare of his dead wife: "Oh, close her eyes! Damn it, shut down those pale blue eyes!" (212).

Despite the crudities of style and general woodenness of dialogue and character, there is clearly more at work here than a simple detective mystery or sensational tale of murder. Delilah on her deathbed is a victim of male sexual manipulation: "[Hank] leaned forward to touch her lips, the coral lipstick with its undertone of purple cyanosis, his expert fingers invoking an old caress." Then, "to his own surprise" Hank hears his voice tremble. Having sexually aroused Delilah he will refuse to make love to her, but only to find himself "struggling against a paroxysm, compound of guilt, anger, remorse that untied his being" (131). The woman, as in so much of Hull's writing, is the primary victim here, but the man who has set himself to destroy her is destroyed along with her.

Hull's most significant legacy, as novelist and as feminist, almost certainly rests with her early stories and novels—notably with *Islanders* and *Heat Lightning*. Yet for the understanding of an unusually prolific and productive career, and not least for her charting of social change as manifested in the family over five decades, her literary output as a whole continues to merit close attention.

If a repeated theme appears in Adriana Spadoni's early fiction as represented by her short stories in *The Masses,* it is their presentation of women as victims of social circumstance. "The Seamstress" (Sept. 1913) is a self-sacrificing figure who gives unswerving devotion to helping the man she loves overcome his alcoholism—in the clear knowledge that, once he is cured, another woman, who has rejected him because of his drinking, will reclaim him. "Real Work" (July 1915) offers a humorous satirical sketch of an elderly woman's uncritical adoration of her elderly husband, whose obsessive cutting of clippings from the newspapers she mistakes for the work of a scholar of genius. "A Hall Bedroom Nun" (June 1916) portrays a lonely single woman who finds vicarious consolation in studying the lives of strangers. In her novels, Spadoni departs considerably from these implicitly femininist themes of women as victims. Like her first novel *The Swing of the Pendulum* (1919), *The Noise of the World* (1921), published five years after her last story appeared in *The Masses,* is a feminine bildungsroman, but not especially a feminist one. Indeed, although the novel's central character happens to be female, the protagonist's quest for existential meaning could equally well, one feels, have been represented as conducted by a man.

At first glance, *The Noise of the World* is not particularly committed to ideals of class struggle, either. Anne, the central character, marries a man who becomes a left-wing labor activist—a commitment which threatens to break up their marriage. Initially sympathetic to the workers' struggle, Anne finds herself increasingly repelled by what she comes to regard as the ugliness of the left-wing labor movement: "It was too loud, too insistent, too hot, like hissing black steam, screaming through a narrow vent" (128). She feels profoundly uncomfortable at a meeting of revolutionary workers (those settings which, one may recall, so stirred and inspired Mary Heaton Vorse, and which seemed so mundane to Max Eastman): [3] "The air, thick with human breath, the shrill voices of boys and girls selling revolutionary pamphlets, the mass weight of their hatred, woke in her a rebellion against the stark ugliness of its expression that took all Anne's control not to express by rising and leaving the hall" (129). In such an atmosphere Anne feels her effort "to believe in the ultimate aim of all this striving shrink and grow cold within her" (128). In the novel's most negative representation of the revolutionary labor movement, it becomes, from Anne's perspective, an anti-life force. Merle, an acquaintance of Anne's, tells how she has aborted a pregnancy, although she had wanted a child, under pressure from her labor organizer husband. Listening to Merle's story, Anne has a vision of "all the babies of the world, the babies thwarted of life, staring at her in the warm blackness of the night" (135). In her view, men like Tom O'Connell are "monomaniac," mad about social justice, "just as mad as any capitalist," and have lost the capacity to think of human beings in their individuality. At her most disillusioned Anne asks herself, "What did it matter whether one went forward or backward, since, in the end all dropped in death . . . (186). She succumbs to a kind of death wish: "Death was the Great Silence, the everlasting Peace" (186).

Yet Anne's rejection of revolutionary commitment is gradually revealed as one movement in a dialectic which takes her from political radicalism to a quasi-mystical experience in a church. She feels carried by "a wave of silence" into "a peace so profound and so real that Anne felt it laving the whole surface of her body. Something within slipped beyond the tight hold of her will, escaped from the encasing body in which she had gripped it, claimed its own and fled into Peace" (179). This experience leads Anne into a quest for what she identifies as "Silence"—and thence to a realization that Silence is merely a by-product, an inseparable opposite and counterpart, of "motion . . . the ever-changing march of the universe" (230). Anne adopts a kind of mystical evolutionism, in which she views this inexorable progress as fulfilling some purpose "hidden from finite sense." At last she is ready to recognize the narrow selfishness of her obsession with personal security, her rejection of political commitments. Of "the chord of the world's pain" clearly audible to her politically and religiously committed friends alike, she has "not grasped a note" (230). Anne at last understands her husband's quest in life as essentially akin to her own: "We both wanted the same thing—a beautiful world, but we tried to find this beauty in different places and there are no different places. There's only one Beauty everywhere" (235).

If *The Noise of the World* deemphasizes both socialist and feminist themes, so, at first glance, does *Mrs. Phelps' Husband* (1924). Indeed, the very title might seem to suggest an antifeminist tract—a story of a hapless male brought under female domination, just as women have traditionally been subjugated by a patriarchal social order. Actually, the novel may be read as a protest against the imprisonment of individuals of both sexes by the conventions of bourgeois society. The unconventional Stuart Phelps is powerfully attracted to the forthright and strong-minded Elinor, until he becomes the "Mrs. Phelps' Husband" of the novel's title, and finds himself compelled to abandon a comfortably bohemian lifestyle in Greenwich Village and move to an elegant modern apartment. Stuart and Elinor socialize with other middle-class professionals: complacent university professors with impeccably conventional opinions, one of whom the high school–educated Stuart insults by presuming to engage him in argument. Stuart finds escape from this stifling environment in an extramarital affair with a young woman less imbued with bourgeois values than his wife—but becomes repentant when Elinor is about to give birth to her and Stuart's child.

Conventional married life has killed Stuart's love for Elinor. He finds himself disgusted by the ugliness of the baby girl she has borne—"the smallest, reddest, ugliest object in the world" (425). Elinor has named the child Elisart—irrevocably binding together her name with Stuart's in the name of the child, who in turn binds Stuart to Elinor. Stuart has to remind himself to display affection to his wife: "He bent toward her. New fathers always kissed the mothers" (426).

Aside from his brief love affair, Stuart's reaction to his growing entrapment in bourgeois married life is one of weary patience. He does not blame Elinor. Nor is the reader invited to—but rather to wonder at the fate of a woman who sees in the weary, repetitive motions of factory workers the lot to which women of all classes are condemned, in the dull monotony of their domestic lives (41–42). Ironically it is those very qualities in Elinor—her independence of mind and strength of will, the "spark of fire" in her character—which have caused her discontent with the stale existence in her middle-class parents' home, and which, in the absence of a feminist consciousness or of any alternative modes of existence, make her the largely unwitting oppressor of her husband.

Not All Rivers (1937) is, like *The Noise of the World*, a *Bildungsroman*—but also a radical novel in the "proletarian," social realist style of the 1930s. Rhoda, the central female character, finds herself dissatisfied with the growing conservatism—and infidelity—of her college professor husband. After divorcing him, she wanders for a while, enjoying the friendship of another woman, until she meets and marries David, a liberal lawyer who defends striking California migrant workers. David is vividly conscious that the world has changed since 1929. "When the stock market crashed," he claims, "it didn't sweep away only the savings of a nation but the very ideal on which this country was founded—the right of every individual to pursuit of life, liberty and happiness" (234). Yet, despite his rhetoric, David still imagines that he can continue to be "a patcher" of the social system, restoring those "rotten spots" in the social fabric that threaten the collapse of the total structure. He remains essentially detached from the class struggle. As a migrant worker tells him, not unkindly, "You've never been on strike; you've never walked a picket line with nothing in your belly. You kin git up in court and talk, and no club cracks down on your skull. Them things make a difference" (315). Only when he has been trapped and beaten up by strike-breaking vigilantes does David understand that the detachment his privileged class status has allowed him is little different from that of a dispenser of charity. He has learned a harsh lesson: "Justice is not inherent in men. It must be fought for, violently fought for" (333).

Rhoda endorses this view: "It was only those who gave without asking any return who found the self-fulfillment that is perfect content. Men and women whose wheel of personal desire revolved within the wheel of a wider purpose . . ." (311). For Rhoda, uneducated by any brutal experience like David's, this conversion is one based on an act of faith. She commits to the workers' cause because her husband has persuaded her to do so. Although Spadoni's fiction is not wholly devoid of feminist themes, in the end her commitment to and celebration of class struggle prove far more compelling than her allegiance to feminism.

As to the feminist convictions of Elsie Clews Parsons there can be little doubt. Parsons' early, speculative feminist sociological writings will no doubt always be most accessible and attractive to the non-anthropologist—works like *The Old-Fashioned Woman* and *Fear and Conventionality*. Her unpublished and uncompleted "Journal of a Feminist" also deserves a wider audience than the few scholars who have consulted it, in view of its exposition of opinions almost as controversial in the 1990s as they were in 1914: the right to abortion, state pensions for the unmarried mother, the acceptability of letting one's children see one naked, part-time employment for women, and the socialization of children as compulsive consumers.[4] The "Journal," in fact, raises most of the hard, still unresolved questions summarized by the provocative question in its final pages: "The problem of sex feminists have now to face is primarily a psychological problem. How are women to live *with* men, not *without* men like the ruthless fighters for institutional freedom, and not in the old way *through* men . . ." (52).

After 1920, however, a dramatic change is apparent in Parsons' style, and even in her subject matter. Her writings after this date consist almost exclusively of works like *Folklore from the Cape Verde Islands* (1923), *Hopi and Zuni Ceremonialism* (1925), *Pueblo Indian Religion* (1939), an edited *Pueblo Indian Journal* (1925)—meticulous, scholarly compilations of the findings from her anthropological field trips. These writings, influenced by the methodology of Franz Boas, are so empiricist, so inductively based in their approach, that to the lay person they may well appear little more than uninterpreted accumulations of raw data. Only very rarely does Parsons offer what seems like implicit comment on her findings. Who but Parsons, in discussing the incidence of transvestism in a Zuni community, would write, "Since Laspeke [a Zuni transvestite well known in his community] no boy in the last twenty years has shown any *promise* of transvestism [emphasis mine]. American influence will work against the trait" (338).[5]

Parsons' overtly feminist and pacifist writings virtually ceased after 1920—but not her feminist and pacifist convictions, nor her commitment to democratic socialism. However, she continued to make important social contributions as president of three professional associations at various times during her career, and as a university teacher and encourager of younger scholars, whose researches she often funded personally. Among her graduate students was Ruth Benedict (who in her turn taught Margaret Mead—an interesting matrilineal succession of major contributors to the science of anthropology). Although Benedict found Parsons' empiricist methodology uncongenial, and came to favor a more theoretical, speculative approach, she nonetheless shared Parsons' feminism and her liberal political views. Moreover, as Benedict's biographer Margaret Caffrey has pointed out, Benedict may have appropriated from Parsons' early sociological writings much of her technique of employing so-called primitive cultures to critique the prejudices and limitations of American industrialized society. Parsons' most significant influence on Benedict seems to lie in this application of cultural analogies to social issues. In her popular sociological writings, Benedict may have drawn "on the example of Elsie Clews Parsons' earlier books like *The Old-Fashioned Woman.* . . . Benedict throughout her life used this type of satirical, consciousness-raising style in her own popular writings."[6]

Anthropologists are generally agreed that Parsons' most significant achievement in the field lies in her work on Pueblo society and culture, notably her monumental two-volume *Pueblo Indian Religion* (1939). In 1942 Franz Boas, in an obituary tribute to Parsons, called the book "a summary of all we know about Pueblo religion" and "an indispensable source book for every student of Indian life." This assessment is seconded (albeit with qualifications) by contemporary scholars, for whom the book is, in Peter Hare's words, "a standard reference work even today" for the exhaustive thoroughness of its detail. *Pueblo Indian Religion* is unusual for its moments of speculative interpretation—such as a section where Parsons considers Hopi and Zuni child-rearing practices. As Boas points out, such speculation once again reveals a preoccupation with "the influence of cultural forms upon personalities, the way in which personalities similar to those found in our own civilization respond to the demands of their culture"—in other words, an implicit revival of concerns more directly expressed in Parsons' earlier, speculative sociological work.[7]

Beyond the anthropological sphere, Parsons' intellectual and social contributions have gone largely unrecognized. Her thinking on social issues, as expressed in her early writings, helped shape the consciousness of her contemporaries. Her ideas on gender socialization and the family remain of interest to this day. Even her anthropological scholarship, in this period when the importance of understanding and appreciating cultural difference begins to be grasped anew, may be of interest to a wider audience than that of the scholarly specialist. But it is for her early work—and for the fearless unconventionality with which she lived her whole life—that feminists will remember and honor her. The boldness and clarity of her thinking, the pungency of her wit, and the breadth of her erudition are as fresh and relevant to the 1990s as to the 1900s. In this context, one recognizes Boas' obituary tribute as more than the rhetoric considered appropriate on such occasions. "Her death is a loss to the nation," Boas wrote (89–90).

The public personae of Louise Bryant are manifold. Perhaps the best known is that of the widow of John Reed who wrote so movingly of a visit to Red Square, and her husband's grave:

> I have been there in the busy afternoon, when all Russia hurries by, horses and sleighs and bells and peasants carrying bundles, soldiers singing on their way to the front. Once some of the soldiers came over to the grave. They took off their hats and spoke very reverently. "What a good fellow he was!" said one. "He came all the way across the world for us." "He was one of ours—." In another moment they shouldered their guns and went on again.
>
> I have been there under the stars with a great longing to lie down beside the frozen flowers and the metallic wreaths and not wake up. How easy it would be![8]

But there is also the playful Bryant of a letter written in happier times, who can parody her usually very serious identification with Ireland and its culture in mock-Irish dialect: "The 17th of Ireland is a grand occasion, indeed"—and the lyrical, sentimental Bryant of her verse.[9] And there are the many voices of Bryant the reporter: sardonic, amused, passionate, analytical.

Few *Masses* women contributors have been so misrepresented, idealized, romanticized, patronized, and disparaged as Louise Bryant—or so overshadowed by the public reputations of the men they married. When Bryant died in Paris in 1936, her *New York Times* obituary described her, in its headlines and in the first line of the article, as "widow of John Reed, the American who became a Soviet hero," and as "the divorced wife" of William C. Bullitt, United States Ambassador to Moscow.[10] This emphasis on Bryant's identity as the wife of more famous men was reinforced more recently by the focus on the "love interest" in Warren Beatty's 1981 film "Reds," accompanied as it was by a deemphasizing of Bryant's career achievements, in favor of an image of her as the devoted, self-sacrificing wife of John Reed. The cover design of a 1982 reprint of Bryant's own account of the Bolshevik Revolution, *Six Red Months in Russia,* which proclaims "Diane Keaton is Louise Bryant in REDS," and describes Bryant in parentheses on the new edition's spine as "Ann Reed," only compounds the confusion.

Even when Bryant's career and writings are discussed in their own right, her critics seem to experience difficulty in striking a balance between hagiography and patronizing dismissal. To the author of an obituary in the

New York Herald Tribune, Bryant is "undoubtedly one of the greatest of women journalists," whose second book on the Bolshevik Revolution, *Mirrors of Moscow,* is "universally acclaimed."[11] In fact, *Mirrors of Moscow* (1913) had received very mixed reviews. The *Times Literary Supplement* charged Bryant with alleged deficiencies in her knowledge of "historical background," and, even more damningly, with inability "to form an independent judgement." Ironically, *The Bookman* found Bryant's vignettes of prominent Bolsheviks lacking in interest, judging them to be too "rigidly truthful." Most disparaging, though, is the *New York Times Book Review,* whose reviewer praises Bryant for her avoidance of bias, for her "personal touches," and for the "note of insouciance" in her writing. But the reviewer's very stress on the personal in Bryant's account of the Bolsheviks is symptomatic of the patronizing sexism of the review as a whole. Instead of "delving into the depths which have swallowed up so many other writers on Russia," the reviewer concludes, "Miss Bryant has been content to write about it in a casual, feminine, chatty way."[12]

Bryant was, before anything, a serious, dedicated radical. She was an active supporter of woman suffrage and socialism in Portland, Oregon, where she worked with her friend Sara Bard Field in the state suffrage campaign and sold subscriptions to *The Masses* long before she ever met John Reed. During and after the First World War she picketed the White House, was jailed, and went on a hunger strike in company with other supporters of the National Woman's Party, and she toured the country to speak against the U.S. invasion of the Soviet Union. Moreover, as a serious professional writer, she was a very different figure from the glamorous dilettante of popular legend. If her verse is generally sentimental and clichéd, her writing for the Provincetown Players undistinguished and conventional, her journalism stands as her enduring achievement. Her articles, like her *Liberator* article on the syndicalist Irish nationalist leader Jim Larkin, or even a piece for *The Nation* on the divorce of Latife Hanoum by the Turkish ruler Kemal Ataturk, are imbued with her concern for social justice.[13] In the last-mentioned article, Bryant finds room to discuss the Turkish woman suffrage movement. Its leaders, she writes, are "brilliant women, superbly educated, tolerant and progressive," offering a marked contrast to the reactionary conservatism of Kemal's former wife. Bryant also comments on the plight of Turkish refugees, which is distracting the suffragists from work for their cause to more immediately pressing material needs. Thanks to Western neglect of the Moslem Turks in favor of Christian wartime refugees, "Forty per cent of the returned refugees died during the first year, mostly from starvation." Such conditions "do not leave women much time to think about suffrage," Bryant writes (232).

The major achievement of Bryant's journalistic career was her reporting from the Soviet Union in the early years of the Bolshevik Revolution. Her privileged access to leading Bolsheviks, her feminism, and her acute sense of the newsworthy—and of the absurd—in human behavior give her first-hand accounts of the events and personalities of a turbulent period a flavor quite unlike that of any other writer. As the events she describes recede in time, her writings become ever more important, as the very individual record of one skilled, intelligent, and close observer.

In *Mirrors of Moscow* Bryant writes of a meeting with Lenin, which she had sought for the purpose of securing a travel permit:

> He simply looked up from his work and smiled.
>
> "I am glad to see there is someone in Russia," he said, "with enough energy to go exploring. You might get killed down there, but you will have the most remarkable experience of your life; it is worth taking chances for." (11)

The energy Lenin describes informed most of Bryant's writing in the Soviet Union, and did indeed produce remarkable results. It took her to the Winter Palace in Petrograd in time to witness the Ministers of the Provisional Government surrendering to the Bolshevik forces (*Six Red Months,* 79–88). It took her to witness fighting between the pro-Bolshevik Petrograd workers and a force of Cossacks loyal to the Whites. The battle took place in the dead of winter:

> A cruel wind swept the streets and hurled the snow against the bleak buildings. It was 25 degrees below zero; I felt ill with cold under my fur coat. And there they came, an amazing, inspired mass in their thin, tattered coats and their pinched white faces—thousands and thousands of them! . . . I saw boys in that army not over ten years of age. . . . For the first time I visualized Washington and his starving, ragged army at Valley Forge. . . ." (178)

This ragged army of workers, untrained, "some armed only with spades," confronted well-armed, highly trained cavalry. "All of them expected to die," writes Bryant of the Petrograd workers. They began to sing "a wailing, melancholy revolutionary song." Bryant "threw discretion to the winds and followed" (179). She watched the rout of the Cossacks—at appalling cost to the Petrograd workers.

Bryant's eyewitness accounts also provide revealing glimpses of less dramatic moments. In *Mirrors of Moscow* she sketches a series of portraits based on interviews with key members of the Bolshevik government: Lenin, Trotsky, Lunacharsky, Dzerzhinsky, and Kollontai.

Of Alexandra Kollontai, Soviet Minister of Welfare, Bryant writes: "Kollontai is like a sculptor working on some heroic figure of woman and always wondering why the slim, inspired, unmaternal figure of her dreams is forever melting back into a heavy, earthy figure of Eve." Although she criticizes Kollontai for her insistence on the public proclamation of feminist ideals which the conservative rural women of Russia find uncongenial, even threatening, Bryant does so with respect and admiration: ". . . if her inspiration, which aims to lift women to the skies, lifts them only from their knees to their feet, then there will be nothing to regret. Civilization, in its snail-like progress, is only stirred to move its occasional inch by the burning desire of those who will to move it a mile" (III).

Bryant's small, observant touches humanize her portraits of these actors in history. A description of the austerity in which most of the early Bolsheviks lived is enlivened by an account of a conversation with Kollontai. Bryant had complimented Kollontai on "a smart little fur toque she was wearing. She laughed and said, 'Yes, one must learn tricks in Russia, so I have made my hat out of the tail of my coat which is already five years old'" (*Mirrors,* 123). Similar humanizing details inform Bryant's report for the *Liberator* of a visit to Lenin's wife Krupskaya—of the books and potted plants in the scrupulously neat one-bedroom apartment, "its size conforming to the strictest regulations for over-crowded Moscow." Krupskaya herself cuts an unpretentious figure, "with her low voice and black dress, her pale face and white, ringless hands." She asks eagerly about Upton Sinclair, whose *Jimmie Higgins* she has just read, and is naively pleased when Bryant suggests that Sinclair would be happy to send her copies of his works. Then the conversation turns to the recent death of John Reed: "She leaned over and touched my hand. 'How difficult it must be!' she said. 'Are you quite alone?'"[14]

Bryant captures some of the absurdities in this period in which the traditional order of things has been turned upside down: a "looting" by Bolshevik soldiers at the Winter Palace, in which the offenders' booty was found to consist of a wax candle, a coat hanger, a blanket, and "a worn sofa-cushion . . ." (*Six Red Months,* 88); stolen goods markets in Petrograd where priceless antiques can be bought at junk sale prices; shops practically empty of food, interspersed with "window after window" full of items citizens either cannot or dare not buy, because of their bourgeois connotations: "flowers, corsets, dog-collars and false hair" (160, 37).

If Bryant's apologetics for the repression of opponents practiced by the Bolsheviks sometimes appear naive, our sense of their naiveté is, after all, informed by hindsight. She dismisses rather too easily the Bolsheviks' continuation, under the threats from enemies domestic and foreign, of the brutally repressive practices of the Czars; she claims that Lenin so controlled the Cheka, or security police, that "when he saw it growing into a power which interfered with the natural development of the country, he at once began to weaken it" (47–48). One may contend in her defense that, if not as critically aware as one might have wished, she was at least no more deluded than more seasoned reporters much less predisposed to idealize the Revolution than was Bryant.

Bryant's professional achievement, after the publication of *Mirrors of Moscow* in 1923, was largely obscured by the miseries which followed her marriage to U.S. diplomat William Bullitt that year. She fought with him to continue her journalistic career, to maintain her independent lifestyle as a liberated feminist, and finally to maintain custody, after their 1930 divorce, of their five-year-old daughter—and lost every one of these battles. Her subsequent unproductive life of illness, drifting, and alcoholism,[15] and her death at the early age of fifty, further buried the memory of all that her early writing had promised. Yet her early legacy—that of a committed leftist, a courageous feminist, a greatly gifted journalist—remains. We only need care to examine it.

Dorothy Day titled the first of her two autobiographies *From Union Square to Rome* (1938). It is a title clearly designed to emphasize the dramatic finality of her break with the past—a move from New York's center of secular radicalism, which was the location of the office of *The Masses* and later of the head office of the U.S. Communist Party, to faith in the teachings of the Catholic Church. In Floyd Dell's recollections, the Day of the *Masses* period was a heedless young freethinker, an adherent of the bohemian lifestyle. To contrast this image with the Day of the Catholic Worker movement, responsible for fifty-odd Houses of Hospitality and a newspaper, writer of pious devotional essays and a candidate for sainthood, is, upon first consideration, to perceive a dramatic change. According to this retrospective version of Day's life, the period of Greenwich Village and *The Masses* was merely a youthful episode on the way to discovery of her true vocation.[16] Yet much of Day's early history, if examined more closely, makes her rediscovery of Catholicism less surprising, most notably in its integration of piety with radical political activism. Even during her Greenwich Village years, while Day was living what she would later refer to as her "disorderly" life, she was reading Tolstoi and finding herself "thoroughly in sympathy with the Christianity he expressed, the Christianity that dispensed with a church and a priesthood." As a child she was given to religious enthusiasm (an enthusiasm not shared by the rest of her family, who were indifferent, though not especially hostile, to religion), and was confirmed in an Episcopalian church in Chicago. During her stay in Greenwich Village, in a further anticipation of her later vocation of Christian charity and activism, she and her friend would occasionally offer a night's lodging to a homeless person met with in one of New York's parks: "Sentimental charity some of the others called it. Mike Gold recognized it as an expression of what he called my religious instinct."[17] While in jail for her part in the White House suffrage picketing and on hunger strike, Day began reading the Bible, and found relief in the reading from her intense physical and emotional distress. It was then, Day writes, that she began to think of her political activism in religious terms: "If we had faith in what we were doing, making our protest against brutality and injustice, then we were indeed casting our seeds, and there was promise of the harvest to come. . . . I prayed and did not know that I prayed" (*Long Loneliness*, 78).

Day's political radicalism may be traced to her membership in a student socialist group at the University of Illinois, where she studied between 1914 and 1916, and to her first job with the New York socialist paper, the *Call*. At about this time she joined the syndicalist Industrial Workers of the World. (She would later describe her political outlook at the time as that of an anarchist.) As a practicing Catholic, she was to reconcile these earlier political views with her newfound (or newly refound) religious faith in work with labor unions, for the civil rights movement, against the Vietnam War, and in aid of migrant farm workers.

Day's commitment to radical activism within a specifically Catholic framework began in December 1932. With Mary Heaton Vorse, Day went as a journalist to cover the Communist Party–led Hunger March of the unemployed into Washington. Day's assignment was from *The Commonweal*, marking the first time she wrote for a Catholic publication. Day and Vorse stayed in dollar-a-night lodgings and ate at lunch wagons "so there was something left over" to donate to the food fund of the hunger marchers. Both women felt that, when the marchers were suffering real deprivation and hardship, "it was not the time for us to be comfortable" (*Long Loneliness*, 158–160). As Day observed the progress of the demonstration in Washington, she felt overwhelmed by a sense that her conversion to Catholicism in 1926—a conversion that had brought about her parting from the dearly loved father of her child—had also isolated her from the political activity around her: "My summer of quiet reading and prayer, my self-absorption seemed sinful as I watched my brothers in their struggle, not for themselves but for others. How our dear Lord must love them, I kept thinking to myself." Day remembered that the first recorded public act of Jesus was the driving of the money changers from the temple (*Long Loneliness*, 161). When the demonstration was over, she went to the national shrine at the Catholic University and prayed that she might be shown some way in which she could serve.

The appearance of Peter Maurin on Day's doorstep upon her return from Washington must have seemed like the answer to her prayers. (He had been sent by the editor of *The Commonweal*.) From Maurin came the basic ideas for the founding of the Catholic Worker movement— discussion groups, Houses of Hospitality for aiding the poor, and "agronomic universities"—communes where workers and intellectuals could

Dorothy Day at St. Thomas Aquinas Church, West Lafayette, Indiana, May 1970. (Courtesy Marquette University Archives.)

exchange skills and experience. What Day brought to this program—drastically modifying it—were her political radicalism and her interest in active struggle for social justice (*By Little,* xxvi). Over the years the Catholic Worker movement grew into a loose organization of several dozen Houses of Hospitality and rural communities, unified ideologically by the *Catholic Worker* newspaper, for which Day wrote dozens of brief editorials.

Day's radical political activism now continued within this framework—not only in her writing, public speaking, and administrative work in the various Houses of Hospitality, but also in direct involvement in strikes, protests, and demonstrations. During the 1930s, she traveled with Mary Heaton Vorse to observe the work of the newly formed Committee (soon to become the Congress) of Industrial Organizations (CIO), which was organizing formerly non-unionized workers in the Pittsburgh steel industry (*Long Loneliness,* 205–207). In May 1936 she arranged accommodation and catering facilities for fifty striking merchant seamen, three of whom stayed after the strike to join the Catholic Worker movement (203). Over the years she was arrested repeatedly, for the last time in California in 1973, when she was seventy-five, during picketing on behalf of the United Farm Workers. To be merely a journalistic observer of social injustice, Day considered—to help in organizing work, to donate to relief funds, or even to pledge oneself to voluntary poverty for life "so that you can share with your brothers" (and Day did all of these)—was still insufficient. One must live with the needy and oppressed, "share with them their sufferings. . . . Give up one's privacy . . ." (*Long Loneliness*, 210).

Not surprisingly, Day did not always see eye-to-eye with the conservative leadership of the Church. She recalls how, in her fact-finding tour of the Pennsylvania steel towns with Mary Heaton Vorse during the 1930s, she quickly learned that the clerical rank and file in these towns could be divided into those who offered their churches as relief centers for striking workers, and those who believed that all organizations of workers were dominated by communists (206). As for the archdiocese of New York City, where the Catholic Worker had its administrative center, Day experienced several conflicts with that body. In the spring of 1951, she was called to the chancery office and told to change the name of *The Catholic Worker*, as it might be interpreted to imply Church endorsement. Day and her fellow workers stood firm and declined to do so. On another occasion, two years previously, Day and *The Catholic Worker* had backed a strike of gravediggers at a Catholic cemetery in New York. When Cardinal Spellman refused to negotiate with the strikers, Day wrote an editorial in *The Catholic Worker* highly critical of his attitude (Coles, *Dorothy Day*, 81).

If Day found her brand of Catholicism was misunderstood by more conservative fellow Catholics, she retained close and loving ties with old leftist friends who did not share her religious beliefs. She regarded Elizabeth Gurley Flynn, for instance, who had joined the U.S. Communist Party in 1937, as "my sister in the deep sense of the word." Flynn, Day wrote, "always did what the laity is nowadays urged to do. She felt a responsibility to do all in her power in defense of the poor, to protect them against injustice and destitution" (*Long Loneliness*, 145–146).

Day was proud, too, that, because she had been eleven times "behind bars in police stations, houses of detention, jails and prison farms," had refused to pay federal income tax, and had never voted, secular anarchists accepted her as one of themselves. And, she added, "I in turn see Christ in them even though they deny Him, because they are giving themselves to working for a better social order for the wretched of the earth" (*By Little*, 351–353). Even the Cuban revolution, which many anarchists regarded with mistrust for the Marxist-Leninist character it gradually assumed over the years, Day regarded as a hopeful sign of awakening of popular consciousness, a victory for justice in no way incompatible with Catholic faith.

"God bless the priests and people of Cuba," she wrote in 1961. "God bless Castro and all those who are seeing Christ in the poor" (*By Little,* 298–302). On the other hand, she well understood the corrupting tendency toward bureaucratic centralism inherent in classic Marxism-Leninism. The rule of the Bolsheviks under Lenin, as Day pointed out, became a dictatorship of the "great mass of dispossessed industrial workers . . . in name only; it was to become a dictatorship by the elite few, by the members of the party" (*Long Loneliness,* 84). Nearer to home, she took a stand on the struggles of less radical U.S. workers' organizations. She believed that the right to strike for a better wage was more than merely compatible with Catholic faith—it was "a good impulse—one could even say an inspiration of the Holy Spirit." Strikers were, she considered, "trying to uphold their right to be treated not as slaves, but as men" (*By Little,* 24).

Pacifism remained as integral a part of Day's convictions, as it had been during the Greenwich Village years, when she had helped select pacifist drawings for *The Masses* and had covered the World War I activities of the Anti-Conscription League. In fact, her direct involvement with pacifist issues intensified over the years. If during the 1930s Day offended conservative Catholics by her sympathy for the cause of the Spanish republican government against Franco's fascist but Catholic rebels, she offended her left-wing friends and supporters even more by her refusal to condone Loyalist use of military force against Franco. In the light of the atrocities committed on both sides in the Spanish Civil War, it did seem "madness," *The Catholic Worker* admitted, to cling to an absolutist Christian pacifism. Yet, *The Catholic Worker* demanded, if the press and the public throughout the world failed to speak "in terms of the counsels of perfection," who would? [18] Their stand during the Second World War was, if anything, even more uncompromising.

During the 1950s, Day was repeatedly arrested for refusal to comply with mandatory air raid drill procedures. During the 1960s, Catholic Worker centers became a refuge and rallying point for those resisting the Vietnam War. Most uncompromising was Day's informing vision of society's complete and utter dependency on the military-industrial complex. In a modern military state like the U.S., Day considered, there was really no such thing as a "civilian population." Everyone who participated in the economy was implicated in militaristic enterprises, if only as a consumer or a taxpayer: ". . . so that you are, in effect, helping to support the state's preparations for war exactly to the extent of your attachment to worldly things of whatever kind" (*By Little,* 111). Hence, a life of voluntary poverty for Day represented not only Christian piety, but an essential strategy for diminishing each individual's complicity with the military-industrial nexus.

Predictably, Day's views on sexuality became much more conservative after her conversion to Catholicism. As a young woman, Day had attended Emma Goldman's lectures on sexual liberation in Greenwich Village. Even at the time, the older Day claims, she was "revolted by such promiscuity" (57). In 1931, when Goldman's autobiography *Living My Life* was published, Day actually refused to read Goldman's account of her long series of love affairs, "because I was offended in my sex" (*Long Loneliness,* 57). Day clearly had no sympathy with or understanding for Goldman's conception of sexual liberation as integral to full political liberation: "Men who are revolutionaries, I thought, do not dally on the side as women do, complicating the issue by an emphasis on the personal" (57). Day later felt deeply ashamed of her only novel, *The Eleventh Virgin* (1924), an autobiographical account of her early radical years, and actually tried to suppress the novel in the years after her conversion by buying up and destroying copies, until a priest to whom she went to confession pointed out the futility of this enterprise.[19]

While very radical in her views on communitarianism, pacifism, and the labor movement, and deeply sympathetic to the left-wing revolutionary movements around the world, Day could be conservative—even reactionary—in her treatment of those who offended her conservative sexual morality. In the late 1960s she forced the eviction from Catholic Worker housing of a group of young people of whose sexual mores and use of drugs she disapproved. (The former seem to have offended Day more than the latter.) She regarded such behavior as "a complete rebellion against authority, natural and supernatural, even against the body and its needs, its natural functions of childbearing." Asked in a 1973 interview on public television what she thought of women's liberation, she responded by talking in the most general of terms about the importance of working for social change through "local politics."[20]

Day's later position on feminism seems ironic on a number of grounds. She fought for a vote for women which, as an anarchist, she chose never to use. She repudiated the love without marriage which had seemed so natural and laudable at the time of her happy relationship with Forster Batterham. She found herself bound by sexual conservatism at a time when the feminism she had championed as a young woman was awakening in a new guise. But it was the brotherhood of man in Christ, rather than feminist sisterhood, that informed all Day's thinking in the later years.

The sheer variety of Mary Heaton Vorse's achievements as novelist, journalist, and activist are difficult to outline concisely, both for their diversity and for the long time span they covered. Between the first decade of the 1900s and the mid-1950s, Vorse never flagged in her commitment to labor's cause. Although never a theoretical feminist in the manner of Elsie Clews Parsons, she retained, along with her left-wing commitments, a deep, abiding sense of solidarity with the sufferings, struggles, and victories of working-class women.

In the early years of her career, Vorse was best known as a writer of fiction. She wrote magazine fiction, a chapter of *The Whole Family* (1908)—a collectively written novel, one of the coauthors of which was Henry James—and *The Autobiography of an Elderly Woman* (1911). In 1917 she published a chapter in *The Sturdy Oak,* another collective novel written to raise funds for the woman suffrage cause. In 1918 she published a comic novel which gives a hilariously exaggerated version of the lighter aspects of the Greenwich Village experience: *I've Come to Stay: A Love Comedy of Bohemia.*

Although Vorse had written articles on social issues in the 1900s, it was only after her radicalization by firsthand experience of labor struggles at Lawrence in 1912 and elsewhere that her labor and other journalism really began to take precedence over her fiction writing. During and after the First World War she covered the refugee situation in Europe, writing pieces like "Les Evacuées," "The Sinistrées of France," "Debatable Lands in Central Europe," and "Milorad." She covered the 1919 Pennsylvania steel strikes for *The Nation* and *Outlook,* and published a book on the subject, *Men and Steel* (1920). After the closing of *The Masses,* Vorse wrote for its successor *The Liberator*—not only stories, but a number of nonfiction pieces, including "Twenty Years," an account of a meeting with radical workers' leaders sentenced to long jail terms after World War One under the Espionage Act, and "Russian Pictures," a powerful account of a night spent talking with fellow train passengers in the newly formed Soviet Union.[21]

The 1920s and 1930s were an immensely productive period in Vorse's career, notably for labor journalism. Her article titled "Waitin' with the Dead," published in *The New Republic* in 1929, is characteristic of much of Vorse's labor reporting in its emphasis not only on group solidarity but on the sufferings of a community subjected to the vigilante violence that, until the passing of the Wagner Act of 1935, was too often the employers' response to peaceful strike action. As often in Vorse's writing, this account of a funeral for strikers shot in the back by deputies in Marion, North Carolina, focuses on the community's women:

> The services were over. . . . The entire company of a thousand people
> filed slowly, one by one, before the dead. Every man and woman,
> every child, looked into the faces of the four murdered fellow-workers.
> Amid the dead silence, Luther Bryson's tiny mother walked before the

coffins. . . . She bent over her son and kissed him, while Randolph
Hall's young widow broke into unrestrained weeping. . . . People went
slowly away in little groups.

"We haven't seen the end of this," men said gravely to one another.
(*New Republic*, 30 Oct. 1929: 288)

During the 1930s Vorse also continued to write nonlabor pieces. Her
article on the Scottsboro case, in which a group of young blacks were
falsely charged with raping a white girl, examines the motives of the young
woman who was induced to lodge the accusation. Vorse regards Victoria
Price and her companions in the context of their homeless, hopeless existence, without even "the promise of lowpaid steady employment." They
have "one thing only—the trains going somewhere, the boxcars for
homes, the jungles for parks. . . . They bum their food, the girls 'pick up
a little change hustling the towns,' and it's all a lot better than the crowded
shacks and the uncertain work in the mills." Vorse's article indicts, not
Victoria Price, but the system which produced her: "If it was intolerance
and race prejudice which convicted Haywood Patterson, it was poverty
and ignorance which wrongfully accused him."[22]

In 1933 Vorse published a series of articles about Nazi Germany. "Germany: The Twilight of Reason," written for *The New Republic*, is a remarkable account of a Nazi book burning, a proceeding conducted not by
storm troopers but by a group of charming, polite, and seemingly intelligent university students. A young student, writes Vorse, "looked at us
with friendly eyes. No doubt dimmed her mind that the book burning
could be considered anything but a splendid act" (14 June 1933: 120). The
innocence of these young people, when contrasted with the terrible creed
to which they have committed themselves, offers, through their very or-
dinariness, disquieting insight into the processes whereby a whole nation
gave itself over to belief in fascism. "We must not underestimate what
has happened," wrote Vorse. "A whole nation has been swung out of its
orbit. People by the thousands have fallen into the incandescent furnace
of National Socialism. Hundreds or thousands of others will be driven
there by necessity. From now on there will only be jobs for National Socialists" (119).

While the 1930s may have been Vorse's most productive decade, culmi-
nating in the publication of *Labor's New Millions* (1938)—her vividly partisan account of the organizing of the Congress of Industrial Organizations—she continued writing into the 1940s and 1950s. Her last book was
Time and the Town, a chronicle of Provincetown, published in 1942. She
wrote articles well into the 1950s, though—two of the most interesting of
which are an intensively documented piece on migrant agricultural work-

Mary Heaton Vorse. (NYT Pictures.)

ers, which reveals all Vorse's old gift for capturing the telling details of her subjects' lives,[23] and an investigative report of corruption on the New York waterfront. In the latter, particularly, Vorse shows the sure instinct of a skilled narrator, introducing her tale of racketeering and murder via the incongruous medium of a conversation between two local priests:

> "Didn't he put Peter Pan in the concrete, Father?" asked the other priest gently.
> "You have it all confused, Father. Peter Pan didn't go in the concrete at all. They found him in the lime and garroted. . . ."[24]

While journalism had, by 1920, become the focus of Vorse's writing career, she continued to write and publish fiction intermittently. Two of her later novels deserve special mention—*Second Cabin* (1928) and her last novel, *Strike!* (1930)—if only for their interest as social history.

Second Cabin was the product of a sea trip home from a visit to the Soviet Union. The novel's title refers to the second-class quarters on board the ship. These are distinguished on the one hand from the first-class accommodation, and on the other from the steerage where the poorer immigrants traveled. The second cabin is notable for the bourgeois respectability of some of its passengers, and the raffish, demi-mondaine character of others. Vorse presents us with an assorted group of these second-cabin passengers: an Irish family, presided over by a wise, capable mother; a lecherous, unprincipled young Italian-American; a group of picture brides en route from Europe to arranged marriages in America, and determined to make best possible use of their remaining days of freedom; a self-styled aristocrat with White Russian connections; and a disillusioned German ex-communist in love with one of the picture brides.

Dee Garrison has called *Second Cabin* a study of "all the barbarities and hypocrisies of the capitalist world assembled in the iron confines of a ship"—and it is that, but it is something more: a study of a new kind of American society in the making. The novel opens and concludes with reflections about the fascination America holds for Europeans of all nations and classes. Many of the passengers, the former communist, Christiansen, reflects in the opening pages, are drawn to America as a seemingly inexhaustible source of wealth that "had flowed like a never-drying river into famished towns and into communities gutted by war and disease which, in 1922, were still hopeless in the face of ruin" (9–10). The closing scene of *Second Cabin* depicts the passengers' excitement at their first sight of New York harbor (318–319).

Second Cabin portrays the prejudices, the snobberies, the conflicting sexual standards of various groups, the political and class antagonisms of those on shipboard—attitudes and behavior identical to those multiplied a millionfold by ethnic and class differences in the United States itself. Thus the naturalized German-American women boast to one another about the modern comforts of their American homes, and their assimilation into American society, excluding "the patient German women" sitting nearby (44–45). The German men wrestle with "vague fears" about starting a new life in what "had suddenly become an enemy country" since the recent war. The few second-cabin passengers whose class position is denoted by their wearing of shawls, rather than hats, look longingly toward the more relaxed milieu of the steerage, where they need not fear social censure: "Here no one was pretending to be anything he was not" (134). Two men from the second cabin get into a fight with the third-class passengers over women (135–138). Later a similar fight breaks out between first- and second-class passengers (305–306). Christiansen voices his disgust at the passengers who give themselves aristocratic airs. To Christiansen, they are a horrible example of what Americans, in abolishing aristocratic titles, imagined they had learned not to adulate but to leave behind (183).

In its focus on groups of middle-class characters and its satiric tone, *Second Cabin* has much in common with some of Vorse's earlier studies of middle-class family life. Although *Second Cabin* is in no sense a protest fiction in the manner of (say) Vorse's short stories for *The Liberator,* it does offer a critique of a society which thrives on class inequities, and which generates rancor, rootlessness, and economic and psychological anxieties. It is clear, too, that the narrator distances herself from the ideological disillusionment of her most socially conscious character. When Christiansen tells an acquaintance that he is "ideologically" a communist, but "through" with membership in any organized movement, the other assures him that this stand will be only temporary. The individual radical, like the radical movement, will recover. Thus Vorse celebrates radicalism without preaching it.

Strike! on the other hand, is overtly polemical—one reason, no doubt, why it is so often cited as a representative example of 1930s realist protest fiction (the so-called proletarian novel). In fact, *Strike!* contains a number of elements which were to become stereotypical in the work of later novelists of the decade: a labor conflict in which unarmed strikers confront armed vigilantes, a preacher sympathetic to labor, a heroic organizer killed by his enemies, a middle-class observer supportive of the strikers' cause. What distinguishes *Strike!* from many of these later works is its author's eye for convincing detail drawn from firsthand observation, a narrative skill essentially akin to that which informs her journalism. Her young women strikers are no idealized heroines (though they are at times heroic), but appearance-conscious, coquettish adolescents, who make up their faces carefully before going out on the picket line. The older generation is represented by Mamie Lewis, a ballad singer who does not burn with any conscious sense of mission, but sings her ballads quite simply because her fellow workers like to hear them. Vorse's character is modeled on Ella May Wiggins, who was shot dead by vigilantes during the Gastonia textile strike of 1929, and whose song "We Leave Our Homes in the Morning" became a classic of Depression-era proletarian culture. The organizer of the strike in Vorse's novel, loosely based on Fred Beal, the organizer at Gastonia, is no radical superman serene in the rightness of his cause, but a "burdened, anxious boy" (57). In short, *Strike!* offers representations of credible, fallible human beings. If *Strike!* is compared with Vorse's report on Gastonia for *Harper's Monthly,* which supplies historical context, dates, and statistics, it is possible to regard the article and the novel as complementary—and *Strike!* as "fictionalized documentary," a novelistic representation of the doomed, heroic fight at Gastonia. Of Vorse's novel, "She tells the truth—and dramatically," Sinclair Lewis wrote.[25]

In 1935 Vorse published her autobiography, *A Footnote to Folly.* The book covers her years of reporting in the United States and Europe, with heavy emphasis on her activities and observations between the turn of the century and the 1920s. Reviewers praised the book as imbued with "a deep and purging indignation," written from "blood and nerves," as Robert Morse Lovett observed in *The New Republic.* A reviewer in *The Nation* remarked that it was a long time since he had read descriptions of children that moved him like those in *A Footnote to Folly.* The *New York Times Book Review* commented that Vorse possessed "an eye that sees vividly and a pen that reports with a clean-cut vitality and lifelikeness," adding surprisingly (after all, this was 1936) that Vorse had "not thought deeply enough" about her subject to appreciate the "very real advances" made in the socioeconomic conditions of the American child. More in keeping with the general tone of reviews of *A Footnote to Folly* was John Chamberlin's assessment in *The New York Times* of the previous year that Vorse had written "a book to be read along with Lincoln Steffens' *Autobiography,* or Floyd Dell's *Homecoming,* as one of the "great documents of liberal America."[26]

That Vorse published her autobiography relatively early in her life was, perhaps, prophetic. Her later reputation was overshadowed both by the red-baiting of the McCarthy period and, ironically enough, by the very success of liberal journalists like herself, in her preferred field of labor journalism, in raising the respectability and prestige of labor unions. As labor organizations increasingly won their battles, securing legitimacy and concrete material gains through the 1930s and 1940s, the role of the partisan labor reporter became increasingly irrelevant. Yet one need only consider a random selection of quotations from Vorse's writings to realize that one is dealing with the record of an extraordinary life: "I went with Joe O'Brien to meet the children of the Lawrence strikers." "I was made delegate for the Suffrage Organization of New York State." "I made my report on Central Europe to Mr. Hoover." "It is midnight already, and Goebbels' voice . . . blares down from a balcony." "I spent most of my time raising money for Russian children." "When I talked to Lenin. . . ." Vorse lived at the center of her times. As a labor activist and strike publicist, she took the hazards of her profession as matter-of-factly as did the strikers themselves. In the course of her long, adventurous life, she was deported from one strike at gunpoint, injured in another, blacklisted by a Congressional committee, and tracked by the Federal Bureau of Investigation for decades. If the authorities regarded Vorse as a dangerous radical, her own formulation of her ideal was a simple, undramatic one: to see working people gain greater control over their own lives. Vorse never joined any political party, retaining independence of mind and action. In the last analysis, what is most radical in her life and work is her unflagging human sympathy, and the naked simplicity of her social vision.

Irwin, Hull, Spadoni, Parsons, Bryant, Day, and Vorse, in their post *Masses* careers, all in varying degrees retained elements of their left-wing radicalism or of their feminism. Irwin continued a feminist as she became less of a leftist, as did Helen Hull. Spadoni, while her later fiction evinces little feminist commitment, returned in the 1930s to support for the cause of organized labor. Parsons remained both a socialist and a feminist, but ceased to write explicitly on political issues. Bryant, although she remained faithful to both her leftist and her feminist ideals, was rendered tragically unable to act on them. Day remained a dedicated and highly effective activist, but relinquished adherence to a feminism about which she had always entertained some misgivings. Of all seven women, only Vorse retained a dual commitment; and even in her writings the stronger emphasis is laid on the fight of workers for self-determination.

Yet in the days of Greenwich Village and *The Masses,* all these women, Day included, found self-evident the compatibility between leftist radicalism and feminism—if not in synthesis, in harmonious coexistence. Arguably, the shifts in their ideological positions thereafter lay in causes beyond the individual—in a decline in and repression of the turn-of-the-century radical movements which had sustained them. The women of *The Masses* participated in a special moment in which thinking individuals were enabled to contemplate the possibility of a redistribution of power. That women might gain control over their own lives and bodies, and that wage workers might gain control over the means of production, could be considered aspirations of a single, broad revolutionary movement. The result was not only a variety of leftist political positions imbued with feminism, but a feminism informed by an awareness of the working-class majority of women that would not be rediscovered until the late 1960s. The women of *The Masses* and their work offer the present a vital legacy. They represent an integral part of the history of feminism in the United States—a part which, if feminism is to have not only a history but a future, we badly need to recover.

Biographical Information about The Masses Women

Barns, Cornelia Baxter

Born in Philadelphia, 1888. Studied at Philadelphia Academy of Fine Arts. Married, 1912, to music critic Arthur Selwyn Garbett. Only son, Charles Garbett, born 1915.

Cornelia Barns began drawing for *The Masses* in March 1913, and joined the magazine's editorial staff in 1914. In 1917 she moved to California for health reasons, but continued to draw, for *The Liberator* (1918–1924), *The New Masses* (1926–1930), *Good Morning, The New York World, The Woman Voter,* and *The Suffragist*. She was art editor and associate editor for the *Birth Control Review* (1921), and during her years in California published daily in the *Oakland Post Enquirer*. She also exhibited in the Salon of American Humorists. Barns was a member of the Socialist Party. She died in 1941.

See:

William L. O'Neill, *Echoes of Revolt: "The Masses," 1911–1917* (1966); Rebecca Zurier, *Art for "The Masses": A Radical Magazine and Its Graphics, 1911–1917* (1987).

Bryant, Louise

Born in Nevada, 1885. Studied at the University of Nevada in Reno, and at the University of Oregon. Married Paul Trullinger in Oregon, 1909. Became a friend of suffragist Sara Bard Field, worked in the Oregon state suffrage campaign (1912), and sold subscriptions for *The Masses*. Divorced Trullinger to marry John Reed in 1916.

After she moved to New York, Bryant published in *The Masses* and wrote for the Provincetown Players. Jailed while picketing the White House in 1917.

Between 1917 and 1918, Bryant covered the Bolshevik Revolution in the Soviet Union. From 1918 to 1919 she worked as a pacifist and Soviet solidarity orator, collaborating closely with Upton Sinclair. In 1920 she returned as a foreign correspondent to the Soviet Union, where she rejoined John Reed, who shortly thereafter fell fatally ill of typhus.

In 1923 Bryant married U.S. diplomat William C. Bullitt (who ten years later became the first U.S. ambassador to the U.S.S.R.). In 1930, the marriage ended in divorce, and Bryant lost custody of her five-year-old daughter. Ill and severely depressed, Bryant settled in Paris, where she died in 1936.

Selected Works:

Nonfiction, *Six Red Months in Russia: An Observer's Account of Russia before and during the Proletarian Dictatorship* ([1918] 1982); *Mirrors of Moscow* (1923). Play, *The Game* (1916). Articles in *The Liberator, The Nation, The Dial, Metropolitan, The New York American.*

See:

Virginia Gardner, *Friend and Lover: The Life of Louise Bryant* (1982); Barbara Gelb, *So Short a Time: A Biography of John Reed and Louise Bryant* (1973). Obituaries, *New York Herald Tribune,* 10 Jan. 1936: 2; *New York Times,* 10 Jan. 1936: 19.

Cleghorn, Sarah Norcliffe

Born in Norfolk, Virginia, 1876. Mother died when she was nine. Studied at Radcliffe College as a special student, 1895–1896, and at Columbia University. First story was published in the *Philistine* in 1897.

Cleghorn taught at the Manumit School for Workers' Children, a progressive institution run on libertarian lines, from 1924 to 1932. For a year, from 1929 to 1930, she taught Narrative Writing at Vassar College. Between 1921 and 1928 she was a contributing editor for *The World Tomorrow.*

During World War I Cleghorn, a Socialist Party member, was involved in party-led pacifist demonstrations. She was active, too, in prison reform. A lifelong Christian socialist, she served on the Women's Committee for Recognition of Soviet Russia (1919–1925), and with the Women's International League for Peace and Freedom. She was vice president of the American Anti-Vivisection Society (1905–1915), of the War Resisters' League, and of the Teachers' Union. In 1932 and 1934, Cleghorn ran as a candidate for the post of Vermont Secretary of State.

Selected Works:

Novels, *A Turnpike Lady* (1907), *The Spinster: A Novel Wherein a Nineteenth Century Girl Finds Her Place in the Twentieth* (1916). Verse collections, *Portraits and Protests* (1917); *Poems of Peace and Freedom* (1945). Autobiography, *Threescore: The Autobiography of Sarah N. Cleghorn* (1936). Devotional writing, *The Seamless Robe: The Religion of Lovingkindness* (1945). Poems in *The Masses, Atlantic Monthly, Scribner's, Harper's, The World Tomorrow.*

See:

Cary Nelson, *Repression and Recovery: Modern American Poetry and the Politics of Cultural Memory, 1910–1945* (1989); also Stanley J. Kunitz and Howard Haycraft, eds., *Twentieth Century Authors: A Biographical Dictionary of Modern Literature* (1942). Obituary, *New York Times,* 5 Apr. 1959: p. 86, col. 3.

Coatsworth, Elizabeth Jane

Born Buffalo, New York, 1893. As a child, traveled worldwide with her family. Received B.A. from Vassar, and M.A. from Columbia (1916). While still in her

twenties, became well known as a scholar of Eastern cultures. In 1929 she married fellow author Henry Beston.
Works:
Verse collections, *Fox Footprints* (1923); *Atlas and Beyond* (1924); *Compass Rose* (1929). Nonfiction, *Here I Stay* (1938); *Country Neighborhood* (1944); *The Creaking Stair* (1949). Coatsworth's tale for children, *The Cat Who Went to Heaven*, won the 1930 Newbery Medal. Autobiography, *Personal Geography* (1976).
See:
Kunitz and Haycraft, *Twentieth Century Authors;* Samuel J. Rogal, *A Chronological Outline of American Literature* (1987).

Conger-Kaneko, Josephine

Born Centralia, Missouri. Studied at Ruskin College in Trenton, Missouri. During early journalistic career was an editor for the socialist *Appeal to Reason*. In 1907 founded her own magazine, *The Socialist Woman*, which in 1909 was renamed *The Progressive Woman*. Married the prominent Japanese socialist Kiichi Kaneko, 1905. Conger-Kaneko's most politically active years coincided with those of the U.S. Socialist Party. After World War I she retired from politics.
See:
Mari Jo Buhle, *Women and American Socialism, 1870–1920* (1981); *Kodansha Encyclopedia of Japan* (1983).

Davies, Mary Carolyn

Born Sprague, Washington. Educated at schools in British Columbia, and at the University of California.
Works:
Play, *The Slave with Two Faces* (1918). Poems, *Youth Riding* (1919); *The Skyline Trail* (1924). Novel, *The Husband Test* (1921). Verse widely cited and anthologized by, among others, Louis Untermeyer, in *The New Era in American Poetry* (1919), and Edwin Markham, in *The Book of American Poetry* (1934).
See:
Who Was Who Among North American Authors.

Day, Dorothy

Born Brooklyn, New York, 1897. Father was a sports reporter. Family moved to Oakland, California, then to Chicago. From 1914 to 1916, attended the University of Illinois, Urbana, where she first joined the Socialist Party. Worked as a reporter for the party's *The Call* in New York, 1916, and joined the Industrial Workers of the World. Engaged in suffragist and pacifist activities. Edited for *The Masses*, in the last year of its existence, then wrote for *The Liberator*. Close friend of Mary Heaton Vorse, Floyd Dell, and Elizabeth Gurley Flynn.

Day formally converted to Catholicism in 1925. In 1932 she joined Peter Maurin in founding the Catholic Worker movement. She was active in innumerable peace and justice struggles until her death in 1980. She is currently a Vatican candidate for sainthood.

The Dorothy Day–Catholic Worker Collection is held at Marquette University, Wisconsin. Father Alex Avitabile has compiled a complete bibliography of Day's writings, including these manuscript holdings (although only a portion of the manuscript holdings is available for public study).

Selected Works:
Novel, *The Eleventh Virgin* (1924). Autobiographies, *From Union Square to Rome* (1938); *The Long Loneliness: The Autobiography of Dorothy Day* (1952). Numerous essays and articles, including almost five decades of editorials for *The Catholic Worker* newspaper. Some of these shorter writings are collected in an anthology, *By Little and by Little: The Selected Writings of Dorothy Day,* edited by Robert Ellsberg (1983).

See:
Robert Coles, *Dorothy Day: A Radical Devotion* (1987); William D. Miller, *A Harsh and Dreadful Love: Dorothy Day and the Catholic Worker Movement* (1973); Mel Piehl, *Breaking Bread: The Catholic Worker and the Origin of Catholic Radicalism in America* (1982).

Deutsch, Babette

Born New York City, 1895. B.A., Barnard College. Wrote poetry for the *North American Review* and *The New Republic,* and on social issues for the *Political Science Quarterly* and *Reedy's Mirror;* also literary criticism for *The Dial.*

In 1921 Deutsch married Avrahm Yarmolinsky, Chief of the Slavonic Division at the New York Public Library. They had two sons.

Deutsch taught poetry courses at the New School for Social Research and, from 1944 onwards, creative writing at Columbia University, which awarded her an honorary doctorate.

Deutsch translated widely from German and Russian. In 1929 she won the *Nation* poetry prize, and was appointed Phi Beta Kappa Poet at Columbia University. For a time she was a member of the Committee for Cultural Freedom, and of the League of American Writers. She died in 1982.

Selected Works:
Poetry, *Banners* (1919); *Honey out of the Rock* (1925); *Fire for the Night* (1930); *Epistle to Prometheus* (1931). Novels, *A Brittle Heaven* (1926); *In Such a Night* (1927); *Mask of Silenus* (1933); *Rogue's Legacy,* a fictionalized biography of François Villon (1942). Also a number of introductions to modern poetry, such as *This Modern Poetry* (1935); and a young adults' biography of Walt Whitman, *Walt Whitman, Builder for America* (1941).

See:
Jean Gould, *American Women Poets: Pioneers of Modern Poetry* (1980); Kunitz and Haycraft, *Twentieth Century Authors;* Dilly Tante, *Living Authors* (1931); William Drake, *The First Wave: Women Poets in America, 1915–1945* (1987).

Dodge (Luhan), Mabel

Born Buffalo, New York, 1879, of wealthy parents. Married Karl Evans in 1900. Had one son before her husband's death in 1903. From 1904 to 1913, was married to Edwin Dodge. An affair with John Reed lasted roughly from 1913 to 1916, when Mabel Dodge married Maurice Sterne.

During the years of her association with Greenwich Village, Dodge conducted her celebrated Fifth Avenue salon, wrote short prose pieces for *The Masses,* and strove to be the inspiration of writers and artists (her conception of woman's proper sociocultural role). In 1917 she traveled with Maurice Sterne to New Mexico, where she would meet and marry the man who transformed her life, Antonio Lujan.

Dodge (who had then taken the name Luhan) dedicated the rest of her life to activities in, and on behalf of, the Pueblo community of Taos. It was at Taos, too, that she wrote *Lorenzo in Taos* (1932), about the stay there of D. H. Lawrence. She died in 1962.

Selected Works:
Nonfiction, *Lorenzo in Taos* (1932); *Taos and Its Artists* (1947). Autobiography: *Intimate Memories* (4 vols., 1933–1937), of which volumes 3 and 4 were republished separately as *Movers and Shakers* (1985) and *The Edge of Taos Desert: An Escape to Reality* (1987).

See:
Winifred L. Frazer, *Mabel Dodge Luhan* (1984); Lois Palkin Rudnick, *Mabel Dodge Luhan: New Woman, New Worlds* (1984).

Dorr, Rheta Childe

Born Omaha, Nebraska, 1866. Became a feminist at the age of twelve, when she heard Elizabeth Cady Stanton and Susan B. Anthony speak, and joined the National Woman Suffrage Association. Studied at the University of Nebraska, 1884–1885. Moved to New York City, 1890, where she studied art, then took up writing. Married John Pixley Dorr, 1892, from whom she divorced in 1898. Thereafter, supported herself and her son by journalism. In 1902, secured a job writing for the woman's page of the *New York Evening Post.* Worked with the Women's Trade Union League and the Association of Social Settlements, and was (briefly) a socialist.

From 1906 to 1907 Dorr was a freelance foreign correspondent. She covered the British suffrage movement, becoming a confidante of Emmeline Pankhurst (1912). In 1914 Dorr was appointed the first editor of the Woman's Party magazine, *The Suffragist.* During this period, she was also a member of the Heterodoxy club.

With the outbreak of World War I, Dorr's political views underwent drastic change. In 1916 she became a Republican, and thereafter, vehemently antipacifist and antisocialist. She died in 1948.

Selected Works:
Nonfiction, *What Eight Million Women Want* (1910); *Inside the Russian Revolution* (1917); *A Soldier's Mother in France* (1918). Autobiography, *A Woman of Fifty* (1924).

Biography, *Susan B. Anthony: The Woman Who Changed the Mind of a Nation* (1928).

Field, Sara Bard

Born 1882, in Cincinnati, into a strictly orthodox Baptist family. Father refused her permission to register at the University of Michigan, since he feared a university education might destroy her religious faith. She later studied at Yale, and at Western Reserve University, Ohio.

In 1900 Field married Albert Ehrgott, and traveled with him for missionary work in the Far East. They returned to the U.S. in 1903. Field became, like her husband, a Christian socialist and, in 1910 after a move to Oregon, active in the campaign which won suffrage for the state in 1912. She also began work as a reporter in 1911.

In 1914, Field was divorced. She thereafter became a key figure in the National Woman's Party, and a leading member of a suffrage delegation that lobbied Woodrow Wilson in December 1915.

Field was remarried in 1935, to a man who had already been her life partner for the previous seventeen years, Charles Erskine Scott Wood. She remained a radical, a pacifist, and a fighter for social causes.

Her book of poems, *Barabbas,* won the gold medal of the Book Club of California. Field died in 1974.

Selected Works:
Verse collections, *Barabbas* (1932); *Darkling Plain* (1936).

Flynn, Elizabeth Gurley

Born in New Hampshire, 1890, into a poor but highly educated working-class family. Father was a socialist activist and orator. Made her speaking debut at age fifteen. First arrest, for public speaking, in New York City at age sixteen. Became a leader and organizer in the Industrial Workers of the World. Wrote labor fundraising appeals in *The Masses.* Heterodoxy member, and lifelong friend of Mary Heaton Vorse. Joined U.S. Communist Party, 1937; elected to the party's National Committee, 1938. In 1940, Flynn's only son died.

From 1955 to 1958, Flynn was imprisoned under the Smith Act. She was elected Communist Party national chair in 1961. When she died in 1964, while on a visit to the Soviet Union, she was buried with full state honors from the Soviet government, and the funeral was attended by twenty-five thousand mourners.

Selected Works:
Autobiographies, *The Rebel Girl: An Autobiography of My First Life, 1906–1926* (1973); *The Alderson Story: My Life as a Political Prisoner* (1963).

See:
Rosalyn Fraad Baxandall, *Words on Fire: The Life and Writing of Elizabeth Gurley Flynn* (1987).

Glaspell, Susan

Born Susan Keating, 1876, in Davenport, Ohio. Ph.B. from Drake University, Ohio, 1899. Married George Cram Cook, 1913. In 1915, she wrote plays for the Provincetown Players.

Cook died in 1924. In 1925, Glaspell probably married Norman Matson; she lived with him until 1931. Glaspell's play *Alison's House* won the Pulitzer Prize in 1930. Glaspell died in 1948.

Selected Works:
Novels, *The Visioning* (1911); *Fidelity* (1915). Plays, *Suppressed Desires* (coauthored by George C. Cook), *Trifles,* and *The People,* all written for the Provincetown Players (1915); *The Verge* (1921); *Inheritors* (1921); *Alison's House* (1930).

Hoyt, Helen

Born 1887, in Connecticut. AB from Barnard College, 1909. Married William W. Lyman, 1921. Associate editor of *Poetry.*

Works:
Verse collections, *Apples Here In My Basket* (1924), *Leaves of Wild Grape* (1929), *The Name of a Rose* (1931).

See:
Who Was Who among North American Writers, 1921–1939 (1976).

Hull, Helen Rose

Born 1888, in Albion, Michigan. Grandfather was a newspaper editor and publisher; parents were teachers. Wrote short stories at the age of nine. Attended Michigan State College, the University of Michigan, and the University of Chicago, from which she received her Ph.B. in 1912. She taught at Wellesley College from 1912 to 1915, at Barnard College from 1915 to 1916, and thereafter as a professor of English and creative writing at Columbia University.

Hull was president of the Authors' Guild, 1949–1952. She had a lifelong relationship with Mabel Louise Robinson. She was a member of the Heterodoxy club, and published her first stories in *The Masses.*

Selected Works:
Novels, *Quest* (1922); *Labyrinth* (1923); *Islanders* (1927); *Heat Lightning* (1932); *Close Her Pale Blue Eyes* (1963). Nonfiction, *Mayling Soong Chiang* (1943); editor, with Michael Drury, of *Writers Roundtable* (1959). Also short stories for *The Masses, Harper's, Seven Arts, Century, Touchstone, Collier's, Saturday Evening Post.*

See:
Patricia M. Miller's sensitively written and informative Afterwords to the Feminist Press editions of *Islanders* (1988) and *Quest* (1990); also Stanley J. Kunitz, ed., *Authors Today and Yesterday* (1933); Kunitz and Haycraft, *Twentieth Century Authors;* Grant Overton, *The Women Who Make Our Novels* ([1928] 1967); Obituary, *New York Times,* 17 July 1971: p. 26, col. 2.

Irwin, Inez Haynes (Gillmore)

Born 1873, in Rio de Janeiro, Brazil, the third youngest of twelve children by her father's two marriages. Father was a prison administrator who had been an actor. Mother, before marriage, had worked in the textile mills in Massachusetts. Became a suffragist at the age of thirteen. After graduating from high school, taught in schools in Boston, 1892–1897. In 1897 married Rufus Hamilton Gillmore; divorced in 1913.

From 1897 to 1900 Irwin was a special student at Radcliffe College, where she majored in English, and joined with Maud Wood Park in founding the National College Equal Suffrage League. After graduation she worked with the labor movement in California, and wrote fiction for popular magazines. In 1911 she became fiction editor of *The Masses*. She and Alice Winter were the first women on the *Masses* editorial board. She married Will Irwin in 1917; he died in 1948.

Irwin was a member of Heterodoxy club. She served on the National Advisory Council of the National Woman's Party, 1918–1920. She was president of the Authors' Guild (1925–1928) and of the Authors' League of America (1931–1933), chair of the Board of Directors of the World Center for Women's Archives, 1935–1940, and vice president of the New York chapter of P.E.N. (1941–1944). Inez Irwin died in 1970.

In 1924, Irwin's short story "The Spring Flight" won the O. Henry Memorial Prize.

Selected Works:
Nonfiction, *The Story of Alice Paul and the National Woman's Party* (1921), *Angels and Amazons: A Hundred Years of American Women* (1933). Novels, *Angel Island* (1914), *The Lady of Kingdoms* (1917), *Gertrude Haviland's Divorce* (1925), *Gideon* (1927), *Family Circle* (1931).

See:
Elaine Showalter's biography in Barbara Sicherman, Edward T. James, Janet Wilson James, and Paul S. Boyer, eds., *Notable American Women;* Kunitz and Haycraft, *Twentieth Century Authors;* Overton, *The Women Who Make Our Novels.*

Lewis, Lena Morrow

Born 1868 in Illinois, daughter of a minister and a Christian evangelist. Active in the early 1890s in the Women's Christian Temperance Union. In 1898 she became secretary of the Illinois Equal Suffrage League. She joined the Socialist Party in 1902, becoming a member of the National Committee in 1905, and of the party National Executive in 1909. She was proud to claim that, in seventeen years of traveling and public speaking for socialism, she had never spent more than fourteen consecutive nights under the same roof. She married fellow socialist Arthur Lewis in 1903.

Lewis remained a socialist when the party split in 1919, and others joined the newly formed Communist Party. In 1925 she was appointed managing editor of the *Oakland Labor World*. She left the Socialist Party in 1936, in protest at its attempted reconciliation with the communists.

See:
Mari Jo Buhle, "Lena Morrow Lewis," in Sally M. Miller, ed., *Flawed Liberation: Socialism and Feminism* (1981).

Lowell, Amy

Born 1874, in Brookline, Massachusetts, into the wealthy Lowell family, who traced their ancestry back to Colonial times. Educated at home and in Massachusetts private schools.

Although Lowell published a book of fairy tales at the age of thirteen, she did not fully realize her talent for poetry until she was nearly thirty. After 1908 she devoted her energies to writing. Lowell published her first volume of verse, *A Dome of Many-Coloured Glass*, in 1912.

Lowell remained a leading figure in literary circles throughout her life, in particular playing a central role in promoting the Imagist movement. She died in 1925.

Selected Works:
Verse collections, *A Dome of Many-Coloured Glass* (1912); *Sword Blades and Poppy Seed* (1914); *Can Grande's Castle* (1918); *Legends* (1921); *Complete Poetical Works* (1955). Essays and criticism, *Six French Poets* (1915); *Tendencies in Modern American Poetry* (1917); *Poetry and Poets* (1930).

See:
Sicherman et al., *Notable American Women;* Richard Benvenuto, *Amy Lowell* (1985).

Marot, Helen

Born 1865 in Philadelphia, fourth of five children, into an old Quaker family. From 1893 to 1896, worked with the University Extension Society of Philadelphia, then as a librarian in Wilmington, Delaware. In 1897 Marot helped to organize a library in Philadelphia for those interested in social problems. In 1899, she began her work as a labor investigator. Her work on the New York Child Labor Committee in 1902 led to the passing by the New York state legislature of the Compulsory Education Act of 1903. In 1905, Marot chaired the Public Education Association of New York, and at the end of the year she became executive secretary of the Women's Trade Union League of New York (1905–1913).

From 1914 to 1920, Marot was active in journalism and labor reporting. A socialist, she was a member of the British Fabian Society. She wrote for *The Masses* from 1914 through 1917, and was a shareholder in the *Masses* cooperative. She was also an editor for the socialist *New Review*. In October 1918, she was an editor for *The Dial* (until 1919).

Selected Works:
Nonfiction, *A Handbook of Labor Literature* (1899); *American Labor Unions* (1913); *The Creative Impulse in Industry* (1918).

See:
Sicherman et al., *Notable American Women; Who's Who of American Women, 1914–1915*. Obituaries, *New York Times,* 4 June 1940; *New York Herald Tribune,* 4 June 1940: 24.

Mastin, Florence Ripley

Born Wayne, Pennsylvania. Daughter of a church minister. Educated at Barnard and Columbia.

Selected Works:
Verse collections, *Green Leaves* (1918); *Cables of Cobweb* (1935). Poems in *Everybody's, Collier's, Pearson's, Saturday Review of Literature.*

See:
Who Was Who Among North American Authors, 1921–1939. Obituary, *New York Times,* 24 Feb. 1968: p. 27, col. 1.

Miller, Alice Duer

Born 1874, Staten Island, New York. Majored in mathematics and astronomy at Columbia University, covering her tuition expenses by freelance writing. Published *Poems* (1896) in collaboration with her sister Caroline. Received her B.A. in 1899; married Henry Wise Miller the same year.

From 1903 to 1907, Miller was a teacher in New York City. From 1916 to 1930, she was a regular contributor to the *Saturday Evening Post.* She also wrote a regular suffrage column, "Are Women People?" for *The New York Tribune* from 1914 to 1917. She chaired the Committee on Resolutions of the National American Woman Suffrage Association in 1916.

Miller authored several collections of satirical verse and fiction. She became a writer of Hollywood scenarios beginning in the 1920s.

Selected Works:
Verse collections, *Are Women People?* (1915); *Come Out of the Kitchen* (1916); *Women Are People!* (1917). Novels, *Ladies Must Live* (1917); *Manslaughter* (1921).

See:
Overton, *Women Who Make Novels* (1967); Sicherman et al., *Notable American Women.* Obituary, *New York Times,* 20 Oct. 1950: 42.

O'Hare, Kate Richards (Cunningham)

Born 1877, in Ada, Kansas, into a prosperous farm family. In 1887 family was financially ruined by drought, and father moved them to Kansas City, Missouri, where he became a machinist.

O'Hare became her father's apprentice in the machine shop and a member of the International Order of Machinists. As a young woman she took part in temperance and Christian evangelist work, though she later lost faith in Christianity.

"Mother" Mary Harris Jones inspired O'Hare's conversion to socialism. In 1901 O'Hare attended a training school for Socialist Party workers. She married a fellow trainee, Patrick O'Hare, the following year, and for the next twenty-six years wife and husband campaigned together for the socialist cause. (Kate divorced Patrick in 1928, to marry Charles C. Cunningham.)

Kate O'Hare coedited the *National Rip-Saw* with her husband. In 1910 she ran for Congress on the Socialist ticket. She served on the Socialist Party's national executive committee numerous times. From 1919 to 1920 she was imprisoned under the Espionage Act for her vocal opposition to United States participation in World War I.

Upon her release O'Hare became a leading figure in the amnesty campaign organized by the Socialist Party for wartime political prisoners. She spent the rest of her life in work for prison reform, and for progressive social causes. These activities included a brief involvement in the socialist Llano del Rio Cooperative colony (1922–1924), campaigning for Upton Sinclair in his 1934 bid for the governorship of California, and an appointment as assistant director of the California Department of Penology during the administration of Governor Culbert Olson. O'Hare died in 1948.

Selected Works:
Novel, *What Happened to Dan* (1940). Nonfiction, *Kate O'Hare's Prison Letters* (1919); *In Prison* (1920).
See:
Sicherman et al., *Notable American Women* (entry under "Cummings").

Ovington, Mary White

Born 1865, in Brooklyn, New York. Attended Parker Collegiate Institute, from 1888–1891, and Radcliffe College from 1891–1893. Ovington was forced to leave Radcliffe when her father's glass and china import business suffered the effects of economic recession. Ovington worked as Registrar of Pratt Institute, Brooklyn, then from 1895 to 1903 as head worker at Greenpoint Settlement. She became vice president of the Brooklyn Consumers' League, and assistant secretary of the Social Reform Club. Ovington joined the Socialist Party of America in about 1905.

From 1903 onwards, Ovington devoted most of her energies to the cause of African-American civil and economic rights. With the encouragement of W.E.B. Du Bois she joined in founding the National Association for the Advancement of Colored People, in which she remained a leader for nearly forty years. As chair of the NAACP in the 1920s, Ovington persuaded the organization to concentrate its efforts on securing equal federal aid for black and white public schools, a campaign which bore fruit in the 1950s. Ovington died in 1951.

Selected Works:
Novel, *The Shadow* (1920). Plays, *The Awakening* (1923); *Phillis Wheatley* (1932). Nonfiction, *Half a Man: The Status of the Negro in New York* (1911); *Portraits in Color* (1927); *The Walls Came Tumbling Down* (1947).
See:
Sicherman et al., *Notable American Women.*

Parsons, Elsie Clews (Worthington)

Born 1875 (? or 1874) in New York City, into a wealthy, conventional family. Attended Barnard College (A.B., 1896). Ph.D., Columbia University, 1899. In 1900 she married Herbert Parsons, later a well-known Republican congressman (1905–1911).

From 1899 to 1902 Parsons was Hartley House Fellow at Barnard, and from 1902 to 1905 she was a lecturer there. Thereafter, she taught at Columbia University and the New School for Social Research.

Parsons was a member of the Heterodoxy club, and collaborated in social activism with other *Masses* contributors and club members: Rose Pastor Stokes, Mary Heaton Vorse, and Mabel Dodge.

She was president of the American Folklore Society (1918–1920), of the American Ethnological Association (1923–1925), and of the American Anthropological Association (1940–1941). From 1918 to 1940, she was associate editor of the *Journal of American Folklore*. A lifelong pacifist and social democrat, Parsons wrote on social issues for *The Dial*, the *New Republic*, the *International Journal of Ethics* and the *Independent*.

Selected Works:
Nonfiction, *The Family: An Ethnographical and Historical Outline* (1906); *Religious Chastity: An Ethnological Study* (1913); *The Old-Fashioned Woman* (1913); *Fear and Conventionality* (1914); *Social Freedom* (1915); *Social Rule: A Study of the Will to Power* (1916); *Hopi and Zuni Ceremonialism* (1933); *Pueblo Indian Religion* (1939); plus numerous studies of the folklore of Mexico, the Sea Islands, and the Cape Verde Islands.

See:
Peter Hare, *A Woman's Quest for Science: Portrait of Anthropologist Elsie Clews Parsons* (1985).

Reely, Mary Katharine

Born 1881, in Spring Grove, Wisconsin. Attended Whitewater Normal School, Wisconsin. From 1906 to 1908, Reely was a social worker at Unity Settlement House in Minneapolis. She then studied for a B.A. at the University of Minnesota (awarded in 1912). Reely later worked for the H. W. Wilson Publishing Company, and as a librarian in charge of book selection for Wisconsin's public libraries.

Reely was secretary of the Madison, Wisconsin, branch of the Women's International League for Peace and Freedom from 1925 to 1933, and a member of the American Association of University Women and of the League of American Pen Women.

Selected Works:
Plays, *Daily Bread* (1919); *Early Ohios and Rhode Island Reds* (1921); *The House Can't Build the Barn* (1927); *Cave Stuff* (1928); *To Be Dealt With Accordingly* (1928); *Trails* (1928). Nonfiction, *Selected Articles on Immigration* (1917).

See:
Durward Howes, Mary L. Braun, and Rose Garvey, eds., *Standard Biographical Dictionary of Notable Women, 1939–40*.

Schwimmer, Rosika

Born 1877, in Budapest, Hungary, into a highly educated, reform-minded Jewish family. As a young woman, Schwimmer worked in a textile factory in order to study labor conditions.

In 1904 Schwimmer helped found the Hungarian feminist and pacifist organization *Feministák Egyesülete* (Feminists' Union). She represented Hungary in the International Neo-Malthusian League, and served on the board of the Hungarian Peace Society. She published fiction, edited a feminist-pacifist journal, and translated Charlotte Perkins Gilman's *Women and Economics* into Hungarian. Between 1904 and 1914 Schwimmer became a leader of the Hungarian suffrage movement, a speaker and writer for the suffrage cause throughout Europe, and a foreign correspondent for several European newspapers. She married in 1911, and was divorced in 1913.

After the outbreak of World War I, Schwimmer took a leading role in international pacifist movements. On a visit to the United States in 1915 she became international secretary of the Woman's Peace Party. In December of that year she persuaded Henry Ford and a group of other socially prominent Americans to sail with her to Europe in the hope of lobbying European statesmen in the cause of peace.

After the war Schwimmer was appointed Hungarian ambassador to Switzerland. In 1919, however, she was deprived of her civil rights after refusing to serve in the government of Bela Kun. In 1920, when the reactionary and anti-semitic Horthy regime took power, Schwimmer fled to the United States. Her application for citizenship was later denied, when she refused to swear to bear arms in defense of the U.S. Schwimmer remained in the United States, however, and continued to be active in peace work. She died in 1948.
See:
Sicherman et al., *Notable American Women.*

Spadoni, Adriana

Very little is known about Spadoni beyond the fact of her Italian ancestry, and that she spent much of her life in Northern California.
Selected Works:
Novels, *The Swing of the Pendulum* (1919); *The Noise of the World* (1921); *Mrs. Phelps' Husband* (1924); *Not All Rivers* (1937). Short stories in *Century, Collier's, Sunset,* the *Outlook.*
See:
Reviews of Spadoni's fiction in *The Dial,* 21 July 1921: 118; *New York Times,* 24 Mar. 1921: 18; *New York Times,* 23 Mar. 1924: 14; *Nation,* 6 Feb. 1937: 163; *New Republic,* 21 Apr. 1937: 338; *New York Times* 14 Feb. 1937: 17. See also Mari Jo Buhle, *Women and the American Left: A Guide to Sources,* for a balanced, appreciative review of *Not All Rivers.*

Stokes, Rose Pastor

Born Rose Wieslander, in Augustow, Poland, 1879. Took her stepfather's name of Pastor. Family moved to Britain, then to the United States, where as an eleven-year-old she worked in a cigar factory. She began writing poetry, and became a regular contributor to the *Jewish Daily News* in 1900, and later an assistant editor for the paper. She married the wealthy James Graham Phelps Stokes in 1905. Both Stokes and her husband worked for the Socialist Party.

Stokes published a number of poems in *The Masses*. She was a member of Heterodoxy, and took part in the Margaret Sanger defense campaigns.

From 1918 to 1920, Stokes was imprisoned for her opposition to United States involvement in the World War. In 1919 she joined the newly formed Communist Party, and wrote for *Pravda* and the *Daily Worker*. She divorced Stokes in 1925 and married V. J. Jerome in 1927. She died in 1933.

Selected Works:
Nonfiction, articles in *The Independent, Everybody's, The Arena, Century*. Play, *The Woman Who Wouldn't* (1916).

See:
Sicherman et al., *Notable American Women;* Obituary, *New York Times,* 21 June 1933: 17.

Untermeyer, Jean Starr

Born 1886, in Zanesville, Ohio. Educated in Ohio schools, and at a private school in New York City. Married Louis Untermeyer, 1907 (divorced, 1951). One son, Richard, who committed suicide in 1927.

Untermeyer had a brief singing career in Europe, 1924–1925. She taught creative literature beginning in 1940 at Olivet College, and from 1948 to 1951 at the New School in New York City. She was a member of the League of American Authors, the Authors' League, the Poetry Society of America, and P.E.N.

Selected Works:
Verse collections, *Growing Pains* (1918); *Dreams Out of Darkness* (1921); *Steep Ascent* (1927); *Winged Child* (1936); *Love and Need: Collected Poems, 1918–1940* (1940). Translations, *Schubert the Man,* by Oskar Bie (1928); *The Death of Virgil,* by Hermann Broch (1945).

See:
Rogal, *A Chronological Outline;* Stanley J. Kunitz and Vineta Colby, eds., *Twentieth Century Authors: First Supplement* (1955). Obituary, *New York Times,* 29 July 1970: 39.

Vorse, Mary Heaton

Born 1874, in New York City. Educated in Europe; studied art in Paris. Married Albert White Vorse, 1898; he died in 1910, leaving children Heaton (b. 1901) and Ellen (b. 1907). Married Joseph O'Brien, 1912; he died in 1915. One son, Joel (b. 1914). In 1920, married Robert Minor. Divorced, 1922. Vorse died in 1966.

Vorse was a contributing editor and cooperative owner of *The Masses,* and a member of Heterodoxy. She was also a suffragist, political activist, fiction writer, labor journalist, and foreign correspondent.

Selected Works:
Fiction, *Autobiography of an Elderly Woman* (1911); *I've Come to Stay: A Love Comedy of Bohemia* (1919); *Second Cabin* (1928); *Strike!* (1930). Nonfiction, *Men and Steel* (1921), *Labor's New Millions* (1938), *Time and the Town* (1942). Autobiography, *A Footnote to Folly* (1935). Numerous stories and articles in *Harper's, Century, The Independent, The New Republic, The New York Times, Outlook, The Nation.*

See:
Dee Garrison, *Mary Heaton Vorse: The Life of an American Insurgent* (1989).

Widdemer, Margaret

Born 1880, Doylestown, Pennsylvania. Daughter of a church minister. Educated at home. Published her first poems locally, at age ten. Librarianship training at the Drexel Institute of Arts and Sciences. Discharged from her first full-time job for errors in work. Turned to full-time free-lance writing. First book, *Factories,* a bestseller.

In 1919 Widdemer married poet Robert Haven Schauffer; they were divorced shortly thereafter. She was a member of Heterodoxy. She received an honorary Litt. D. from Bucknell University in 1931, and an honorary M.A. from Middlebury College in 1973. She gave numerous talks and lectures on writing, as well as a lecture series, "Do You Want to Write?" on NBC radio. Widdemer received the *Literary Review* prize for best satire in 1922, and for best lyric in 1923. In 1919 Widdemer shared the Poetry Society of America prize for the best book of poems for 1918 with Carl Sandburg. She died in 1978.

Selected Works:
Verse collections, *Factories* (1915); *Old Road to Paradise* (1918); *Cross-Currents* (1921); *Collected Poems* (1928). Novels, *Angela Comes Home* (1942); *Red Cloak Flying* (1950); *Lady of the Mohawks* (1951); *The Golden Wildcat* (1954). Nonfiction, *Basic Principles of Fiction Writing* (1953).

See:
Who's Who among North American Authors; Overton, *The Women Who Make Our Novels;* Kunitz and Haycraft, *Twentieth Century Authors.*

Wilkinson, Marguerite Bigelow

Born 1883, in Halifax, Nova Scotia. When a small child, family moved to the United States. Studied English at Northwestern University. In 1909 married James G. Wilkinson, a New York State school principal. She died while swimming off Coney Island, New York, in January 1928.

Selected Works:
Verse collections, *In Vivid Gardens* (1911); *By a Western Wayside* (1912); *The Passing of Mars* (1915); *Golden Songs of the Golden State* (1917); *The Way of the Makers* (1925); *Citadels* (1928). See also *The Dingbat of Arcady* (1923), a humorous travelogue.

See:
Stewart Wallace, ed., *A Dictionary of North American Authors Deceased before 1950* (1951); *National Cyclopedia of American Biography, 1892–1947* (1984); *Who Was Who among North American Authors;* Kunitz and Haycraft, *Twentieth Century Authors.* Obituaries: *New York Times,* 15 Jan. 1928: 29; *Poetry,* Mar. 1928: 332–334.

Winter, Alice Beach

Born 1877, Green Ridge, Missouri. Studied at St. Louis School of Fine Arts, 1892–1898. In 1904, went to New York for further study. Married Charles Allen Winter, 1904.

Winter was an active member of Branch One of the Socialist Party. She was widely known as a society portrait painter and magazine illustrator for *Collier's, Century, Scribner's,* and *Metropolitan,* among other periodicals.

With Inez Haynes Irwin, Winter was among the first *Masses* editors to resign in 1916, after a dispute between the magazine's artists and writers.

In 1931, Winter moved to Gloucester, Massachusetts, where she exhibited her work and produced materials for public education projects, as well as murals for city public buildings. She died in 1970.

See:

O'Neill, *Echoes of Revolt;* Zurier, *Art for the Masses.*

Notes

Chapter 1. Women Are People

1. Susan Glaspell, *The People*, in *Plays* (1920), 33–34.

2. Mabel Dodge, *Movers and Shakers* (1936), 143–144. Because she is best known as Mabel Dodge, she will be referred to here by that name, rather than by her later married name, Mabel Dodge Luhan.

3. From Inez Haynes Irwin's unpublished autobiography, "Adventures of Yesterday," 282. Inez Haynes Irwin Papers. Although her name was Inez Haynes Gillmore at the time *The Masses* was published, she will be referred to here by her later married name, Irwin, by which she is better known.

4. Alice Duer Miller, *Come Out of the Kitchen* (1916).

5. See Nancy Cott, *The Grounding of Modern Feminism* (1987), 211; William L. O'Neill, *Everyone Was Brave: A History of Feminism in America* (1969), 271.

6. Leslie Fishbein, *Rebels in Bohemia: The Radicals of "The Masses"* (1982), 31.

7. William L. O'Neill, *Echoes of Revolt: "The Masses," 1911–1917* (1966), 303.

8. Max Eastman, *Enjoyment of Living* (1948), 400.

9. For Mary Sanford's letter see *The Masses*, Mar. 1916: 20; for George Bernard Shaw's criticism, see "Correspondence" in *The Masses*, Oct. 1917: 16. For John Dos Passos' recollections, see *The Best of Times* (1966); for Charlotte Perkins Gilman's support of *The Masses*, see Eastman, *Enjoyment*, 467.

10. Dorothy Day, *By Little and by Little: The Selected Writings of Dorothy Day* (1983), 148; *The Long Loneliness: The Autobiography of Dorothy Day* ([1952] 1959), 69.

11. Inez Haynes Irwin, "The Confessions of an Alien," *Harper's Bazaar*, Apr. 1912: 170–171, 210 (published, of course, under the name Inez Haynes Gillmore).

12. For statistics on left-wing periodicals of the turn of the century, see James Weinstein, *The Decline of Socialism in America, 1912–1925* (1967), 84–87.

13. Judith Schwartz, *Radical Feminists of Heterodoxy: Greenwich Village 1912–1940* (1982); Rebecca Zurier, *Art for "The Masses": A Radical Magazine and Its Graphics (1911–1917)* (1987).

14. Mary Heaton Vorse, *A Footnote to Folly: The Reminiscences of Mary Heaton Vorse* (1935), 41.

15. Floyd Dell, *Homecoming: An Autobiography* (1933), 296.

16. Ethel Lloyd Patterson, "Lena Morrow Lewis: Agitator," *Masses*, July 1911: 13.

17. Both Elsie Parsons and Dorothy Day remained assiduous contributors until the very last year of publication.

18. For the invention of this apt epithet, I am indebted to my friend Gordon Koestler.

19. Max Eastman, *Enjoyment*, 407; *Love and Revolution: My Journey through an Epoch* (1964): 23.

20. Cary Nelson, *Repression and Recovery: Modern American Poetry and the Politics of Cultural Memory, 1910–1945* (1989): 206.

21. Floyd Dell, "Adventures in Anti-Land," *Masses* Oct./Nov. 1915: 5–6. Dell shuddered in mock-horror at the "scientific" evidence offered by medical specialist Sir Almroth Wright of woman's supposedly biologically determined psychic instability, and hence—in the eyes of the anti-suffrage lobby—her unfittedness to vote.

22. See Mary White Ovington's story "The White Brute," *Masses*, Oct./Nov. 1915: 17–19, and discussed in chapter 5; Rosika Schwimmer's article "News from the Front," *Masses*, May 1915: 10, and discussed in chapter 4; and Susan Glaspell's obituary poem "Joe," *The Masses*, Jan. 1916: 9.

23. On the distribution of socialist literature, see Richard Fitzgerald, *Art and Politics: Cartoonists of "The Masses" and "Liberator"* (1973): 127, 189. On the campaign in support of Margaret Sanger, see chapter 2. On the organization of women workers, see, e.g., William Mailly, "The Working Girls' Strike," *Independent*, 23 Dec. 1909: 1416–1418. On the Paterson Pageant, see Dodge, *Movers and Shakers*, 203–312; Lois Palken Rudnick, *Mabel Dodge Luhan: New Woman, New Worlds* (1984), 86–87. On the woman suffrage campaign, see chapter 4.

24. For accounts of the Heterodoxy experience, see Inez Haynes Irwin, "Adventures," 416–423; Dodge, *Movers and Shakers*, 144. For a fictionalized account, see Helen R. Hull, *Labyrinth* (1923), 237.

25. Elizabeth Gurley Flynn to Mary Heaton Vorse, 18 Sept. 1939. Mary Heaton Vorse Collection.

26. An example of the kind of advice and support Flynn gave Vorse in this relationship is Flynn's admonition, which Vorse quoted to Minor: "Mary any woman can love him requiringly!" Mary Heaton Vorse to Robert Minor, 1920 (n.d.). Vorse Collection.

27. See, e.g., Babette Deutsch's letter to Vorse, dated 30 Mar. 1956, reporting how much she was enjoying *Time and the Town*: "I keep interrupting A. [her husband, Avrahm Yarmolinsky] to regale him with snatches of it. My admiration for you grows—and that it can't!" Vorse Collection.

28. For a fuller account of these activities, see Rudnick, *Mabel Dodge Luhan*, 176–181, 261–265.

29. Virginia Gardner discusses this aspect of Bryant's association with Greenwich Village in *Friend and Lover: The Life of Louise Bryant* (1982).

30. Dorothy Day gives amusing descriptions of this ménage in her novel *The Eleventh Virgin* and in her autobiography, *The Long Loneliness* (67).

31. Max Eastman, *Venture* (1927). Eastman's central character, an upper-class young man on his way to becoming a radical, thinks of the character representing Flynn as "the Mother-general" (239).

32. Art Young to Mary Heaton Vorse, 8 Dec. [no year given]. Vorse Collection.

33. For accounts of the first *Masses* trial (the second involved Eastman, Dell, Art Young, and John Reed, and resulted in the acquittal of all the defendants), see Eastman, *Love and Revolution*, 83–91; Louis Untermeyer, *From Another World* (1939); and Floyd Dell's report in *The Liberator*, June 1918.

34. Dorothy Day, *From Union Square to Rome* (1938), 80.

35. See, e.g., Vorse's story "The Hopper," *Liberator*, Apr. 1920: 34–38, about the nightmarish struggle of a veteran, newly returned from World War I, to support his family; or her "Fraycar's Fist," *Liberator*, Aug. 1920: 17, 20–24, about a steelworker.

36. Dorothy Day, "Girls and Boys Come Out to Play," Review of *Janet Marsh* by Floyd Dell, *Liberator*, Nov. 1923: 30–31; "A Coney Island Picture," *Liberator*, Apr. 1918: 46. Mary White Ovington, "Bogalusa," *Liberator*, Jan. 1920: 31–33. Helen Keller, "In Behalf of the IWW," *Liberator*, Mar. 1918: 13.

37. See Mary Heaton Vorse, "Twenty Years," *Liberator*, Jan. 1921: 10, 12–13. See also "The Silent Defense in Sacramento," Jean Sterling's moving account of a trial of California Wobblies, in *Liberator*, Feb. 1919: 15–17.

Chapter 2. Patriarchy

1. Elsie Clews Parsons, "Journal of a Feminist" (no date), 51. Elsie Clews Parsons Papers.

2. Parsons expressed particular admiration for Alice Duer Miller in her handling of personal relationships. Miller, she wrote, did not "really know what jealousy is like." Letter to Herbert Parsons, 27 July 1909. Parsons Papers.

3. For H. L. Mencken's appreciation of her work, see Peter H. Hare, *A Woman's Quest for Science: Portrait of Anthropologist Elsie Clews Parsons* (1985), 20.

4. For an extended discussion of Parsons' relationship with her husband, and of her own childrearing practices, see Hare, *A Woman's Quest*, 53–75, 77–87.

5. Elsie Clews Parsons, "Marriage and Parenthood: A Distinction," *International Journal of Ethics* 25 (1915): 514–517.

6. Elsie Clews Parsons, "When Mating and Parenthood Are Theoretically Distinguished," *International Journal of Ethics*, 26 (1916): 207–216.

7. Parsons, *Old-Fashioned Woman*, 9. This atmosphere of post-Victorian repression supplies a context for a poem like Helen Hoyt's "Menaia," discussed in chapter 1 of this book.

8. "How They Are Voting," *New Republic*, 21 Oct. 1940: 554.

9. "Thoroughly commercialized, [a woman's] price may be extremely low. . . . In Chicago, the brothel charges are fifty cents, one dollar, five dollars, half going to the prostitute and half to the keeper of the house. Jane Addams tells the story of a Chicago factory girl who tried in vain for seven months to save enough for a pair of shoes. Twice during this time she had her old shoes resoled. When they became too worn out to stand a third soling, and she had but ninety cents towards a new pair, she gave in and, to use her own phrase, 'sold out for a pair of shoes.' " (Parsons, *Old-Fashioned Woman*, 197–198).

Parsons further compares the prostitute's income to that of the unskilled wage worker: "In a recent comparison of the earnings of Chicago working girls and prostitutes its commercialized value is plainly expressed. The average employee in a department store earns $7 a week; the average income of one hundred prostitutes, described in the Vice Commission's Report, ranged from $50 a week to, in exceptional cases, $100" (199).

10. Everett Wheeler, *The Case Against Woman Suffrage*, quoted by Floyd Dell in "Last But Not Least—," *Masses*, July 1915: 22.

11. Alice Duer Miller's column in the *Tribune*, like her book, was titled "Are Women People?" This was a question which Elsie Clews Parsons addressed in similarly ironic terms in her book *Religious Chastity: An Ethnological Study* ([1913] 1975): "Christian churchmen once debated the question whether or not women had souls, a controversy which now and again appears to be still unsettled" (279).

12. Floyd Dell returned a poem on prostitution to a contributor, pointing out that the magazine was already inundated with poems on the subject (Zurier, *Art,* 26).

13. Emma Goldman, *Anarchism and Other Essays* (1910), 217. Note that contemporary feminist Gayatri Spivak, in a provocative critique of orthodox Marxist thinking on the question of women's relation to production, views female reproduction as, in itself, an aspect of production: "The possession of a tangible place of production in the womb situates the woman as an agent in any theory of production." *In Other Worlds: Essays in Cultural Politics* (1987), 79.

14. Contraception was discussed and practiced more freely in France, where Sanger found that "recipes" for simple contraceptives were handed down within families over generations. Margaret Sanger, *Autobiography* (1938), 76.

15. Heywood Brown and Margaret Leech, *Anthony Comstock: Roundsman of the Lord* (New York: Albert and Charles Boni, 1927), 15–16.

16. Cornelia Barns also drew for the *Birth Control Review*. One of her cartoons for the *Review* links the fight for birth control to the woman suffrage issue. This drawing, "The New Voter at Work," shows a sturdy woman sweeping away a heap of garbage labeled "Charity Destitutes," "Child Labor," and so on, with a broom labeled "Birth Control" (*Birth Control Review*, Feb.–Mar. 1918: 9).

For access to this material I am indebted to Alice Sheppard, who has written a number of papers and articles on the artistry of the New Woman cartoonists. See, e.g., "There *Were* Ladies Present! American Women Cartoonists and Comic Artists in the Early Twentieth Century," *Journal of American Culture* 7 (1984): 34–38.

17. "Emma Goldman's Defense," *Masses*, June 1916: 27. Whereas Goldman viewed birth control as a tool that working women could use to combat poverty, Eastman warned that birth control might also be coopted by the ruling classes, who would make of it "a palliative, a method of promoting contentment in Poverty" ("Revolutionary Birth-Control," *Masses*, July 1915: 21).

18. Although *The Masses* throughout its brief existence remained supportive of and in close contact with both Emma Goldman and Margaret Sanger, relations between them and Max Eastman were not without strain. Eastman admitted that, despite a certain mutual respect between Goldman and himself, he "never liked Emma Goldman very well." Eastman angered and disappointed her when, having undertaken to speak at a meeting in Carnegie Hall to celebrate Goldman's release

from jail, he refused to appear on the same platform with Goldman's fellow activist Ben Reitman. Eastman, who in any case regarded all anarchists as "kindergartners in the school of revolutionary thinking," objected to what he viewed as Reitman's "juvenile" tactic of "shocking people with crude allusions to their sexual physiology." However, Reitman was at the time under indictment, and later jailed, for distributing birth control information. Thus, in Goldman's possibly oversimplified view, Eastman, in refusing to be associated with Reitman at so crucial a moment, had "permitted personal dislikes to stand in the way of what [Eastman] claimed to be his 'high ideal.' " Goldman, *Living My Life* (1931), 571–572.

Eastman's relationship with Sanger went somewhat more smoothly. Although Sanger largely disregarded Eastman's advice on the conduct of her defense in the 1914 *Woman Rebel* case, she and Eastman remained on friendly terms. When in 1917 he started *The Liberator* as a successor to *The Masses*, he consulted Sanger as someone possessing editorial experience in dealing with government censorship: "She wrote . . . assenting to my view, and I was happy because of my admiration for her" (*Love and Revolution*, 70).

19. An opponent of birth control argued in a letter to *The Masses* that the use of contraception would create a "morbid atmosphere" in the home (Apr. 1915: 24).

20. "Women Appeal to Mayor," *New York Times*, 29 Jan. 1917: 1, 6. As *The New York Times* reported on January 25, 1917, it was a socialist, New York Assemblyman Abraham Shiplacoff, who made the first attempt to introduce a bill—drafted with the aid of the National Birth Control League—into the New York State legislature that would have legalized the distribution of printed birth control information.

Initially a socialist, Sanger later parted company with the Socialist Party. For a detailed account of the relations between Margaret Sanger and the U.S. Socialist Party, see Mari Jo Buhle, *Women and American Socialism, 1870–1920* (1981), 268–280.

21. Emily Taft Douglas, *Margaret Sanger: Pioneer of the Future* (1970), 222. On February 19, 1916, *The New York Times* had reported that the court hearing Margaret Sanger's case had dropped proceedings against her. Since Mrs. Sanger "was not a disorderly person and did not make a practice of publishing such articles" as those in *The Woman Rebel*, "the Government had considered there was room for reasonable doubt" ("Drops Mrs. Sanger's Case," 12).

Because of the risk involved, Floyd Dell treated all requests to *The Masses* for information on birth control methods with great caution: "These letters, as associate editor, I answered, saying that we were forbidden by law to give the information; then, as a private individual, I carefully turned over all these letters to other private individuals, who mailed this information to the women; and in this lawbreaking I cheerfully and conscientiously participated" (*Homecoming*, 252).

22. Charlotte Perkins Gilman, *Herland*, ed. Ann J. Lane (New York: Pantheon Books, 1979). As Lane explains, *Herland* was serialized in 1915 in Gilman's monthly magazine *The Forerunner*. Lane was the first to edit and publish in book form this utopian fable of a world inhabited entirely by women.

23. Ursula Le Guin considers that Irwin's representations of male and female behavior patterns in *Angel Island* are, in some respects, "powerfully conventional," particularly with regard to the women's preoccupation with personal adornment

(Introduction, *Angel Island*, 1988, viii–ix). This is, I believe, to misunderstand Irwin's evolutionary conception of feminism. In fact, the most "evolved" and strong-minded of the women, Julia, largely spurns such frivolity (175–176).

Chapter 3. Labor

1. Josephine Conger-Kaneko, "Women Suffrage and Socialism," *Masses*, Aug. 1911: 16. Conger-Kaneko was probably best known as the editor, in the years before World War I, of the magazine *Socialist Woman*. Apart from "Women Suffrage and Socialism," she wrote two other pieces for *The Masses:* a short sketch called "The Dream of Mirah" (Nov. 1911: 9), and an article entitled "Kathleen Kelly" (11), about a victim of the Triangle factory fire of 1911.

2. Of the nineteenth-century protest writers, Thomas Hood ("The Song of the Shirt," *Poems*, 1897) and Charles Kingsley *(The Water Babies*, 1863) in England and Edward Zane Carroll Judson *(Mysteries and Miseries of New York*, 1848) in the United States seem likely influences on these women's work. See Alice Kessler-Harris, *Out to Work: A History of Wage-Earning Women in the United States* (1982), 66.

3. Eloise Robinson's poem seems to owe more than a little to Dante Gabriel Rossetti's "The Blessed Damozel" (*Ballads and Sonnets*, 1881), where a soul in heaven (though a lovelorn maiden, not a factory child) feels herself to be an alien in the new environment.

4. Florence Kiper Frank, "Where Sympathy Pays," *Masses*, May 1915: 14.

5. According to estimates by Kessler-Harris, only 3 to 6.6 percent of women employed in U.S. industry between 1900 and 1920 were members of trade unions (*Out to Work*, 152).

6. Babette Deutsch's verse collection entitled *Banners* (1919) contains a number of poems that celebrate the Revolution, including "Banners," "June 1917," and "Zorka."

7. The "Ludlow Massacre" arose out of the Colorado coal strike of 1913–1914. Eleven thousand miners, employees of the Colorado Fuel and Iron Corporation, owned by the Rockefellers, went on strike to protest pay and conditions as well as the killing of an IWW leader who had been organizing among them. In April 1914, eight months after the miners' eviction from company housing, the National Guard attacked the miners' tent colony at Ludlow with machine guns and set fire to the tents.

8. Rose Pastor Stokes (born Rose Harriet Wieslander in 1879), who emigrated to the U.S. from Poland in 1890, worked in cigar and shirtwaist factories in Cleveland before securing a job as editor's assistant at the *New York Jewish Daily News*. She, and the wealthy reformer James Graham Phelps Stokes, whom she married in 1905, formally joined the Socialist Party in 1906. See Philip Foner, *History of the Labor Movement in the United States* (1965), 4:175.

9. See, e.g., Upton Sinclair's *They Call Me Carpenter* (1922), in which Christ is imagined returning to the Los Angeles of the early 1920s, where his disciples are drawn from strike leaders and socialists, and the Last Supper takes place at the local offices of the Socialist Party.

10. Cleghorn, *Threescore*, 182. "The complete abolitionist," Robert Frost called

Sarah Cleghorn in his 1936 introduction to *Threescore* (xi). Probably her most famous lines are a single quatrain on child labor:

> The golf links lie so near the mill
> That almost every day
> The laboring children can look out
> And see the men at play
>
> (*Threescore*, xi)

11. Most of Adriana Spadoni's *Masses* contributions are less autobiographical, such as "A Rift of Silence" (Feb. 1913: 12–13) or "Real Work" (July 1915: 5, 7–8, 10). See also chapter 6.

12. Dee Garrison, ed., *Rebel Pen: The Writings of Mary Heaton Vorse* (1985), 22.

13. Crystal Eastman, telegram to Mary Heaton Vorse, 26 Nov. 1919. Vorse Collection.

14. Vorse makes explicit the allusion to Ella May Wiggins as the original of Mamie Lewis in *Strike!* by attributing to her fictional character the most famous of Wiggins' ballads, "We Leave Our Homes in the Morning":

> We leave our homes in the morning,
> We kiss our children good-by,
> And while we slave for the bosses,
> Our children scream and cry . . .
>
> How it grieves the heart of a mother
> You every one must know,
> But we can't buy for our children
> Our wages are too low. . . .
>
> (*Strike!* 90)

15. Mary Heaton Vorse, "The Trouble at Lawrence," *Harper's Weekly*, 16 Mar. 1912: 10; "The Mining Strike in Minnesota: From the Miners' Point of View," *Outlook*, 30 Aug. 1916: 1044–1045; "The Case of Adolf," *Outlook*, 2 May 1914: 27–31 (reprinted in Garrison, *Rebel Pen*, 36–43).

16. Vorse, *Footnote to Folly*, 135. Elizabeth Gurley Flynn had written to Vorse: "So far we seem to have failed to get any worthwhile publicity. Carlo [Tresca], Jo Schmidt, and nine others, are in jail here in Duluth since July 3rd, charged with first degree murder. It is terribly serious. . . . They will be tried in September. They are concentrating the fight on Carlo—as the brains of the crowd, etc. Mary dear, there never was a time when we needed our writer friends to get busy, more than right now, if . . . a few of our best men are to be saved from the penitentiary . . . "(135).

For a full account of the strike, based on a number of press accounts, including those of Vorse, see Foner, *Labor Movement*, 494–517.

17. Elizabeth Gurley Flynn wrote a separate appeal for legal defense funds for the accused in the Mesaba Range case: "The Minnesota Trials," *Masses,* Jan. 1917:

8. On the role played by the press in the case, and the eventual fate of the Mesaba Range defendants, see Foner, *Labor Movement*, 515–517, and Elizabeth Gurley Flynn, *The Rebel Girl: An Autobiography of My First Life, 1906–1926* (1973), 216.

18. During the Lawrence textile strike, Vorse reported on the strike and, "because the leaders were in jail and because Elizabeth Flynn was shorthanded," also functioned as "part of the movement, a sort of assistant to the leaders. . . . I spoke from platforms. I was identified in the eyes of the community . . . "(*Footnote to Folly*, 148).

19. Helen Marot wrote an account of the cloakmakers' strike of 1910 for *The Outlook*: "A Moral in the Cloakmakers Strike," 17 Sept. 1910: 99–101. See also William Mailly, "The Working Girls' Strike," *Independent*, 23 Dec. 1909: 1416.

The National Labor Defense Counsel was founded in 1916 to provide non-unionized workers with access to legal aid. In December, Marot, along with Fremont Older, Dante Barton, Lincoln Steffens, and the new organization's Secretary-Treasurer, Ida Rauh, appealed in *The Masses* for donations to the Counsel's funds (Dec. 1916:29).

20. Marot ignores here a widespread form of discrimination by American Federation of Labor executives toward women: their apathy toward the organizing of new trade union groups, whose applications for affiliation could be rejected or ignored by the parent body. See Kessler-Harris, *Out to Work*, 157.

21. Marot calls for the setting up of training schools in which students would participate actively in manufacturing, accounting procedures, and the development and marketing of new products, with a view to "the development of a creative impulse in the individual" and to the development of "industry as a socially productive enterprise" (*Creative Impulse*, 112–137).

22. "Even the temporary gains wrenched by trade unionism from a capitalism unprepared to meet the crisis created by the war are to be nullified by an internal militarism which will keep down wages at the point of the bayonet, and an external militarism which will protect the American capitalist in his desertion of the American labor market for more profitable fields in other countries" (Helen Marot, "Immigration and Militarism," *Masses*, Apr. 1916: 21).

23. Inez Haynes Irwin, *Angels and Amazons: A Hundred Years of American Women* (1933): 309–323.

24. Jones retells several of these stories in her autobiography: Mary Harris Jones, *The Autobiography of Mother Jones* (1925).

25. Inez Haynes Irwin, "The A.F. of L. Convention: An Impression," *Masses*, Feb. 1916: 8.

26. Inis Weed and Louise Carey, "I Make Cheap Silk," *Masses*, Nov. 1913: 7.

Chapter 4. The War and Suffrage

1. For a personal account of one prominent socialist's divergence from (and eventual reconciliation with) the Socialist Party over the war issue, see Upton Sinclair's autobiography.

2. In Eleanor Flexner's classic history of the fight for women's rights in the U.S., *Century of Struggle: The Woman's Movement in the United States* (1959), she gives a useful account of the NAWSA's stand on the war. See also O'Neill, *Everyone*

Was Brave. In O'Neill's words, although the NAWSA "would do only enough war work to make its patriotism credible," all the same, the war did prove "enormously popular with middle-class women" (185).

3. The National Woman's Party (which at first called itself the Congressional Union) initially split from the National American Woman Suffrage Association (NAWSA) in 1914, over the question of strategy. The NAWSA favored lobbying of and conciliation toward the Democratic administration then in power; the Woman's Party preferred to bring pressure to bear by ostracizing and embarrassing the administration. When the Woman's Party began picketing the White House in 1917 (an action viewed as disruptive and unpatriotic in wartime, as well as harmful to the suffrage cause), the NAWSA openly denounced the Woman's Party action. See Robert Booth Fowler, *Carrie Catt: Feminist Politician* (1986), 202.

4. See the biographical sketch of Rosika Schwimmer in Barbara Sicherman et al., eds., *Notable American Women: The Modern Period* (1980).

5. When the United States entered World War I, Vorse, out of dire financial need, accepted a job with the propaganda department, the U.S. Committee on Public Information. The job, which was secured for her by Inez Irwin's second husband, Will Irwin, required Vorse to write pamphlets on the rights of small Eastern European nations. See Dee Garrison, *Mary Heaton Vorse: The Life of an American Insurgent* (1989), 115.

6. Elizabeth Waddell, "What of the Night," *Masses*, Mar. 1917: 6.

7. Miriam Allen de Ford, in "The Singing Mouth," *Masses*, Feb. 1916: 14. Here is a longer excerpt:

> Holy rebellion breathes within our air
> We are dream-goaded to a prophet's deed
> And aspiration is made sharp with hope!
> Still singing mouth, thy voice shall be a cry
> To urge us to the sacred wrath of war. . . .

This qualified approval of violence in the cause of labor occurred frequently among those connected with *The Masses*. For example, in *The Long Loneliness*, Dorothy Day explained her position as follows: "I was pacifist in my views—pacifist in what I considered an imperialist war though not pacifist as a revolutionist" (87).

8. Later Louise Bryant would travel to the Soviet Union and write an account of the Bolsheviks and their revolution, *Six Red Months in Russia: An Observer's Account of Russia before and during the Proletarian Dictatorship* ([1918] 1982).

9. Mabel Dodge, "The Secret of War," *Masses*, Nov. 1914: 9. Dodge offered her article to the Woman's Peace Party for reprinting because one of the party's leaders had read and praised it. See Rudnick, *Mabel Dodge Luhan*, 102.

10. In April 1914, President Wilson ordered troops landed at the Mexican port of Veracruz. The Mexican president, Victoriano Huerta, who was not recognized by the United States, had taken power the previous year. Early in 1914, the Mexican authorities had arrested a group of U.S. Marines. Although the Mexican government quickly ordered their release and apologized, the Wilson administration de-

manded that the Mexicans also fire a twenty-one-gun salute, out of respect for the U.S. flag. When the Mexicans did not comply with this demand, U.S. troops landed in Veracruz. Seventeen Americans were killed in this expedition, and sixty-three wounded. Shortly afterwards, the U.S. government succeeded in forcing Huerta out of power.

11. In December 1915, the Wilson administration proposed to Congress a comprehensive national defense plan. The plan, which was enacted into law the following year, called for unprecedented increases in the national military budget.

12. Sara Bard Field, "San Francisco and the Bomb," *Masses*, Oct. 1916: 16. During a Preparedness parade in 1916 in San Francisco, a bomb exploded, killing nine people and injuring a number of others. The bombing became a pretext for the arrest and conviction of two prominent labor leaders, Billings and Mooney, on murder charges, and for attempts to destroy San Francisco's powerful and well-organized labor movement. Field's article concentrates particularly on the latter aspect of the incident.

13. Margaret Widdemer, "War-March," *Masses*, Aug. 1915: 17. The context for Waddell's poem is the wartime clamp-down on civil liberties—notably, the passing of the Espionage Act of 1917.

14. The idea of war toys as conducive to militarism in the rising generation was a matter of concern to contemporary British pacifists also. In this context, see the story "The Toys of Peace" by Saki (H. H. Munro), which satirizes the anti–war toy lobby (in *The Short Stories of Saki* [H. H. Munro], 1930: 439–446).

15. For a survey of opinion on the suffrage question among "prominent women" of the period, see Barbara Kuhn Campbell, *The "Liberated" Woman of 1914* (1976), 132–137. Not surprisingly, Campbell finds particularly strong support for suffrage among women in the professions; 69 percent of professional women were pro-suffrage, or active in the suffrage movement, and only 3 percent were opposed (134–135).

16. For accounts of Rheta Childe Dorr's argument with Wilson, see Inez Haynes Irwin, *The Story of Alice Paul and the National Woman's Party* (1921), 187–190, and Dorr's autobiography, *A Woman of Fifty* (1924), 291–296. Dorr challenged the President on his contention that each state should vote separately for suffrage and called attention to the preferred alternative, that of an amendment to the Constitution, initiated by Congress, which she called on the President to support. Wilson, annoyed at being, as he put it, "cross-examined" by this impertinent nonvoting citizen, left the room in a huff, without further ceremony. Dorr was unflustered by the scandal her boldness caused among aides and onlookers, and even among her fellows in the suffrage delegation. She told the other suffragists: "'This will be a front page story on every newspaper in the country tomorrow morning.' And of course it was" (*Woman of Fifty*, 296).

Sara Bard Field also had an opportunity to confront President Wilson on the suffrage question. For an account of this meeting, see Irwin, *Story of the Woman's Party*, 62.

17. See Irwin, *Angels and Amazons*, 356; "Adventures," 454.

18. Day dated the beginnings of her conversion to Catholicism from this hunger strike (*Loneliness*, 77–81).

19. These perceptions had their effect on the way extreme anti-suffragists re-

garded women's alleged unfitness to vote, particularly in the context of the nation's growing preoccupation with war. For example Henry A. Wise Wood, president of the Aero Club of America, is on record as having told a congressional committee on woman suffrage that it was "a damnable thing" to "weaken ourselves by bringing into the war the woman, who has never been permitted in the war tents of any strong, virile, dominating nation" (O'Neill, *Everyone Was Brave*, 56).

20. The *Masses* item which discusses the indecency accusation is by "H. B." (probably Howard Brubaker). "Provincial Suffragists," *Masses*, Nov. 1913: 11.

21. More than sixty years later, Miriam Allen de Ford told an interviewer, "It sounds very radical to get out on a soapbox and stand on a street corner, but everybody did it . . . quite conservative political candidates would. That was the day of the soapbox." Sherna Gluck, ed., *From Parlor to Prison: Five American Suffragists Talk about Their Lives* (1975), 147.

22. Grace Potter, "Breaking Up the Home," *Masses*, Dec. 1911: 13. Mary Katharine Reely, another *Masses* contributor, seems to invite contrast with Potter in her half-serious contention that women, in dealing with a male-dominated world, are at their most empowered when their feet are most firmly planted on the hearth-stone. See Reely's sketch in *The Masses* entitled "The Helpmeet" (July 1914: 12) as well as a later work, the short play *Cave Stuff: A Play in Two Episodes* (1928), in which the implications of this position become unambiguously reactionary. In the later work, Reely portrays a group of men and women stranded on a desert island. While the men never give up longing to return to civilization, the women lapse contentedly into a domestic existence in which they wield power over the men.

23. On Louise Bryant's arrest, see Irwin, *Story of the Woman's Party*, 404. On Dorothy Day's imprisonment, see *Long Loneliness*, 60–61.

24. Miriam Allen de Ford's suffragist mother sent her at fourteen to represent the family's contribution to the movement; see Gluck, *Parlor to Prison*, 132–133. About joining the IWW, she wrote, "It was about that time, at my husband's suggestion, really, that I decided that the way to express my opposition to the war would be to join the IWW." (157). De Ford was a member for only one year.

25. An example of Alice Duer Miller's pacifist writing, which invites comparison with Pauline Barrington's "Toy Guns," is the poem "Playthings":

Perhaps another season
We shall not give our boys
Such very warlike playthings,
Such military toys. . . .

(*Are Women People?* 81)

26. In *A Woman of Fifty*, Rheta Dorr complains that although the thought of Germany's invasion of Belgium "disturbed my sleep," her friends at the Heterodoxy women's club (many of whom were *Masses* contributors) were neutral, pacifist, or even, she alleges, pro-German in their views on the war. Moreover, in Dorr's view, "all were too absorbed in the fascinating study of 'ourselves' to care . . . about what happened to the rest of the world" (309). In her account of the experiences of *A Soldier's Mother in France* (1918), Dorr remarks with approval that the American sol-

diers at the front have all lost "what theories they ever had about internationalism" (62). Dorr calls for opponents of U.S. intervention to be imprisoned as "camp followers of the Hun," in the interests of national security (245).

27. For Carrie Chapman Catt's pro-war stand, and her attitude to the National Woman's Party, see O'Neill, *Everyone Was Brave*, 125; Fowler, *Carrie Catt*, 202.

28. Sarah N. Cleghorn, "The Mother Follows," *Masses*, Aug. 1917: 47. For the support expressed by Jane Addams for a pro-suffrage argument along these lines— a support fairly unusual among NAWSA officeholders—see Aileen S. Kraditor, *The Ideas of the Woman Suffrage Movement, 1890–1920* (1965), 43–74.

29. *The Masses* printed an extract from Goldman's *Mother Earth* editorial with the sardonic title "Anti-Suffrage Papers Please Copy" (Jan. 1916: 20).

30. Vorse, *Footnote to Folly*, 169. As Jane Marcus has pointed out, the militant suffrage movement, at least in Britain, actually provided an ideal training for war relief work at the front. See her essay, "Corpus/Corps/Corpse: Writing the Body in/at War," in Helen M. Cooper, Adrienne Munich, and Susan Squier, eds., *Arms and the Woman: War, Gender and Literary Representation* (1989). The editors of this volume cite Virginia Woolf's "Thoughts of Peace in an Air Raid" as part of their strategy to challenge and deconstruct traditional stereotypes of warlike men and peaceable women: "Rather than the mother arming the hero, Woolf's essay offers the anticanonical proposition that mothers should disarm the hero by turning over to men the mothering role" (22).

Chapter 5. Ethnicity

1. Pastora San Juan Cafferty, Barry R. Chiswick, Andrew M. Greeley, and Teresa A. Sullivan, *The Dilemma of American Immigration: Beyond the Golden Door* (1983), 29. See pages 29–48 of this book for a concise summary of the debates on immigration in the years before U.S. entry into World War I, and of the legislation passed as a result.

2. Edward A. Ross, "Racial Consequences of Immigration," *Century*, Feb. 1914: 616. Ross, a professor of sociology at the University of Wisconsin, wrote a series of articles for *Century* in which he wavers between two lines of thinking. First, he asserts that the particular groups of immigrants currently entering the United States are inferior to their compatriots left behind. Second, he makes a number of claims about the "excitable" blood of the Southern European and the dangerous consequences of interracial marriage, which appear to be based on as-sumptions of the congenital inferiority of virtually all other races to Northern Europeans. The *Century*'s editors praised Ross' article "Racial Consequences" for "frankly and fearlessly" stating the possible consequences of admitting to the United States " 'sub-common' " millions of "the least desirable nationalities re-cently pouring into our land" (615).

3. Republican Congressman E. A. Hayes, as reported in the *Congressional Rec-ord*, 13 March 1906, 40:3749–3753; reprinted in Mary Katharine Reely, ed., *Selected Articles on Immigration* (1917), 268.

4. W. Z. Ripley, "Races in the United States," *Atlantic Monthly*, Dec. 1908: 747. The article concludes with a statement by Ripley at his most "liberal," where he concedes, first, that all human beings are, in the last analysis, human; and sec-

ond, that even "inferior" races may catch up, someday, with the Northern European: "It is only in their degree of physical and mental evolution that the races of men are different" (759).

5. Reprinted in Reely, ed., *Articles on Immigration*, p. 271.

6. Elizabeth Gurley Flynn, "The Minnesota Trials," *Masses*, Jan. 1917: 8; Mary Heaton Vorse, "Accessories before the Fact," *Masses*, Nov. 1916: 6–7, 22.

7. Mary Heaton Vorse, "Behind the Picket Lines," *Outlook*, 21 Jan. 1920: 107–109.

8. Mary Heaton Vorse, "Courage," *Liberator*, Mar. 1923: 11–13.

9. See John Collier's introduction to the final part of Mabel Dodge's autobiography, which was republished separately in 1987, titled (significantly) *The Edge of Taos Desert: An Escape to Reality*, xix–xxv.

10. For an account of the resentment aroused by Elsie Clews Parsons' monograph *Taos Pueblo* (1936), see Hare, *A Woman's Quest*, 162.

11. Elsie Clews Parsons, ed., *A Pueblo Indian Journal 1920–1921* (1925), 10. In his introduction to Dodge's *Edge of Taos Desert*, John Collier possibly overstates the case when he claims that Parsons "made no mention of human superiority" in her descriptions of Pueblo society, although when one compares her level tone with Dodge's poetic, rapturous accounts of Indian life, one may certainly observe a contrast in their manners of expressing admiration (xix).

12. Dee Garrison deals interestingly with this fairly brief interlude in Vorse's adventurous and varied career in *Mary Heaton Vorse*, 267–270.

13. Revealingly, in a transcript of a radio broadcast ("Why I Write about American Family Life," 1), Helen Hull speaks of "inferior races," whom she regards as analogous with children. Helen Rose Hull Papers.

14. Helen Marot, "Immigration and Militarism," *Masses*, Apr. 1916: 21. Elihu Root had served as Secretary of War and Secretary of State under successive Republican administrations. At the time of the anti-immigrant speech to which Marot alludes, he was President of the Carnegie Endowment for International Peace.

15. In her *Woman's Body, Woman's Right: A Social History of Birth Control in America* (1974), Linda Gordon gives a brief but interesting history of the concept of "race suicide" in turn-of-the-century America (136–158).

16. Elsie Clews Parsons, "Facing Race Suicide," *Masses*, June 1915: 15. Parsons *did* regard the decline in the birth rate of upper-class families as a regrettable trend, but for reasons unconnected with ethnicity—or genetic heredity. Parsons says she regrets that uneducated people have more children than those who are more "culturally developed." While this statement is certainly open to charges of snobbery, Parsons' overall argument in the last chapter of *The Family* (1906) indicates to what extent Parsons, who had herself been a mother for five years, adhered to what Gordon calls "the motherhood mystique" (*Woman's Body*, 143).

17. Jean Starr Untermeyer, "Church Sociable," *Liberator*, Mar. 1918: 12. Reprinted in Untermeyer, *Love and Need: Collected Poems, 1918–1940* (1940).

18. Elizabeth Hines Hanley, "Chivalry," *Masses*, June 1916: 5; Inez Haynes Irwin, "Stray Thoughts on Chivalry," *Masses*, Oct./Nov. 1915: 22. Leo Frank was posthumously pardoned in 1982; see John D. Buenker and Edward R. Kantowicz, eds., *A Historical Dictionary of the Progressive Era, 1890–1920* (1988), 165.

19. Inez Irwin's *Gideon* (1927) offers an illustration of the difficulty, even for the

well intentioned, of transcending racist stereotypes. Laurel Hallam, one of the novel's most thoroughly sympathetic characters—who, we are told, has traveled widely in Africa—makes up a story for guests at a party which seems to owe more to the Hollywood legend of Tarzan than to any travel experience. In Mrs. Hallam's story, a white man is in danger of being sacrificed to the god of the "natives" at the behest of a witch doctor/priest.

20. As a founder and leader of the Catholic Worker movement, Day was later to work actively on behalf both of the civil rights movement of the 1960s, and of Cesar Chávez's United Farm Workers.

21. As Dee Garrison explains, *Second Cabin* is loosely based on Vorse's observations of shipboard life among a group of middle-class passengers during her voyage back from the Soviet Union in 1922 (*Mary Heaton Vorse*, 209).

The racial and cultural stereotypes of Vorse's earlier writing are greatly modified in *Second Cabin* by the treatment of individual characters. The novel's Irish family, for instance, though treated comically, is recognizably a group of disparate individuals: a wise, practical mother, a truculent brother, and an ungainly daughter—who, in the course of the voyage, unexpectedly blossoms into a social success. The character of Christiansen, the young German who falls in love with the young picture bride Elsa, is one of the most satisfyingly complex that Vorse ever developed.

Chapter 6. Keeping the Faith?

1. For a rebuttal of *Nation* reviewer John Smertenko's view that the ending of Helen Hull's *Islanders* represented a "hat trick," see the Afterword by Patricia McClelland Miller, 331.

2. Helen Hull, "Why I Write about American Family Life," 2, 1, 4. Hull Papers.

3. In Eastman's *Venture*, the hero observes an outdoor strike meeting of the IWW and experiences "a feeling not far from disappointment. . . . How simple and straight-out and perfectly intelligible and not at all exciting it was!" (233).

4. Elsie Clews Parsons, "Journal of a Feminist," 106, 44, 28, 55, 72. Parsons Papers.

5. Elsie Clews Parsons, "The Last Zuni Transvestite," *American Anthropologist* 41 (1939): 338–340.

6. Margaret Caffrey, *Ruth Benedict: Stranger in This Land* (1989), 185–198, 96, 159.

7. Franz Boas, obituary tribute to Elsie Clews Parsons, *Science*, 23 Jan. 1942: 89–90; Peter Hare, *A Woman's Quest*, 163.

8. Louise Bryant, "Last Days with John Reed," *Liberator*, Feb. 1921: 11–12.

9. Louise Bryant, letter to Edna Kenton, Mary Heaton Vorse, and others, 15 Mar. 1917 (Vorse Collection). Also see Bryant's poems in *The Masses*. In "Lost Music," for example, Bryant writes of "the desert, / Breathless with eager silence / That out-beauties sound" (Apr. 1917: 37).

10. "Louise Bryant, 41, Journalist, Dead," *New York Times*, 10 Jan. 1936: 19. She was actually fifty years old.

11. "Louise Bryant, 41, American Writer, Dies in Paris Hospital," *New York Herald Tribune*, 10 Jan. 1936: 2.

12. Review of *Mirrors of Moscow, Times Literary Supplement*, 26 Apr. 1923: 279; Katharine Sergeant Angell, "The Soviet Leaders," *Nation*, 9 May 1923: 548–549; Review of *Mirrors of Moscow, The Bookman*, June 1923: 464; "Machiavellian Muzhiks of Moscow," *New York Times Book Review*, 11 Mar. 1923: 3.

13. Louise Bryant, "Jim Larkin Goes to Jail," *Liberator*, June 1920: 13–16; "A Turkish Divorce," *Nation*, 26 Aug. 1925: 231–232.

14. Louise Bryant, "The First Woman of Russia," *Liberator*, Nov. 1921: 20.

15. For a thoughtful analysis of this period of Bryant's life, see Gardner, *Friend and Lover*.

16. Dorothy Day's autobiography also deemphasized her earlier sympathy for birth control activism.

17. Robert Coles, *Dorothy Day: A Radical Devotion* (1987), 34, 27, 81.

18. "On Use of Force," *Catholic Worker*, Sept. 1938: 1.

19. See Robert Coles' account of an interview with Day in his *Dorothy Day*, 36–38.

20. Day's comment about what she regarded as modern-day promiscuity is quoted by William D. Miller, *A Harsh and Dreadful Love: Dorothy Day and the Catholic Worker Movement* (1973), 337. She was asked about her views on the women's movement by Bill Moyers in a documentary entitled *Still a Rebel* ("Bill Moyers' Journal," PBS, 20 Feb. 1973).

21. Mary Heaton Vorse, "Twenty Years," *Liberator*, Jan. 1921: 10–13; "Russian Pictures," *Liberator*, July 1922: 20–23.

22. Mary Heaton Vorse, "How Scottsboro Happened," *New Republic*, 10 May 1933: 356–358.

23. Mary Heaton Vorse, "America's Submerged Class: The Migrants," *Harper's Bazaar*, Feb. 1953: 86–93.

24. Mary Heaton Vorse, "The Pirate's Nest of New York," *Harper's Bazaar*, Apr. 1952: 27.

25. Sinclair Lewis, "A Novel for Mr. Hoover," *Nation*, 29 Oct. 1930: 474.

26. Robert Morss Lovett, "Mary Vorse Remembers," *New Republic*, 1 Jan. 1936: 232; Harold E. Stearns, "Suffer Little Children," *Nation*, 15 Jan. 1936: 80, 82; Florence F. Kelly, "A Decade in the Life of Mary Heaton Vorse," *New York Times Book Review*, 12 Jan. 1936: 6; John Chamberlin, Review of "A Footnote to Folly," *New York Times*, 16 Dec. 1935: 25.

Bibliography

Material Published in *The Masses*

Articles

Anderson, Frances. "War's Hinterland." June 1914: 34–35.
"Anti-Suffrage Papers Please Copy." Jan. 1916: 20.
Bryant, Louise. "The Poets' Revolution." July 1916: 29.
————, and John Reed. "News From France." Oct. 1917: 5–8.
Conger-Kaneko, Josephine. "Kathleen Kelly." Nov. 1911: 11.
————. "Women Suffrage and Socialism." Aug. 1911: 16.
Dell, Floyd. "Adventures in Anti-Land." Oct./Nov. 1915: 5–6.
————. "Criminals All." Oct./Nov. 1915: 21.
————. "Last But Not Least." July 1915: 22.
————. "The Nature of Woman." Jan. 1916: 6.
Dodge (Luhan), Mabel. "The Secret of War." Nov. 1914: 8–9.
Dorr, Rheta Childe. "Adv." July 1913: 15.
"Do You Believe in Patriotism?" Mar. 1916: 12.
Eastman, Max. "Birth-Control." July 1916: 27.
————. "Revolutionary Birth-Control." July 1915: 21–23.
————. "Revolutionary Progress." Nov. 1916: 21.
Eaton, Jeannette. "The Woman's Magazine." Oct./Nov. 1915: 19.
"Emma Goldman's Defense." June 1916: 27.
Field, Sara Bard. "Do You Believe in Patriotism?" Mar. 1916: 12.
————. "San Francisco and the Bomb." Oct. 1916: 16.
Flynn, Elizabeth Gurley. "Do You Believe in Patriotism?" Mar. 1916: 12.
————. "Joe Hill." Dec. 1915: 17.
————. "The Minnesota Trials." Jan. 1917: 8.
Hanna, Esther. "Amusement." Feb. 1914: 3.
H. B. "Provincial Suffragists." Nov. 1913: 11.
[Irwin], Inez Haynes (Gillmore). "The A.F. of L. Convention: An Impression." Feb. 1916: 8.
————. "As Mars Sees Us." Aug. 1912: 12.
————. "At the Industrial Hearing." Mar. 1915: 8–9.
————. "Do You Believe in Patriotism?" Mar. 1916: 12.

———. "Shadows of Revolt." July 1915: 7–8.
———. "Stray Thoughts on Chivalry." Oct./Nov. 1915: 22.
Lewis, Lena Morrow. "Jeffersonianism vs. Social Democracy." Apr. 1912: 17.
———. "The Sex and Woman Questions." Feb. 1912: 9, 16.
———. "Working Class Politics in America." Dec. 1911: 7.
Lowell, Carlotta Russell. "*The Masses* and the Negro." Letter to the Editors. May 1915: 6.
Marot, Helen. "Actors and Teachers." June 1916: 16.
———. "Immigration and Militarism." Apr. 1916: 21.
———. "Railroads and Revolution." Nov. 1916: 5.
———. "Revolution and the Garment Trade." Aug. 1916: 29.
———. "The Revolutionary Spirit at Seattle." Jan. 1914: 16.
Marvin, Gertrude. "Anthony and the Devil." Feb. 1914: 16.
McKeehan, Irene. "Adieu, Plaisant Pays de France." June 1917: 45.
McKenna, Edmond. "Art and Humor." June 1915: 10–12.
O'Hare, Kate Richards. "Booze and Revolution." Apr. 1915: 21.
Ovington, Mary White. Letter to the Editor (Re "The White Brute"). Jan. 1916: 20.
Parce, Lida. "Woman Suffrage: Why?" Dec. 1911: 12.
Parsons, Elsie Clews. "Engagements." Nov. 1916: 14.
———. "Facing Race Suicide." June 1915: 15.
———. "It Costs." Oct. 1917: 35.
———. "Marriage: A New Life." Sept. 1916: 27–28.
———. "Privacy in Love Affairs." July 1915: 12.
Patterson, Ethel Lloyd. "Lena Morrow Lewis: Agitator." July 1911: 13.
Potter, Grace. "Breaking Up the Home." Dec. 1911: 13.
Schwimmer, Rosika. "News from the Front." May 1915: 10.
Spadoni, Adriana. "Foreladies." Mar. 1917: 5–6.
"A Strange Meeting." Apr. 1917: 21–24.
"Suffrage and Sedition." Aug. 1917: 42.
Van Saanen, Marie Louise. "The Game." May 1916: 9.
Vorse, Mary Heaton. "Accessories before the Fact." Nov. 1916: 6–7, 22.
Weed, Inis, and Louise Carey. "I Make Cheap Silk." Nov. 1913: 7.
"A Wife's Troubles." Dec. 1916: 38.

Fiction

Conger-Kaneko, Josephine. "The Dream of Mirah." Nov. 1911: 9.
Dodge (Luhan), Mabel. "The Eye of the Beholder." Oct. 1917: 10–11.
———. "The Parting." Oct. 1916: 8.
———. "The Quarrel." Sept. 1916: 16–17.
Forbes, Helen. "The Hunky Woman." May 1917: 12–13.
Frank, Florence Kiper. "In the Pride of His Youth." July 1912: 9–10.
Hanley, Elizabeth Hines. "Chivalry." June 1916: 5.
Hull, Helen R. "Mothers Still." Oct. 1914: 14–15.
———. "Till Death . . ." Jan. 1917: 4, 6.
———. "Usury." Sept. 1916: 7–8.
———. "Yellow Hair." Feb. 1916: 15.

[Irwin], Inez Haynes (Gillmore). "The Classmates." Mar. 1911: 13–15, 18.

———. "Henry." Dec. 1911: 15–17.

———. "The Other Way." June 1912: 15–16, 19.

Ovington, Mary White. "The White Brute." Oct./Nov. 1915: 17–19.

Patterson, Ethel Lloyd. "Things for Dolls." Jan. 1912: 12–13.

Pearl, Jeanette D. "Pride." June 1917: 15.

Reely, Mary Katherine. "Barriers." Feb. 1914: 8.

———. "The Helpmeet." July 1914: 11.

Spadoni, Adriana. "A Hall Bedroom Nun." June 1916: 6.

———. "Real Work." July 1915: 6, 7–8, 10.

———. "A Rift of Silence." Feb. 1913: 12–13.

———. "The Seamstress." Sept. 1913: 15–16.

Vorse, Mary Heaton. "The Day of a Man." May 1912: 8, 18.

———. "The Happy Woman." Apr. 1915: 18–19.

———. "The Story of Michael Shea." Nov. 1913: 16.

———. "Tolerance." Feb. 1914: 12–15.

———. "The Two-Faced Goddess." Dec. 1912: 12–14.

Weil, Dorothy. "A New Woman?" Jan. 1916: 17–18.

Wyatt, Phyllis. "The Checked Trousers." June 1917: 17.

Illustrations

Barns, Cornelia. "Anti-Suffrage Argument No. 187." Mar. 1913: 12.

———. Circus Scene (untitled). Nov./Dec. 1917: Cover.

———. "The Flight of the Innocents." July 1916: 13.

———. "Lords of Creation." May 1913: 7.

———. "Mrs. Callahan, the Irish . . ." Nov. 1914: 24.

———. "My Dear, I'll Be Economically Independent . . ." Mar. 1915: 7.

———. "Patriotism for Women." Nov. 1914: 7.

———. "Requiem." Feb. 1916: 20.

———. "Shop Talk." Aug. 1913: 14.

———. "Tonight Will Be Army and Navy Night." Aug. 1917: 11.

———. "Twelve-Thirty." Jan. 1915: 15.

———. "Voters." Dec. 1915: 4.

———. "Where Ignorance Is Bliss." Feb. 1914: Cover.

Grieg, Elizabeth. "At the City Hospital." Feb. 1914: 13.

———. "Look at That Suffragette, Madge. . ." Oct./Nov. 1915: 19.

———. "What Every Young Woman Ought to Have Known." Apr. 1915: 23.

———. "What's Your Name?" Aug. 1916: 11.

Robinson, Boardman. Picketing Suffragist (untitled). Oct. 1917: 17.

Winter, Alice Beach. "Discrimination." Feb. 1913: 8.

———. "Look What I Gotta Carry." Dec. 1912: 17.

———. "Puzzle: Find the Race Problem." Mar. 1914: 20.

Poetry

Aldis, Mary. "The Barber Shop." Apr. 1916: 23.

Apotheker, Nan. "In the Hallway." Sept. 1917: 42.

Barrington, Pauline B. "Toy Guns." May 1916: 13.
Bell, Josephine. "Mighty Fires." June 1917: 43.
———. "A Tribute." Aug. 1917: 28.
Bradley, Mary. "A Stranger in the City." Mar. 1917: 40.
Bryant, Louise. "Lost Music." Jan. 1917: 43.
———. "Sensations." Apr. 1917: 37.
Bull, Nina. "In Answer to a Critic." Oct./Nov. 1915: 4.
Burr, Jane. "Nigger Tilly." Apr. 1916: 6.
Bu Zard, Claire. "A Question." June 1917: 47.
Cleghorn, Sarah N. "And Thou Too, America?" June 1916: 8.
———. "Comrade Jesus." Apr. 1914: 14.
———. "The Masquerader." Jan. 1914: 19.
———. "The Mother Follows." Aug. 1917: 47.
Coatsworth, Elizabeth J. "The Coolie Ship." Nov./Dec. 1917: 43.
Davies, Mary Carolyn. "The Dream Bearer." July 1916: 23.
———. "To the Women of England." Apr. 1916: 7.
———. "When the Seventeen Came Home." July 1914: 17.
Day, Dorothy. "Mulberry Street." July 1917: 49.
De Ford, Miriam Allen. "The Singing Mouth." Feb. 1916: 14.
Deutsch, Babette. "Extra." Nov./Dec. 1917: 37.
———. "Ironic." June 1917: 48.
Eaton, Jeannette. "Rebellion." Aug. 1917: 23.
Field, Mary. "Justice." June 1916: 14.
Fitch, Ruth. "Chinese Music." July 1917: 45.
Flexner, Hortense. "The Fire-Watchers." Sept. 1913: 17.
———. "The Winds of Spring." May 1915: 18.
Frank, Florence Kiper. "Where Sympathy Pays." May 1915: 14.
Gibson, Lydia. "Artemis." Mar. 1915: 11.
———. "Children of Kings." May 1914: 21.
———. "Children Playing." Apr. 1917: 42.
———. "Lies." Oct. 1913: 15.
Glaspell, Susan. "Joe." Jan. 1916: 9.
Gruening, Martha. "Prepared." Mar. 1916: 13.
Henke, Mary Isabelle. "Brother of Poets." Nov./Dec. 1917: 41.
Hoyt, Helen. "Comparison." Sept. 1915: 16.
———. "Golden Bough." Aug. 1916: 14.
———. "Menaia." Sept. 1915: 16.
Lowell, Amy. "The Grocery." June 1916: 17.
———. "The Poem." Apr. 1916: 21.
Mastin, Florence Ripley. "The Dream." June 1916: 16.
Miller, Alice Duer. "To Everett P. Wheeler." Oct./Nov. 1915: 9.
Mixter, Florence K. "A Greek Coffee House." Aug. 1917: 13.
Patton, Miriam Keep. "The Clock." May 1917: 3.
Reynolds, Lucy. "A Good Man." Dec. 1914: 19.
———. "Oh, That's Different!" Dec. 1914: 19.
———. "The Old Mother's Death." Dec. 1914: 19.
Robinson, Eloise. "Sweat-Shop Flowers." Sept. 1917: 37.

Sangster, Margaret. "Proportionately." Nov./Dec. 1917: 3.
Simmons, Laura. "Blades of Grass." Oct. 1917: 42–43.
Smith, Edith. "The Mills of the Rich." July 1912: 8.
Snow, Jane. "The Married Woman Speaks." Aug. 1917: 47.
Stokes, Rose Pastor. "Paterson." Nov. 1913: 11.
Untermeyer, Jean Starr. "Sonya." Sept. 1916: 17.
———. "Zanesville." Oct. 1916: 20.
Waddell, Elizabeth. "The Dear Little Bullet." Apr. 1915: 24.
———. "The First Gun." Sept. 1915: 8.
———. "For Lyric Labor." Sept. 1917: 39.
———. "The Job." Feb. 1916: 18.
———. "Making a Safe." Aug. 1917: 42.
———. "The Sword of Flame." Dec. 1913: 3.
———. "The Tenant Farmer." Aug. 1916: 8.
———. "What of the Night." Mar. 1917: 6.
Widdemer, Margaret. "War-March." Aug. 1915: 17.
Wilkinson, Marguerite. "Woman Returning." Oct./Nov. 1915: 6.

Other Works by *Masses* Contributors

In Books

Bryant, Louise. *The Game*. In *The Provincetown Plays* (First Series). New York: Shay, 1916.
———. *Mirrors of Moscow*. New York: Seltzer, 1923.
———. *Six Red Months in Russia: An Observer's Account of Russia before and during the Proletarian Dictatorship*. 1918. Reprint. London: Journeyman, 1982.
Cleghorn, Sarah N. *The Ballad of Gene Debs*. North Montpelier, Vt.: Driftwind, 1928.
———. *Portraits and Protests*. New York: Holt, 1917.
———. *The Seamless Robe: The Religion of Lovingkindness*. New York: Macmillan, 1945.
———. *The Spinster: A Novel Wherein a Nineteenth Century Girl Finds Her Place in the Twentieth*. New York: Holt, 1916.
———. *Threescore: The Autobiography of Sarah N. Cleghorn*. New York: Smith and Haas, 1936.
———. *A Turnpike Lady*. New York: Holt, 1907.
Day, Dorothy. *By Little and by Little: The Selected Writings of Dorothy Day*. Edited by Robert Ellsberg. New York: Knopf, 1983.
———. *The Eleventh Virgin*. New York: Boni, 1924.
———. *From Union Square to Rome*. Silver Spring, Md.: Preservation of the Faith Press, 1938.
———. *The Long Loneliness: The Autobiography of Dorothy Day*. 1952. Reprint. New York: Image Books, 1959.
Dell, Floyd. *Homecoming: An Autobiography*. New York: Farrar, 1933.
Deutsch, Babette. *Banners*. New York: Doran, 1919.
———. *A Brittle Heaven*. New York: Greenberg, 1926.

———. *Collected Poems, 1919–1962.* Bloomington: Indiana University Press, 1963.

Dodge (Luhan), Mabel. *The Edge of Taos Desert: An Escape to Reality.* Vol. 4 of *Intimate Memories.* New York: Harcourt Brace, 1937. Reprinted separately. Albuquerque, N. Mex.: University of New Mexico Press, 1987.

———. *Movers and Shakers.* Vol. 3 of *Intimate Memories.* New York: Harcourt Brace, 1936. Reprinted separately. Albuquerque, N. Mex.: University of New Mexico Press, 1985.

Dorr, Rheta Childe. *A Soldier's Mother in France.* Indianapolis: Bobbs-Merrill, 1918.

———. *Susan B. Anthony: The Woman Who Changed the Mind of a Nation.* New York: Stokes, 1928.

———. *What Eight Million Women Want.* Boston: Small, 1910.

———. *A Woman of Fifty.* New York: Funk, 1924.

Eastman, Max. *Enjoyment of Living.* New York: Harper, 1948.

———. *Love and Revolution: My Journey through an Epoch.* New York: Random, 1964.

———. *Venture.* New York: Boni, 1927.

Flynn, Elizabeth Gurley. *The Rebel Girl: An Autobiography of My First Life, 1906–1926.* New York: International Publishers, 1973.

Glaspell, Susan. *Plays.* Boston: Small, 1920.

Hull, Helen R. *A Circle in the Water.* New York: Coward-McCann, 1943.

———. *Close Her Pale Blue Eyes.* New York: Dodd, 1963.

———. *Hawk's Flight.* New York: Coward-McCann, 1946.

———. *Heat Lightning.* New York: Coward-McCann, 1932.

———. *Islanders.* 1927. New York: Feminist Press, 1988.

———. *Labyrinth.* New York: Macmillan, 1923.

———. *Last September.* Edited by Patricia McClelland Miller. Tallahassee, Fla.: Naiad, 1988.

———. *Quest.* 1922. New York: Feminist Press, 1990.

———. *The Surrey Family.* New York: Macmillan, 1925.

Hull, Helen R. and Michael Drury, eds. *Writers Roundtable.* New York: Harper, 1959.

Irwin, Inez Haynes (Gillmore). "Adventures of Yesterday." Unpublished autobiography. Inez Haynes Irwin Papers.

———. *Angel Island.* 1914. Reprint, with introduction by Ursula Le Guin. New York: New American Library, 1988.

———. *Angels and Amazons: A Hundred Years of American Women.* New York: Doubleday, 1933.

———. *Family Circle.* Indianapolis: Bobbs-Merrill, 1931.

———. *Gertrude Haviland's Divorce.* London: Harper, 1925.

———. *Gideon.* New York: Burt, 1927.

———. *The Lady of Kingdoms.* New York: Doran, 1917.

———. *The Story of Alice Paul and the National Woman's Party.* Fairfax, Va.: Denlinger's, 1921.

Marot, Helen. *American Labor Unions.* 1914. Reprint. New York: Arno, 1969.

———. *The Creative Impulse in Industry.* New York: Dutton, 1918.

Miller, Alice Duer. *Are Women People?* New York: Doran, 1915.

———. *Come Out of the Kitchen.* New York: Doran, 1916.

———. *Women Are People!* New York: Doran, 1917.

Ovington, Mary White. *Half a Man: The Status of the Negro in New York.* 1911. Reprint. New York: Schocken, 1969.

———. *The Shadow.* New York: Harcourt, 1920.

———. *The Walls Came Tumbling Down.* 1947. Reprint. New York: Arno, 1969.

Parsons, Elsie Clews. *The Family: An Ethnographical and Historical Outline.* New York: Putnam's, 1906.

———. *Fear and Conventionality.* New York: Putnam's, 1914.

———. *Folklore from the Cape Verde Islands.* Cambridge, Mass.: American Folklore Society, 1923.

———. *Hopi and Zuni Ceremonialism.* Menasha, Wisc.: Collegiate Press, 1925.

———. *The Old-Fashioned Woman.* New York: Putnam's, 1913.

———. *Pueblo Indian Religion.* 2 vols. Chicago: University of Chicago Press, 1939.

———. *Religious Chastity: An Ethnological Study.* 1913. New York: AMS Press, 1975.

———. *Social Freedom.* New York: Putnam's, 1915.

———. *Social Rule: A Study of the Will to Power.* New York: Putnam's, 1916.

———. *Taos Pueblo.* Menasha, Wisc.: George Bauta, 1936.

———, ed. *A Pueblo Indian Journal 1920–21.* Menasha, Wisc.: Collegiate Press, 1925.

Reely, Mary Katharine. *Cave Stuff: A Play in Two Episodes.* Boston: Baker, 1928.

———. *Daily Bread and Other Plays.* New York: Wilson, 1919.

———, ed. *Selected Articles on Immigration.* White Plains, NY: Wilson, 1917.

Spadoni, Adriana. *Mrs. Phelps' Husband.* Indianapolis: Bobbs-Merrill, 1924.

———. *The Noise of the World.* New York: Boni, 1921.

———. *Not All Rivers.* 1937. New York: AMS Press, 1976.

———. *The Swing of the Pendulum.* New York: Boni, 1919.

Untermeyer, Jean Starr. *Love and Need: Collected Poems, 1918–1940.* New York: Viking, 1940.

Untermeyer, Louis. *From Another World.* New York: Harcourt, 1939.

Vorse, Mary Heaton. *Autobiography of an Elderly Woman.* 1911. Reprint. New York: Arno, 1974.

———. *A Footnote to Folly: The Reminiscences of Mary Heaton Vorse.* New York: Farrar, 1935.

———. *Growing Up.* New York: Boni, 1920.

———. *I've Come to Stay: A Love Comedy of Bohemia.* New York: Century, 1919.

———. *Labor's New Millions.* 1938. New York: Arno, 1969.

———. *Men and Steel.* New York: Boni, 1920.

———. *Rebel Pen: The Writings of Mary Heaton Vorse.* Edited by Dee Garrison. New York: Monthly Review Press, 1985.

———. *Second Cabin.* New York: Liveright, 1928.

———. *Strike!* New York: Liveright, 1930.

———. Chap. 8 of *The Sturdy Oak.* Edited by Elizabeth Jordan. New York: Holt, 1917.

———. *Time and the Town: A Provincetown Chronicle.* New York: Dial, 1942.

———. *The Whole Family: A Novel by Twelve Authors*. New York: Harper, 1908.
Young, Art. *On My Way: Being the Book of Art Young in Text and Picture*. New York: Liveright, 1928.

In Periodicals

Barns, Cornelia. "The New Voter at Work." *Birth Control Review*, Feb.–Mar. 1918: 9.
Bryant, Louise. "Communist Jail-Keepers." *Liberator*, June 1921: 12–14.
———. "The First Woman of Russia." *Liberator*, Nov. 1921: 20–21.
———. "Jim Larkin Goes to Jail." *Liberator*, June 1920: 13–16.
———. "Last Days with John Reed." *Liberator*, Feb. 1921: 11–12.
———. "A Turkish Divorce." *Nation*, 26 Aug. 1925: 323.
Day, Dorothy. "A Coney Island Picture." *Liberator*, Apr. 1918: 46.
———. "Girls and Boys Come Out to Play." Review of *Janet March*, by Floyd Dell. *Liberator*, Nov. 1923: 30–31.
———. "On Use of Force." *Catholic Worker*, Sept. 1938: 1.
Dell, Floyd. "The Story of the Trial." *Liberator*, June 1918: 9–11.
Irwin, Inez Haynes (Gillmore). "The Confessions of an Alien." *Harper's Bazaar*, Apr. 1912: 170–171, 210.
———. "Just before the Drive." *Liberator*, May 1918: 10–13.
———. "The Marysville Strike." *Harper's Weekly*, 4 Apr. 1914: 18–20.
Marot, Helen. "Demobilizing the Trade Unions." *Liberator*, Jan. 1919: 28–32.
———. "A Moral in the Cloakmakers' Strike." *Outlook*, Sept. 1910: 99–101.
———. "The War Labor Board." *Liberator*, Dec. 1918: 12–15.
———. "A Woman's Strike—An Appreciation of the Shirtwaist Makers of New York." *Proceedings of the Academy of Political Science in the City of New York*, 1910: 127–128.
Ovington, Mary White. "Bogalusa." *Liberator*, Jan. 1920: 31–33.
Parsons, Elsie Clews. "Feminism and Sex Ethics." *International Journal of Ethics* 26 (1916): 462–465.
———. "The Last Zuni Transvestite." *American Anthropologist* 41 (1939): 338–340.
———. "Marriage and Parenthood: A Distinction." *International Journal of Ethics* 25 (1915): 514–517.
———. "Notes on Zuni." *Memoirs of the American Anthropological Association* 4 (1917). Reprint. New York: Kraus Reprint, 1964.
———. "On the Loose." *New Republic*, 27 Feb. 1915: 101.
———. "A Pacifist Patriot." *Dial* 68 (1920): 367–370.
———. "Penalizing Marriage and Child-Bearing." *Independent*, 18 Jan. 1906: 146–147.
———. "When Mating and Parenthood Are Theoretically Distinguished." *International Journal of Ethics*, Jan. 1916: 207–216.
Untermeyer, Jean Starr. "Church Sociable." *Liberator*, Mar. 1918: 12.
Vorse, Mary Heaton. "America's Submerged Class: The Migrants." *Harper's Magazine*, Feb. 1953: 86–93.
———. "Behind the Picket Lines." *Outlook*, 21 Jan. 1920: 107–109.
———. "The Case of Adolf." *Outlook*, 2 May 1914: 27–31.

———. "Civil Liberty in the Steel Strike." *Nation,* 15 Nov. 1919: 633–635.

———. "Courage." *Liberator,* Mar. 1923: 11–13.

———. "Debatable Lands in Central Europe." *New York Times Magazine,* 6 July 1919: 7, 13.

———. "Deer Dance in Taos." *Nation,* 13 Aug. 1930: 178–179.

———. "Les Evacuées." *Outlook,* 10 Nov. 1915: 622–626.

———. "The Extra Thousand." *Harper's Magazine,* June 1911: 101–109.

———. "Fraycar's Fist." *Liberator,* Aug. 1920: 17, 20–24.

———. "Gastonia." *Harper's Magazine,* Nov. 1929: 700–710.

———. "Germany: The Twilight of Reason." *New Republic,* 14 June 1933: 117–121.

———. "Getting the Jews Out of Germany." *New Republic,* 19 July 1933: 255–258.

———. "Grantham's Limitations." *Scribner's,* Nov. 1908: 521–532.

———. "The Hopper." *Liberator,* Apr. 1920: 34–38.

———. "How Scottsboro Happened." *New Republic,* 10 May 1933: 356–358.

———. "Locked Out." *Liberator,* Feb. 1921: 5–8.

———. "The Madelon Viera." *Atlantic Monthly,* Jan. 1910: 80–89.

———. "Milorad." *Harper's Magazine,* Jan. 1920: 256–262.

———. "The Mining Strike in Minnesota: From the Miners' Point of View." *Outlook,* 30 Aug. 1916: 1044–1045.

———. "The Pirate's Nest of New York." *Harper's Magazine,* Apr. 1952: 27–37.

———. "Profits and Dreamers: The R.A.I.C." *Nation,* 21 Dec. 1922: 713–714.

———. "Protection of Nursing Mothers." *Success,* Oct. 1911: 13–14, 24–25.

———. "The Quiet Woman." *Atlantic Monthly,* Jan. 1907: 80–89.

———. "Russian Pictures." *Liberator,* July 1922: 20–23.

———. "The Sinistrées of France." *Century* 71 (1917): 445–450.

———. "The Steel Strike." *Liberator,* Jan. 1920: 36–40.

———. "The Troubles at Lawrence." *Harper's Weekly,* 16 March 1912: 10.

———. "Twenty Years." *Liberator* Jan. 21: 10–13.

———. "Waitin' with the Dead." *New Republic,* 30 Oct. 1929: 287–288.

Memoirs, Biographies, and Reviews

Angell, Katharine Sergeant. "The Soviet Leaders." *Nation,* 9 May 1923: 548–549.

Baxandall, Rosalyn Fraad, ed. *Words on Fire: The Life and Writing of Elizabeth Gurley Flynn.* New Brunswick, N.J.: Rutgers University Press, 1987.

Benvenuto, Richard. *Amy Lowell.* Boston: Twayne, 1985.

Boas, Franz. Obituary tribute to Elsie Clews Parsons. *Science,* 23 Jan. 1942: 89–90.

Bourne, Randolph. "A Modern Mind." *Dial* 62 (1917): 239–240.

Caffrey, Margaret M. *Ruth Benedict: Stranger in This Land.* Austin: University of Texas Press, 1989.

Chamberlin, John. Review of *A Footnote to Folly. New York Times,* 16 Dec. 1935: 25.

Coles, Robert. *Dorothy Day: A Radical Devotion.* Reading, MA: Addison-Wesley, 1987.

Dos Passos, John. *The Best of Times: An Informal Memoir.* New York: New American Library, 1966.

Douglas, Emily Taft. *Margaret Sanger: Pioneer of the Future.* New York: Holt, 1970.

Fowler, Robert Booth. *Carrie Catt: Feminist Politician.* Boston: Northeastern University Press, 1986.

Frazer, Winifred L. *Mabel Dodge Luhan.* Boston: Twayne, 1984.

Gardner, Virginia. *Friend and Lover: The Life of Louise Bryant.* New York: Horizon, 1982.

Garrison, Dee. Introduction to *Rebel Pen: The Writings of Mary Heaton Vorse.* Edited by Dee Garrison. New York: Monthly Review Press, 1985.

———. *Mary Heaton Vorse: The Life of an American Insurgent.* Philadelphia: Temple University Press, 1989.

Gelb, Barbara. *So Short a Time: A Biography of John Reed and Louise Bryant.* New York: Norton, 1973.

Gluck, Sherna, ed. *From Parlor to Prison: Five American Suffragists Talk about Their Lives.* New York: Octagon, 1975.

Goldman, Emma. *Living My Life.* New York: Knopf, 1931.

Hare, Peter H. *A Woman's Quest for Science: Portrait of Anthropologist Elsie Clews Parsons.* Buffalo, NY: Prometheus, 1985.

Jones, Mary Harris. *The Autobiography of Mother Jones.* Chicago: Kerr, 1925.

Kelly, Florence Finch. "A Decade in the Life of Mary Heaton Vorse." *New York Times Book Review,* 12 Jan. 1936: 6.

Kempton, Murray. *Part of Our Time: Some Ruins and Monuments of the Thirties.* New York: Simon and Schuster, 1955.

Lewis, Sinclair. "A Novel for Mr. Hoover." *Nation,* 29 Oct. 1930: 474.

"Louise Bryant, 41, American Writer, Dies in Paris Hospital." Obituary. *New York Herald Tribune,* 10 Jan. 1936: 2.

"Louise Bryant, 41, Journalist, Dead." Obituary. *New York Times,* 10 Jan. 1936: 19.

Lovett, Robert Morss. "Mary Vorse Remembers." *New Republic,* 1 Jan. 1936: 232.

"Machiavellian Muzhiks of Moscow." *New York Times Book Review,* 11 Mar. 1923: 3.

Mailly, William. "The Working Girls' Strike." *Independent* 67 (1909): 1416–1418.

"Mary Heaton Vorse, a Novelist and Champion of Labor, Dead." Obituary. *New York Times,* 15 June 1966: 47.

Miller, William D. *A Harsh and Dreadful Love: Dorothy Day and the Catholic Worker Movement.* New York: Liveright, 1973.

"Miss Helen Marot." Obituary. *New York Times,* 4 June 1940: 24.

Piehl, Mel. *Breaking Bread: The Catholic Worker and the Origin of Catholic Radicalism in America.* Philadelphia: Temple University Press, 1982.

Review of *Mirrors of Moscow,* by Louise Bryant. *The Bookman,* June 1923: 464.

Review of *Mirrors of Moscow,* by Louise Bryant. *Times Literary Supplement,* 26 April 1923: 299.

Rudnick, Lois Palken. *Mabel Dodge Luhan: New Woman, New Worlds.* Albuquerque, N. Mex.: University of New Mexico Press, 1984.

Sanger, Margaret. *Autobiography.* New York: Norton, 1938.

Sheppard, Alice. "There *Were* Ladies Present! American Women Cartoonists and Comic Artists in the Early Twentieth Century." *Journal of American Culture* 7 (1984): 34–38.

Sinclair, Upton B. *Autobiography.* New York: Harcourt, 1962.

Stearns, Harold. "Suffer Little Children." *Nation,* 15 Jan. 1936: 80, 82.

Further Background Material

Aaron, Daniel. *Writers on the Left: Episodes in American Literary Communism.* 1961. Reprint. New York: Oxford University Press, 1971.

Brown, Heywood, and Margaret Leech. *Anthony Comstock, Roundsman of the Lord.* New York: Albert and Charles Boni, 1927.

Buenker, John D, and Edward R. Kantowicz, eds. *A Historical Dictionary of the Progressive Era, 1890–1920.* New York: Greenwood, 1988.

Buhle, Mari Jo. *Women and American Socialism, 1870–1920.* Urbana, IL: University of Chicago Press, 1981.

———. *Women and the American Left: A Guide to Sources.* Boston: Hall, 1983.

Cafferty, Pastora San Juan, Barry R. Chiswick, Andrew M. Greeley, and Teresa A. Sullivan. *The Dilemma of American Immigration: Beyond the Golden Door.* New Brunswick: Transaction, 1983.

Campbell, Barbara Kuhn. *The "Liberated" Woman of 1914.* Michigan: University of Michigan Press, 1976.

"Clarissa S. Ware." Obituary. *Liberator,* Oct. 1923: 7.

Cott, Nancy. *The Grounding of Modern Feminism.* New Haven: Yale University Press, 1987.

Crane, Stephen. *Maggie, A Girl of the Streets.* 1893. Reprint. New York: Norton, 1979.

Drake, William. *The First Wave: Women Poets in America, 1915–1945.* New York: Macmillan, 1987.

"Drops Mrs. Sanger's Case." *New York Times,* 19 Feb. 1916: 12.

Eastman, Crystal. "In Communist Hungary." *Liberator,* Aug. 1919: 5–9.

Flexner, Eleanor. *Century of Struggle: The Woman's Movement in the United States.* Cambridge, MA: Belknap, 1959.

Foner, Phillip. *History of the Labor Movement in the United States.* Vol. 4. New York: International Publishers, 1965.

———. *Women and the American Labor Movement.* New York: Free Press, 1979.

Gilman, Charlotte Perkins. *Herland.* Edited by Ann J. Lane. New York: Pantheon, 1979.

———. *Women and Economics.* 1898. Reprint. New York: Source Book Press, 1970.

Goldman, Emma. *Anarchism and Other Essays.* 1910. Reprint. Port Washington: Kennikat, 1969.

Gordon, Linda. *Woman's Body, Woman's Right: A Social History of Birth Control in America.* New York: Grossman, 1974.

Gould, Jean. *American Women Poets: Pioneers of Modern Poetry.* New York: Dodd, 1980.

Hood, Thomas. *Poems.* Edited by Alfred Ainger. London: Macmillan, 1897.

"How They Are Voting." *New Republic,* 21 Oct. 1940: 553–554.

Judson, Edward Zane Carroll. *Mysteries and Miseries of New York: A Story of Real Life.* New York: Berford, 1848.

Keller, Helen. "In Behalf of the IWW." *Liberator,* Mar. 1918: 13.

Kessler-Harris, Alice. *Out to Work: A History of Wage-Earning Women in the United States.* New York: Oxford University Press, 1982.

Kingsley, Charles. *The Water-Babies*. London: Macmillan, 1863.

Kraditor, Aileen S. *The Ideas of the Woman Suffrage Movement, 1890–1920*. New York: Columbia University Press, 1965.

Marcus, Jane. "Corpus/Corps/Corpse: Writing the Body in/at War." *Arms and the Woman: War, Gender and Literary Representation*. Edited by Helen M. Cooper, Adrienne Munich, and Susan Squier. Chapel Hill: University of North Carolina Press, 1989: 124–168

Miller, Sally M., ed. *Flawed Liberation: Socialism and Feminism*. Westport, Conn.: Greenwood, 1981.

Nelson, Cary. *Repression and Recovery: Modern American Poetry and the Politics of Cultural Memory, 1910–1945*. Madison: University of Wisconsin Press, 1989.

Norris, Frank. *The Octopus*. Garden City, N.Y.: Doubleday, Doran, 1901.

O'Neill, William L. *Everyone Was Brave: A History of Feminism in America*. Chicago: Quadrangle, 1969.

Ortiz, Alfonso, ed. *New Perspectives on the Pueblos*. Albuquerque, N. Mex.: University of New Mexico Press, 1972.

Ripley, W. Z. "Races in the United States." *Atlantic Monthly*, Dec. 1908: 745–759.

Ross, Edward A. "American and Immigrant Blood." *Century*, Dec. 1913: 225–232.

———. "Immigrants in Politics." *Century*, Jan. 1914: 392–398.

———. "Racial Consequences of Immigration." *Century*, Feb. 1914: 615–622.

Rossetti, Dante G. *Collected Poems*. Edited by Oswald Doughty. New York: Dutton, 1961.

Saki [H. H. Munro]. *The Short Stories of Saki*. Edited by Christopher Morley. New York: Viking, 1930.

Schwartz, Judith. *Radical Feminists of Heterodoxy: Greenwich Village 1912–1940*. Lebanon, N.H.: New Victoria Publishers, 1982.

Sinclair, Upton. *They Call Me Carpenter: A Tale of the Second Coming*. Pasadena, Calif.: Sinclair, 1922.

Spivak, Gayatri C. *In Other Worlds: Essays in Cultural Politics*. New York: Methuen, 1987.

Sterling, Jean. "The Silent Defense in Sacramento." *Liberator*, Feb. 1919: 15–17.

Weinstein, James. *The Decline of Socialism in America, 1912–1925*. New York: Monthly Review Press, 1967.

"Women Appeal to Mayor." *New York Times*, 29 Feb. 1917: 16.

Books about *The Masses*

Fishbein, Leslie. *Rebels in Bohemia: The Radicals of "The Masses," 1911–1917*. Chapel Hill: University of North Carolina Press, 1982.

Fitzgerald, Richard. *Art and Politics: Cartoonists of "The Masses" and "Liberator."* Westport, Conn.: Greenwood, 1973.

O'Neill, William L. *Echoes of Revolt: "The Masses," 1911–1917*. Chicago: Quadrangle Books, 1966.

Taggard, Genevieve, ed. *May Days: An Anthology of Verse from "Masses"-"Liberator."* New York: Boni and Liveright, 1925.

Zurier, Rebecca. *Art for "The Masses": A Radical Magazine and Its Graphics, 1911–1917*. 1987. Reprint. Philadelphia: Temple UP, 1988.

Biographical Dictionaries

Howes, Durward, Mary L. Braun, and Rose Garvey, eds. *The Standard Biographical Dictionary of Notable Women, 1939–40.* Los Angeles: American Publications, 1939.
Kodansha Encyclopedia of Japan. Tokyo: Kodansha Ltd., 1983.
Kunitz, Stanley J., ed. *Authors Today and Yesterday.* New York: Wilson, 1933.
Kunitz, Stanley J., and Howard Haycraft, eds. *Twentieth Century Authors: A Biographical Dictionary of Modern Literature.* New York: Wilson, 1942.
Kunitz, Stanley J., and Vineta Colby, eds. *Twentieth Century Authors: First Supplement.* New York: Wilson, 1955.
National Cyclopedia of American Biography, 1892–1947. Clifton, N.J.: J. T. White, 1984.
Overton, Grant. *The Women Who Make Our Novels.* 1928. Reprint. Freeport, N.Y.: Books for Libraries Press, 1967.
Rogal, Samuel J. *A Chronological Outline of American Literature.* New York: Greenwood, 1987.
Sicherman, Barbara, Edward T. James, Janet Wilson James, and Paul S. Boyer, eds. *Notable American Women: The Modern Period.* Cambridge, MA: Belknap, 1980.
Tante, Dilly. *Living Authors.* New York: Wilson, 1931.
Wallace, Stuart, ed. *A Dictionary of North American Authors Deceased Before 1950.* Toronto: Ryerson, 1951.
Who's Who of American Women. Chicago: A. N. Marquis, 1964–1965.
Who Was Who among North American Authors, 1921–1939. Detroit: Gale Research, 1976.

Manuscript Collections

Dorothy Day: Dorothy Day–Catholic Worker Collection, Marquette University Archives, Marquette, Wisc.
Mabel Dodge (Luhan): Mabel Dodge Luhan Papers, Beinecke Rare Book and Manuscript Library, Yale University, New Haven, Conn.
Sara Bard Field: Sara Bard Field Papers, Huntington Library, San Marino, Calif. *Also* Bancroft Library, University of California, Berkeley.
Helen R. Hull: Helen Rose Hull Papers, Rare Book and Manuscript Library (Butler Library), Columbia University, New York.
Inez Haynes Irwin: Inez Haynes Irwin Papers, Schlesinger Library, Radcliffe College, Cambridge, Mass.
Elsie Clews Parsons: Elsie Clews Parsons Papers, Library of the American Philosophical Society, Philadelphia. *Also* Oral History Collection, Columbia University, New York.
Mary Heaton Vorse: Mary Heaton Vorse Collection, Walter Reuther Library (Archives of Labor History and Urban Affairs), Wayne State University, Detroit. *Also* "Reminiscences of Mary Heaton Vorse," Oral History Collection, Columbia University, New York; materials on Mass Consumers' League, Schlesinger Library, Radcliffe College, Cambridge, Mass.

Index